nty

Managing Legal Uncertainty

Elite Lawyers in the New Deal

Ronen Shamir

DUKE UNIVERSITY PRESS   *Durham and London 1995*

© 1995 Duke University Press
All rights reserved
Printed in the United States of America on acid-free paper ∞
Typeset in Minion by Keystone Typesetting, Inc.
Library of Congress Cataloging-in-Publication Data
appear on the last printed page of this book.

To Yonit

Contents

Preface

This book is about lawyers in the early years of the New Deal. Yet it is more than a historical account. The setting—the Great Depression years of the early 1930s—is discussed here as a reflective present that attracted echoes from the past and summoned reminders for the future. From the perspective of the law, the New Deal saw a dramatic shift in the discourse on law and within law. I speak about echoes from the past because the practices of the present (i.e., the New Deal) were premised upon philosophical and theoretical discussions that had been in the process of materializing since the second half of the nineteenth century. Concretely, philosophical pragmatism had a tremendous impact on the legal-realist movement that reshaped the face of the law during the New Deal. It was in the New Deal that legal realism, heretofore confined to academic circles, became the active program of the administration's legal-policy agenda.

Those aspects of pragmatism that shaped legal realism declined in the postwar years. Yet given the resurgence of pragmatism in contemporary legal and social theory, the discussions, or at least the general mood of the book, may also summon reminders for the future. To some extent, reading the book with an eye to pragmatist philosophy may become quite an ironic endeavor. Many critics of pragmatism in the pre- and postwar years, most notably Frankfurt School adherents, tended to emphasize pragmatism's reductionist empiricism and untamed behaviorism and accused it of providing intellectual justifications for corporate capitalism in general and the instrumentally rational and de-humanized administered state in particular. This book will show that, iron-ically, critics from the Right and defenders of the old order attacked the carriers of legal realism for the very same reason: helping to promote a monstrous bureaucratic and interventionist state.

Yet there are also ironies of a different, and perhaps more significant, order. The present-day resurgence of pragmatism is based on the rediscovery of prag-matism's sensitivity to social indeterminacy, chaos, and contingency, and hence to methods of inquiry and interpretation that are hospitable to hermeneutics,

deconstruction, and contextualization. As we shall see, many in the legal profession in the 1930s both were aware of these tendencies and publicly condemned them for creating an aura of uncertainty and instability in the law. In
this respect, the elite corporate lawyers who are the protagonists of this book
displayed deep understandings of pragmatism—in its legal-realist guise—to
which Frankfurt School critics had been largely oblivious. On the other hand,
immersed in a state of sometimes near panic, these lawyers could not perceive
and anticipate the dialectical aspects of legal realism and its pragmatist prem-
ises. Although the realists and their allies within the expanding New Deal-
administered state spoke in the name of public mobilization and revitalization,
their practical involvement with the administration contributed to the further
development of a culture of experts and to the consolidation of the new man-
agerial class. This was the process, of course, that so worried latter-day Frankfurt School critics. The irony, however, is that what elite lawyers regarded as
a deprofessionalization process ultimately enhanced their own professional
powers. In the last instance, it is precisely these aspects of the New-Deal-in-the-
law that lead me to speak about "managing legal uncertainty": having to confront a new situation whose consequences could not be anticipated, controlled,
and intelligently assessed.

Thus, as a sociologist with interests in history, political theory, and the
sociology of knowledge and its carriers (i.e., professions), I explore a restricted
aspect of the New Deal with theoretical questions in mind. Although the final
product is a work in history, I nonetheless owe readers the modest confession
that the project originated as an intellectual exercise in sociological theories
that I had entertained in my doctoral dissertation. The traces of such interests,
admittedly and deliberately, are still evident throughout the study.

I should also say that the focus of the work on the upper echelons of the legal
profession may have obscured some of the fundamental realities of the period.
The book portrays intense and passionate struggles and debates over the face of
the nation, the fate and direction of the republic, the meaning of the Constitution, the place of government in society, and the role of law as a mechanism of
social control. These debates took place in the shadow of a severe social crisis.
The New Deal, above and beyond its marked intellectual upheavals, philosophical turning points, academic earthquakes, and ideological thunderstorms—all
types of moments of suspense that create a fascinating era—was for many
American citizens a time of despair, hunger, misery, shame, violence, and dark-
ness. All this is recorded in this book in a very indirect, remote, and oftentimes
dim manner. I discuss actions and intentions that had or could have had
practical and immediate implications for the lives of many. But the distance

ideas and dispositions had to travel before materializing into practices that produced either relief or more pain is hardly covered in this work. I owe a debt of gratitude to a reader of this book who drew my attention to this point. I can only respond by saying that this is the price I pay for mostly looking at the preoccupation of people who—regardless of their intentions and sympathies— were rather comfortably sheltered from the truly harsh realities of the day. This does not mean, however, that I discuss detached ideas and people who were isolated in ivory towers. This would have implied that only some people—in this case the unprivileged—may paradoxically claim the privilege of having been there, of having truly experienced the New Deal. Rather, my simple point is that any moment in history is simultaneously experienced by people whose perspectives on events may be fundamentally at odds. This book, for better or worse, focuses on the experiences of the privileged: successful academics at elite institutions, influential policy makers, and wealthy corporate lawyers.

For the elite stratum of the American legal profession, the New Deal became a battleground for the implementation of new ideas, or, conversely, a time for counterattacks and vehement trench defensive. The struggles, to be sure, were cast in the sharp vocabularies of good versus evil, moralists versus pragmatists, careful versus careless, foundationalists versus relativists, or reformers versus reactionaries. Far from claiming an objective standpoint, I nonetheless have tried to escape these dichotomies. Crudely put, there are no good and bad fellows in my account, only social actors whose differential locations within a given grid of power relations help to explain much of their doings and ideas. The title of this work also reflects this position. Both lawyers who fought for what they perceived as the integrity of the legal system and adversaries who held to entirely different conceptions of the law under the sometimes similar ideo- logical banner of working for the "public good" were in fact operating within conditions of uncertainty. Some were uncertain about the future of their own professional standing, others about the positions they were supposed to ad- vance in the midst of the turmoil, and all about the consequences of the administration's policies and experiments. The book, in this respect, is about discursive practices that are shaped by, and in turn shape, the indeterminate and uncertain universe of law and of legal interpretation.

I began my research for this book as a doctoral fellow at the American Bar Foundation in Chicago. During the many hours spent at the adjacent North- western Law School—overlooking Lake Michigan from the upper-floor com- fort of its beautiful library—I occasionally imagined myself as a sailor without a compass. Words of Salmon Rushdie's *Haroun and the Sea of Stories* repeatedly floated in my mind: "Different parts of the Ocean contained different sorts of stories, and as all the stories that had ever been told and many that were still in the process of being invented could be found there, the Ocean of the Streams of Story was in fact the biggest library in the universe. And because the stories were held here in fluid form, they retained the ability to change, to become new versions of themselves, to join up with other stories and so become yet other stories."

I cannot possibly begin to thank the friends, colleagues, and readers who shared my moments of reflection, doubt, enthusiasm, and anxiety in the course of writing this book. Many, at this point or another, assisted me in weaving together the streams of this story. I owe a particular debt of gratitude to Arthur Stinchcombe, whose insights, comments, and intellectual authority were invaluable in bringing the abstract idea and the written word closer together. I thank Robert Nelson, whose experience and knowledgeable observations were invaluable. I am deeply thankful to Allan Schnaiberg, whose willingness to engage me in long discussions about the work has provided me with an often-needed sense of direction. Conversations and consultations with Arthur, Bob, and Allan, all of whom directed my doctoral dissertation, were a vital part of the process through which my work assumed its focus and later was revised and written as this book. I also deeply thank Robert Jerome Glennon, who read the manuscript with care and provided comments that significantly contributed to my ability to proceed with the work. Finally, I thank the American Bar Foundation—both its colleagues and its administrative staff—for allowing me to enjoy a lively and highly productive intellectual atmosphere. The two-year Professionalism Fellowship which was granted me by the ABF also provided the funds necessary for undertaking this project, and for this I am deeply thankful.

quodcumque suis mutatum finibus exit, continuo hoc mors est illius quod fuit ante. Which being translated forgive my clumsiness, is "Whatever by its changing goes out of its frontiers,"—that is, bursts its banks,—or, maybe, breaks out of its limitations,—so to speak, disregards its own rules, but that is too free, I am thinking . . . "that thing," at any rate, Lucretius holds, by doing so brings immediate death to its old self.
—Salman Rushdie,
Satanic Verses

1 Introduction

Two general observations are shared by most students of the New Deal: first, that it marked the most significant shift in American history from a relatively "weak" and abstemious federal state to the modern regulatory state—that the New Deal represented a quantum leap in national-government involvement in the economy; and second, that the New Deal did not challenge the basic principles of the free-market economy and ended up reproducing and securing the foundations of corporate capitalism. The declared agenda of the New Deal's administration was to pull the United States out of the depression by facilitating renewed economic confidence and not by transforming the distributive principles of the system as a whole.

Yet the New Deal administration was in no way committed to a single political philosophy. Economic recovery, as far as the administration was concerned, necessitated different, if not conflicting, experiments. The sense of disorientation that this spirit of experimentation created was well captured in a letter that Justice Louis Brandeis wrote to Felix Frankfurter, then a law professor at Harvard: "Franklin D. Roosevelt's readiness to experiment is fine. But I am at times reminded of the Uncle from India's answer to the Private Secretary. When asked by his housekeeper 'Do you believe in spirits?' 'Yes,' said he, 'in moderation.'"[1] Brandeis's wishes notwithstanding, the New Deal often resembled a disarrayed response to "a variety of pressures and forces pushing the government in all . . . directions. The result was an amalgam of conflicting policies and programs, one that might make some sense to the politician, but little to a rational economist."[2] Consequently, the New Deal was described by its contemporaries in almost every conceivable way: a communist conspiracy, a capitalist strategy , a socialist plan, fascism in disguise, an enlightened-liberal reform, corporatism in action, and a dictatorship in the making. To some extent, these sharp differences in perception have not subsided. Although sometimes engaged in asking a different type of question, sixty years later a host of political scientists, legal historians, sociologists, public policy analysts, philosophers, jurists, labor historians, and economists still establish respectable academic careers debating the origins and fate of the New Deal.

It seems that the New Deal so fascinates researchers because it was an era of profound crisis. A crisis, to paraphrase Gramsci, consists precisely in the fact that the old is dying and the new is yet to be born. "In this interregnum," he wrote, "a great variety of morbid symptoms appears."[3] It is in such times that what usually remains hidden under the calm waters of what is taken for granted is exposed. Established truths, accepted dogmas, and unavoidable arrangements lose their objective character and are recontextualized, revealing the relations of domination, cooperation, inequality, privilege, suspicion, and trust that underlie them. It is in such times that old alliances break apart and new coalitions are formed and that society's most basic discursive and nondiscursive formations are formulated and experienced with exceptional clarity. Above all, a crisis is a suspended moment in which everything seems possible. New definitions of the situation may be born, new terms with which to negotiate the unstable flux that sociologists term the "social order" are introduced, and new possibilities of action, however contained within existing patterns, condition old institutions and allow one to imagine uncharted seas. A crisis, then, is when old certainties have to be defended and uncertainties knock on the door of established structures. It is the necessity to deal with uncertainty, to manage it, so to speak, that interests me in this book.

My intention in this book is neither to explain the New Deal nor to attempt any comprehensive account of it. I treat the New Deal as a process whose various aspects were shaped and negotiated on many sites. The whole, from the perspective I offer here, is an indeterminate aggregation of activities, projects, local struggles, and processes that take place in various, not necessarily coordinated, arenas. Accordingly, I focus on one particular site in which the New Deal was shaped, manipulated, debated, and conceptualized, and in this particular site, I mainly concentrate on one particular group. Insofar as the New Deal represented a quantum leap in involvement of the national government in the economy, this was largely accomplished by invoking a novel discourse on law and within law. In this respect, the *New York Times* adequately captured the mood of the times when it described the New Deal as an era in which Americans discussed the Constitution around the breakfast table. Law, to put it somewhat more concretely, was a primary medium through which the federal government constituted new arrangements and operationalized its economic and social programs. In the New Deal, as Guido Calabresi aptly puts it, the United States became a "nation governed by written laws."[4] For Americans, the growing emphasis on the merits of intensive legislation at the national level as a form of social and economic planning collided with old judicial traditions and with what seemed to be fundamental constitutional maxims. It is the debates around and within the juridical arena that I discuss in this book.

Law, however, is not only a system of authoritative commands constituting the language of the state but also a body of knowledge, which is shaped by the various groups of experts who comprise the legal profession. Judges, academic jurists, government lawyers, and a host of practitioners in private practice participate in the discursive game of lawmaking. Laws as texts are raw materials that assume practical and theoretical meaning only in the course of ongoing work by these various carriers of the law. Courts, for example, are reactive instititions. Judges "find" laws, interpret statutes, and contextualize relevant precedents only in reaction to a legal process in which practitioners enjoy considerable gatekeeping powers. Practitioners are thus able not only to retain a considerable measure of control over the agenda of courts but are also capable of acting as solution finders, rationalizers, and innovators.[5] In fact, Weber articulated theoretical and empirical links between the work of lawyers and the direction of legal developments as early as the beginning of the century. In Weber's scheme, the role of autonomous legal experts who enjoyed a measure of immunity from political and economic interests was crucial for the development of law as a heuristically consistent and self-referential system: "The increased need for specialized legal knowledge created the professional lawyer," Weber argued, and lawyers, in turn, had considerable influence on the "formation of law through 'legal invention.'"[6] Accordingly, Weber's treatment of various types of legal thought (i.e., formally rational and substantively rational legal systems) went hand in hand with his analysis of the various subgroups that comprised the legal profession.[7]

The role of lawyers in the New Deal, let alone the role of courts and legislators, has not been overlooked by students of the period. The New Deal is often remembered as an era of open and bitter confrontation between the Supreme Court and Roosevelt's administration. In this context at least, considerable attention has also been given to the role played by government lawyers and legal experts in the direct and indirect service of the state. The role of these lawyers in drafting, shaping, formulating, and defending the avalanche of new statutes and, in general, the reliance of the administration on legal expertise as means to advance its reform-driven agenda has been recorded in detail.[8] Yet it is a curious omission that, despite abundant literature on the rise of an elite stratum of lawyers in private practice in America, few attempts have been made to provide an in-depth analysis of these lawyers in one of America's most crucial periods.[9] One purpose of this book is to partially fill this void by concentrating on the response of the bar's elite practitioners to the New Deal. In speaking about these elite lawyers I have in mind what turned out to be a rather small but well-organized and coordinated group of corporate lawyers who ran some of the nation's biggest and most prosperous law firms and, concurrently, had considerable control over the collective activities of the bar due to their control of the bar's major associations. This elite, in short, both provided legal advice to the nation's leading corporations and business enterprises and presented itself as the voice of the legal profession as a whole.

In the New Deal, as we shall see, elite lawyers often found themselves in an awkward position. On the one hand, many understood that they were witnessing an era of new opportunities and new markets for legal services. It can be seen in retrospect that the New Deal created the modern law firm, with its highly specialized capabilities and a structure that resembled the structure of the corporations it represented. On the other hand, the New Deal frequently positioned lawyers in the role of an oppositional vanguard, not a typical position for a profession that is usually recognized for its prudence and conservatism. The literature that deals with the role of lawyers in the New Deal routinely treats them as a group of reactionaries whose overt hostility to the New Deal simply reflected the interests of their clients in resisting various legislative measures. A notable exception is Auerbach, who discussed the response of elite lawyers to the New Deal as part of his broader study of the history of the American legal profession. Auerbach noted that elite lawyers had their own distinct reasons to abhor some of the New Deal's tendencies. In particular, he emphasized the fact that the administration facilitated the emergence of a new counterelite of Jews, Catholics, and second-generation immigrants—heretofore generally excluded from the circles of Wall Street lawyers—who achieved positions of power and influence that they had never enjoyed before. Auerbach concluded, therefore, that xenophobia and ethnic considerations constituted part of the reason that elite lawyers often displayed outright hostility towards the New Deal. Yet even Auerbach routinely referred to the Wall Street lawyer as, first and foremost, a mouthpiece for capitalists.[10]

Let it be immediately said that I have no argument with the observation that corporate clients had a significant impact on the way lawyers shaped and articulated their response to the New Deal. The conception of corporate lawyers as hired guns who are by and large subservient to clients' expectations and needs is a powerful and well-founded view.[11] Yet it seems to me that an approach that attributes the practices of lawyers solely to the demands of clients risks an exaggerated reduction that fails to distinguish the role of lawyers in their diret capacity as legal counsel from their role *qua* professionals who are concerned with their own distinct interests. First, in their relations with clients, lawyers are sometimes able to shape the needs of clients and to define their horizon of expectations. Further, subservience to clients can hardly account for the fact that the activities of some lawyers in opposition to New Deal legislation far exceeded their strict obligations to clients. I will show that a network of prominent lawyers not only challenged New Deal legislation in courts and in Congress but also wrote articles in popular and professional publications, addressed numerous audiences, and mobilized the American Bar Association to produce reports and resolutions in which the legal philosophy of the New Deal was condemned. The readiness of some lawyers to engage in such public activities and to openly challenge an administration that enjoyed wide public support cannot be explained solely on grounds of representation functions.

In this study, therefore, I wish to complement the view of lawyers as servants with an approach that tries to avoid the pitfall of reductionism to which the former is prone. This approach is premised on the idea that law as knowledge is also a mechanism of social closure. The Weberian notion of social closure, says Parkin, refers to "the process by which social collectivities seek to maximize rewards by restricting access to resources and opportunities to a limited circle of eligibles."[12] In this respect, the claim of specialized knowledge and expertise is the principle by which professionals secure their own market advantages. In the case of lawyers, the discourse on law and within law constitutes the knowledge base of the profession. Law as knowledge allows its possessors to restrict entry into the profession, to insist on self-regulation, to consolidate relations with consumers, to develop a market monopoly, and to control the pace and direction of legal developments.[13] It is precisely the intersection of law as the language of the state and a currency of professional expertise that has to be taken into account in evaluating the fragile project of the formation of the distinct boundaries that are assumed by law's self-appointed guardians. And it is precisely the treatment of law as a professional currency that is often lacking in the analysis of the role of lawyers in the New Deal. The treatment of law as a medium and lawyers as the rather passive carriers of this medium resulted in a situation in which both the government lawyers who pushed the reform agenda of the state and the corporate lawyers who often tried to block it were at least implicitly assumed to be mere executioners, in spite of the recognition that lawyers' own views and methods shaped the fate of law. The challenge and the purpose, in other words, is to offer an analysis that takes into account the fact that the legal services that corporate lawyers offer are mediated through a legal field in which lawyers are positioned and to which they are linked through a complex web of institutional networks and normative assumptions. From the

point of view of the "field," as this book strives to show, the practices of
corporate lawyers in the New Deal are rendered more problematic, yet nonetheless more comprehensible, than the way in which they have so far been
portrayed.

The conception of professional work as the typical actions and ideas that are
produced and assumed in a given structured field—a legal or juridical field in
the present case—has been systematically developed by the French sociologist
Pierre Bourdieu.[14] The concept of the field captures the conditions of competition and conflict, yet at the same time cooperation and mutual dependence, to
which the various players in the field are subjected. Metaphorically, as Bourdieu's English translator has noted, the field is like a magnet, which exerts forces
of attraction and repulsion upon all those who come within its range.[15] The
idea of a field, in itself a metaphor, presupposes a pervasive set of ideas, norms,
procedures, and practices that, however unstable they might be, structure the
range of possibilities for the relevant actors within it and mark the boundaries
of their legitimate action. The field, in this sense, both constrains and enables
action; it is shaped by the practices of actors and at the same time gives shape
and meaning to various discursive and nondiscursive practices that are realized
within it. The theoretical value of the concept lies in the fact that it anchors
symbolic systems of meaning in the concrete practices of their carriers and,
consequently, articulates a blueprint for analyzing the way a given discourse is
produced within a social universe that has its own internal division of labor,
structured hierarchies, and differential positions. The interaction of ideas with
differential positions gives the concept the analytic ability to transcend the
often arbitrary separation between tracing the history of intellectual production and tracing the trajectory of those who produce knowledge. This analytic
framework, in other words, refuses the reduction of professional work to external interests that supposedly dictate the courses of action taken by the producers of knowledge and, at the same time, escapes the radical abstraction of
idealist approaches.

Bourdieu's description of the legal field posits that it is "the site of a competition for monopoly of the right to determine the law."[16] The imagery of the legal
field as a site of competition is based on the idea of an internal division of
juridical labor that potentially pits "sole practitioners against members of large
firms, or, on another level, the partisans of more scholarly approaches against
those favoring more 'practical' approaches to resolving legal issues."[17] Further,
the competition that the concept of the field presupposes is often directly
related to the process by which new ideas about law are generated, the boundaries of the field are constituted, and the content and scope of that symbolic

system of meaning *and* that symbolic capital we call law are determined. From this point of view, Bourdieu argues, the sociological analysis is also able to set itself free from jurisprudential debates about law that are cast in terms of formalism (which asserts the absolute autonomy of law) versus instrumentalism (which thinks of law as a tool in the service of dominant groups). Neither view, Bourdieu argues, adequately captures the significance of rooting these competing views in the context of the field. Both, in other words, commit the error of rendering the legal profession absent from the analysis of law. This point, as I will try to show, is particularly important in analyzing an era which is typically described as a "revolt against formalism"[18] on the one hand and as a struggle between legal experts in the service of different masters on the other. From the point of view of the field, however, the analysis should emphasize the interaction between ideas about law and the differential histories, positions, and tasks of various segments of the legal profession. The intellectual interest in a given worldview, in other words, is "always simultaneously an interest in the social struggles within the field."[19]

Consider, for example, the New Deal debates concerning the appropriate ways of interpreting the Constitution. Nathan Isaacs, of Harvard Law School, talked, in the terminology of the times, about a contest of interpretation between "verbalists" and "realists, or whatever they call themselves."[20] The former, he argued, strained words in their attempt to remain within the boundaries of the original intent of the Constitution's framers, while the latter, he complained, strained principles in their advocacy of the idea that the constitutional text should be given sufficient flexibility to respond to changing social conditions. This formulation may thus be easily grasped in terms of a debate between formalists and instrumentalists. Let us attempt to take this distinction a step further. Consider Foucault's discussion of disciplines and commentaries as two distinct ways of thinking of the Constitution as a source for "truth-to-be-invented" and for "truth-to-be-discovered," respectively. The treatment of a text as a basis for further elaborations, Foucault argues, is the organizing principle of "disciplinary discourse": "What is supposed at the point of departure is not some meaning which must be rediscovered, nor an identity to be reiterated; it is that which is required for the construction of new statements. For a discipline to exist, there must be the possibility of formulating—and of doing so ad infinitum—fresh propositions."[21] This principle, which comes remarkably close to the treatment of the Constitution as a text in flux, is opposed to the principle of commentary, which in turn fairly corresponds to a verbalist position. The commentary principle produces a discourse that retains a special type of relationship to the original text: "On the one hand, it permits us to create new discourses ad infinitum. . . . On the other hand, whatever the techniques employed, commentary's role is to say finally, what has silently been articulated deep down . . . it gives us the opportunity to say something other than the text itself, but on condition that it is the text itself which is uttered and, in some ways, finalised. . . . The novelty lies no longer in what is said, but in its reappearance."[22]

Foucault's treatment of these principles as representing different modes in which the *social organization* of a given discourse is assembled opens the door to what Bourdieu has in mind in articulating the concept of the field. Accordingly, the principle of commentary historically corresponds to a legal field organized around the authority of courts to look "backward" and offer authoritative readings of past precedents. As we shall see, it was around the dominance of courts in the field's internal hierarchy that lawyers in private practice constructed their own privileged professional standing and pursued their particular version of law as a science. The disciplinary principle, on the other hand, *at a particular historical juncture*, allowed legal academics to reformulate the boundaries of legal discourse and thereby to escape a perceived structural marginality within the legal field. This latter formulation requires a caveat: it is by no means an essentialist one. I do not argue for a necessary correspondence between interpretive flexibility and academic positions, and I do not suggest that all players who share similar positions in a given field necessarily hold similar views. The point is that we should try to identify contingent links between given structural positions and given discursive and nondiscursive practices that intersect and feed each other at a given point in time. With this hypothesis in mind, the analytic concept of the field provides potential solutions to some of the shortcomings of conventional jurisprudence, the sociology of law, and the sociology of the legal profession. It avoids on the one hand the underdetermination that results from reducing ideas about law to conditions external to the field and on the other the overdetermination that comes with the analysis of lawyers' conceptions of law as free-floating systems of ideas.

The concept of the field, in general, is in agreement with the variant in sociology that moved away from studies that, in spite of the early contributions by Weber, embraced the self-definitions of their objects of study and portrayed professions as collegial bodies of experts who used their expertise in order to solve society's problems and to advance the common good. In particular, the assertions of professional groups that social closure guaranteed impartial and effective systems of training and service, that professional work differed from mere commercial activities because of its altruistic nature and high ethical standards, and that the material and symbolic rewards accorded to professionals reflected the social affirmation of their value to society were largely accepted at face value in early studies.[23] Since the early 1970s, such studies have been criticized for neglecting explanations that indicated "that any given reward structure is the result of arrogation by groups with the power to secure their claims and create their own system of legitimation" and, in general, for ignoring the exlusionary dimension of professional practice and the mystification of professional knowledge that came with the carefully constructed distance between the expert and the client.[24] The "new" school of professionalism, in short, conceptualized professionalization as a process whereby some occupational groups were able to monopolize secured markets for their services and to pursue a status-seeking collective mobility project.[25] Accordingly, the collegial image that professions strove to present has also been challenged by new studies that expose the stratified organization of professional practice, the often conflict-ridden division of professional labor, the uneasy coalitions between various professional segments, and the enforced internal professional hierarchies that have resulted in an unequal distribution of professional rewards. In studies of the legal profession this approach notes, similarly to Bourdieu's model, the profound differences between various segments of the profession: city lawyers and rural lawyers, sole practitioners and lawyers in large law firms, partners and associates, self-employed lawyers and salaried lawyers, lawyers in private practice and lawyers in the service of the state, commercial lawyers and lawyers for a cause, legal practitioners and legal academics, and so on.[26]

In the 1980s, Richard Abel persuasively demonstrated the relevance of the new approach to empirical analyses of the American legal profession.[27] Carefully collecting and considering available data on lawyers, Abel follows Larson in asserting that the process of professionalization involves three basic mechanisms through which lawyers pursue a collective yet elite-biased project of market control and status enhancement: professional control over the production of producers, which aims at supervising the number, quality, and identity of new entrants to the profession; over the production by producers, which aims at securing established zones of practice, protecting them from external invasions, and autonomously regulating internal competition; and the creation of demand, which aims at ensuring an ongoing flow of legal "needs" that can be supplied by the ever-growing profession. It is in relation to this last element that the interaction between professional practices and law as a professional resource becomes particularly obvious. For whatever reasons, however, the effect of the ongoing need to generate demand by defining and redefining various problems and areas of practice as matters of the law is marginal to Abel's model. For example, Abel's discussion of the creation of demand mainly notes the attempts of lawyers to institutionalize the right to legal defense in criminal cases and to encourage state subsidies of legal aid to the indigent.[28] Yet the soundness of a market for legal services can hardly be secured by expanding it to low-income groups. The most lucrative and prestigious areas of legal practice are oriented toward the needs of corporations and wealthy individuals. It is the ability of lawyers to innovate in these areas that is crucial, as Nelson demonstrated in his study of big law firms, to maintaining market capacities.[29]

My point is, in short, that even some of the most advanced studies of the legal profession still display little effort to show how professional knowledge is developed and negotiated in the course of its manipulation as a professional resource. In the case of law this omission is particularly grave, because, as I previously argued, law is both the lawyers' currency of social closure and the means by which authorities regulate economic, political, and social relations.[30] It is here that Bourdieu's concept of the field seems to fill a gap and to overcome the unwarranted conceptual separation between lawyers' practices and the pace and direction of legal change. Following Bourdieu, I submit that a fusion between the study of law and the sociology of the legal profession is required. Philip Lewis poignantly articulated this conceptual necessity: "Much of what sociologists write about lawyers de-emphasizes the part they play in the legal system and that system's influence on them because it draws on bodies of thought that apply not just to lawyers but also to other occupations . . . Such approaches may be a healthy reaction to professional ideologies that regard the form and activities of the profession as entirely determined by the law and its demands. Yet, the critique may go too far. Where the legal system is significant in society, so may be the part lawyers play in it."[31] My purpose in this book, therefore, is to escape two pitfalls: that which reduces lawyers to mere hired guns and that which thinks of their role as being determined simply by abstract ideas. Rather than explaining the activities of corporate lawyers in the New Deal by reference to clients' demands, I look for structural homologies between the two. However, instead of describing the debates of the times in terms of struggles of ideas, I look for the correspondence between ideas and practices, always with a careful eye to the assumptions that are shared by otherwise warring factions within the legal field. The result, as we shall see throughout this book, is far from unambiguous. The combined focus on the internal dynamic of the legal field and on the external pressures by clients, politicians, and the popular mood ultimately produces an account that takes a considerable step away from the simple treatment of corporate lawyers as uncompromising challengers of the New Deal. Rather, my account tries to be sensitive to the dilemmas, inconsistencies, concerns, interests, and traditions that jointly produced what

I somewhat artificially describe as the response of corporate lawyers to the New Deal.

In chapter 2 I discuss the response of corporate lawyers to the enactment and subsequent implementation of the National Industrial Recovery Act of 1933. The act was one of the main pillars of the early New Deal and as such received wide attention from supporters and critics alike. An attempt to satisfy the demands of both capital and labor, the act ultimately failed on both counts and was eventually struck down by the Supreme Court as unconstitutional. I discuss the uneasy and often confused treatment of the act by corporate lawyers and argue that it reflects the complex set of pressures to which they had to respond: demands of clients, pleadings of politicians, public opinion, "scientific" legal ideas, and distinct concerns that had been bred by the particular location of corporate lawyers within the legal field.

In chapter 3 I discuss the efforts of lawyers to articulate a collective position on various New Deal measures and on the New Deal legislative program as a whole. My framework of analysis emphasizes what I label the "representation dilemma" of lawyers. In order to effectively serve clients and to establish their own reputations as professional experts who may legitimately take part in shaping public-policy decisions, lawyers must seek ways to symbolically distance themselves from the direct interests they represent. This chapter considers the degree to which lawyers succeeded in this project. I show that the representation functions of lawyers repeatedly frustrated their ability to defend their own vision of law, and that the various distancing mechanisms they employed in order to overcome their suspected position did not seem to have a significant effect. The particular episodes that I consider cast serious doubts on the ability of lawyers to invoke their professional expertise in order to command moral authority and shape public opinion.

In chapter 4 I analyze the events that followed the decision of the Supreme Court to strike down the National Industrial Recovery Act. Some of the administration's legal advisers responded to the decision by mounting a frontal attack on the Court's judicial prerogatives, and this attack in turn triggered a vigorous defense of judicial authority by the leaders of the organized bar. Having at their disposal the authoritative statements of the Court in its recent decision, many corporate lawyers confidently asserted the unconstitutionality of other New Deal measures as well and assertively commanded a critique of the New Deal's legal agenda in general. This chapter focuses on the efforts of corporate lawyers to promote a collective response to the New Deal and at the same time to firmly draw a line between law and politics. However, I show that these efforts were not based on a naive, formalist vision of law. Rather, they were generated by the understanding that the ability to retain the *symbolic* separation between these two universes of discourse was crucial for maintaining an aura of impartial expertise and for protecting the profession's social and economic privileges.

I end this part of the book with a short excursus in which the network of corporate lawyers who assumed the role of the profession's leaders is systematically located. I show that a rather limited group of senior partners in big urban corporate firms controlled the committees of the leading bar associations, cooperated in launching well-calculated attacks on specific laws, and orchestrated oral and written campaigns against what they perceived as the New Deal subversion of judicial authority.

In chapter 5 I discuss the response of lawyers to the rapid development of administrative regulatory practices. I analyze the administrative arena as a space where the dichotomy of law and politics was dissolved, thereby creating a boundary problem that triggered renewed struggles over the power and influence of lawyers. It is within this expanding space that I identify the conflicting interests and distinct concerns of various segments of the legal profession. The struggle over the fate of administrative practice pitted practitioners against academics, lawyers in private practice against lawyers in the service of the state, and solo practitioners against corporate law firms. In particular, I focus on the attempts of the leaders of the bar to block the expansion of the administrative process and to bring controversies back into the judicial system. I describe this campaign as part of the larger effort to redraw the boundaries between law and politics, and I argue that this drive was one of the major forces that shaped the policies of the bar in the New Deal. Chapter 5 is followed by a theoretical excursus that situates the case of lawyers and administrative law in the context of contemporary theories of the legal profession.

In chapter 6 I move from an analysis of the rhetoric and action of corporate lawyers to that of their declared "enemies," namely, government lawyers and legal academics who provided justifications for the administration's legal agenda. In previous chapters I discussed some of the typical inclinations and the general spirit of experimentation that characterized those legal experts who aligned themselves with President Roosevelt's administration. In this chapter I develop a more systematic evaluation of these tendencies and trace the relationship between the new ideas about law and the position of their carriers within the legal field. I submit that to describe the animosity between the bar's leaders and the emergent group of academic thinkers who advocated a new approach to law in terms of a struggle between liberals and conservatives—that is, in terms of external idea-shaping forces—would miss the degree to which reform-minded attitudes on the one hand and attachments to the status quo on the other hand had their own dynamic and sources within the legal field. The purpose of this chapter, therefore, is to consider the new body of thought as it was embedded, determined, and expressed in concrete practices. Specifically, I focus my attention not only on the widely recognized *instrumental* connection between the so-called academic legal realists and the New Deal's administration but also on the *conceptual* bond that linked the two together.

Chapter 7, the final chapter, is written not as a summary and conclusion but as an attempt to elaborate on various theoretical issues touched upon throughout the book. In particular, I further develop and offer a suggested theoretical framework for considering the question of law and politics, the theme of law's autonomy, and the class- and state-centered treatments of law and lawyers. However, I do bring to conclusion here one of the central theses of this book: To the extent that corporate lawyers acted as a capitalist vanguard, they did so by defending their own perceived autonomous domain and not because they necessarily embraced the particular values of their clients. It was the structural bias of this self-conceived autonomous system of law, and not substantive ideological inclinations, that created the bond between laissez-faire capitalism and the court-centered legal system that I discuss in this work. Corporate lawyers, tied to their representation functions, adhered to a unifying professional paradigm that served them in the double capacity of consolidating their privileged role as experts and of securing their own privileged position within the legal field. I also conclude that academic legal realists, who were free from representation functions, indeed transcended the boundaries of the unifying paradigm of the field. However, my point is that the transgression of the unifying paradigm was not necessarily a result of a principled dissatisfaction with the social order in general. Rather, it was first and foremost an expression of a certain sense of blocked opportunities that legal academics experienced under a unifying paradigm that marginalized the role of academic experts within the legal field. On the basis of these formulations I conclude the work with a broad outline of the processes of convergence that ultimately keep ardent adversaries within the boundaries of a shared legal field.

2 Subservience to $18,000 Functionaries: Lawyers and the National Industrial Recovery Act

Introductory Note

How do lawyers respond to a major piece of legislation which is, on the one hand, constitutionally doubtful and, on the other hand, enjoys wide public support and the at least silent approval of their clients? How, in other words, do lawyers resolve the tension between what they perceive as an "anti-lawyers anti-law" law and what they perceive as both a popular and a business-backed statute? By way of exploring this terrain, this chapter seeks to describe the hesitant, incoherent, and tactically restrained response of lawyers to the 1933 National Industrial Recovery Act (NIRA).

The NIRA was the central pillar of the early New Deal. Enacted in June 1933 and declared unconstitutional by the Supreme Court in 1935, the statute sought to enhance economic recovery by increasing the public's purchasing power and by imposing some measure of control over conditions of production and commerce. The underlying economic philosophy of the NIRA was that the depression was a result of cutthroat competition in industry and commerce. In order to correct the evil, the act provided for the creation of business "codes of fair competition" to be promulgated by trade associations and industrial groups and brokered by the administration. Further, the NIRA recognized the right of labor to organize and bargain collectively with employers and in exchange offered business a considerable relaxation of antitrust legislation.[1] Thus embodying a corporatist approach to economic recovery, competing interest groups could look to the NIRA to safeguard some of their long-sought objectives.[2]

The NIRA as an Unconstitutional Law

The most striking fact about the NIRA was that even its drafters and staunchest supporters did not believe that it could survive a constitutional test. It was passed with the implicit understanding among the administration's senior legal advisers that since it would be in effect only two years, judicial review by the

Supreme Court might be avoided. Two prominent government lawyers, Donald Richberg, the general counsel of the National Recovery Administration (NRA), which had been created by the act, and Homer Cummings, the United States attorney general, were so convinced that the NIRA was unconstitutional that the former constantly attempted to avoid judicial review and the latter refused to defend it before the Supreme Court.[3]

Felix Frankfurter, at the time a law professor at Harvard and one of President Roosevelt's most trusted advisers, also harbored grave doubts about the ability of the NIRA to successfully pass the Court's judicial review. In fact, it seems that constitutional doubts were nowhere "greater than among the lawyers who looked for Frankfurter for leadership."[4] Charles Wyzanski, one of the NIRA's drafters, wrote Frankfurter that the codemaking process went "so far beyond the bounds of constitutionality that it would be useless" to test it in the courts.[5] Frankfurter, however, was determined "to lend his best support" to the NIRA and urged the NRA to avoid tests on constitutionality while the statute was tried, amended, and modified in the course of its administration.[6] The decision to go about with a plan perceived to be unconstitutional was thus based on a tacit understanding that in order to enhance recovery one had to operate, at least to some extent, outside the established boundaries of constitutional discourse.

Constitutional doubts were also evident in the way New Dealers articulated their public defense of the act. In general, the NIRA could be challenged or defended on the basis of three constitutional considerations: delegation of legislative power, the commerce clause, and the due process clause.[7] Yet most defenders did not try to establish a solid constitutional defense of the act on these bases. Instead, the defense of the act rested on a "state of emergency" reasoning, according to which hard times required extraordinary measures. The unavoidable result of this line of reasoning, as Thurman Arnold aptly observed, was that the supporters of the NIRA developed an "unconstitutional habit of thought about constitutional issues."[8]

Milton Handler, for example, wrote an early defense of the NIRA in the August 1933 issue of the *American Bar Association Journal*: "Candor demands the admission," wrote Handler, "that for the statute . . . to be sustained . . . requires a change of attitude on the part of the Supreme Court no less revolutionary than the law itself."[9] Yet the "doubtful features of the new law" could be justified on grounds of emergency: "Unprecedented conditions required unprecedented action. The emergency created a mist in which the familiar contours of the landmarks of constitutional decision seemed blurred or even lost."[10] Charles E. Clark, who also admitted the NIRA's constitutional flaws, took his arguments a step further and "advised" the Court not to "take the responsibility of wiping it out of existence."[11] The Court, Clark argued, should not pass judgment on the NIRA because it was "not in a position to exercise leadership in an economic and social emergency."[12]

Other defenders of the law coupled the general state of economic emergency with political rhetoric that justified the NIRA as a defensive measure against a communist revolution. David Podell, one of the NIRA's drafters, addressed the American Bar Association's Committee on Commerce and explained that "a year ago the grave danger and the real source of danger to our national economy lay in the fact that our legitimate labor organizations were being by degrees demoralized and the Communistic groups and Red agitators and Left Wingers were eating into the very heart of these organizations. . . . The labor provisions of the law, he explained, were designed to 'revitalize the legitimate labor organization.' "[13] Donald Richberg, the general counsel of the NIRA, which oversaw the administration of the NIRA, addressed the New York State Bar Association and painted a particularly grim picture: "Those who delight in meaningless distinctions between the power to prevent, and the power to deal with, a catastrophe may argue that until millions of revolutionaries were on the march, and blood had flowed copiously in the streets of many cities, there would be no legal justification for the exercise of federal authority."[14]

Very few New Deal supporters, therefore, embarked on a straightforward legal defense of the NIRA's constitutionality.[15] One exception was Thurman Arnold's "The New Deal Is Constitutional," which exposed the intellectual fragility of arguments that rested on emergency reasoning. Radicals, liberals, and conservatives alike, according to Arnold, were trapped in an unsound habit of thought: thinking of the Constitution as a text that fundamentally prevented social change and assuming that the only justification for departing from the constitutional straitjacket required the vague basis of self-defense in time of danger, analogous to the powers of the government in time of war. Arnold, in contrast, sought to demonstrate that the Supreme Court was well equipped to articulate constitutional constructions in accord with the new legislation. Turning the constitutional debate upside down, Arnold argued that "no actual dilemma between logic and expediency faces the Supreme Court if it supports the government. The fact is that the logic of the cases is in favor of the recent legislation, that new doctrine and new terminology are necessary only if the acts are held unconstitutional, and that resort to economics and sociology is required only of those who oppose the legislation."[16]

In other words, Arnold understood the internal contradictions that characterized the defense of the NIRA. On the one hand, many of the academics and government lawyers who defended the law were associated, or at least identified, with a legal-realist approach that emphasized the flexibility and uncertainty of law in general and the Constitution in particular. On the other hand, when confronted by concrete legislation, they struggled to situate it within the framework of established constitutional doctrines, or, alternatively, adopted a defensive posture that avoided direct confrontation with these established doctrines. These contradictions, as we shall see, surfaced again in the response to the *Schechter* decision of the Supreme Court and, to some extent, in the response to the constitutional attack on the National Labor Relations Act. Arnold's, at any rate, remained an almost isolated voice. The NIRA, even in the eyes of those who supported the "experiment," raised severe constitutional problems.

Explicit Opposition

The administration's legal advisers thus provided lawyers in private practice with ample ammunition should they wish to launch a full-scale attack on the NIRA in the name of the Constitution and the rule of law. Further, lawyers in private practice had very good reasons to oppose the act, not only because of its doubtful constitutionality but also because, on a more concrete level, the NIRA had been designed as an "anti-lawyers" law. The NRA was probably the most far-reaching and complex administrative agency the American system of government had heretofore known. It was responsible for sponsoring codes and agreements, formulating basic codes of fair competition, interpreting existing codes, and issuing compliance regulations. In these capacities, the NRA was invested with the authority to hold hearings on negotiated codes, to approve codes, to allow changes in approved codes, and to formulate procedural rules that governed its own activity.[17]

From a lawyer's perspective, the administrative features of the act were very troublesome. The NRA's sweeping discretionary powers were explicitly designed to avoid legalistic methods and to escape judicial review. Its explicit policy was to discourage the participation of lawyers in negotiations over codes of fair competition and to insist on the nonlegalistic character of the NRA's hearings. Richberg outlined this philosophy on the eve of the first hearing of the cotton textile code: "These [public hearings] are not judicial investigations nor, strictly speaking, legislative investigations, but rather in the nature of administrative inquiries for the purpose of adequately advising the administration of the NRA of the facts upon which the exercise of administrative authority must be predicated. . . . No representative of a private interest favoring or opposing a code has any legal right to control or direct the presentation of evidence or the procedure in a public hearing. . . . These hearings will not be appropriate for the presentation of arguments upon issues of law." [18]

The NRA hearings and code-drafting processes were described in terms of a "forum for co-operation," where adversarial approaches and legalistic arguments were not only unnecessary but also undesired. Accordingly, the procedures of the NRA strongly stated that "although the employer may be represented by counsel, if he so desires, there is no necessity for this," and Hugh Johnson, the NRA's outspoken director, simply advised businessmen to "leave their attorneys at home." [19] Thus, while there were some indications that these administrative methods pleased businessmen, they were certainly offensive to lawyers. If the NIRA symbolized the new administration's disregard for established constitutional principles, the NRA, with its lack of judicial review procedures and combined legislative and judicial functions, symbolized the administration's systematic subversion of the "autonomy of law," at least as elite lawyers came to think of this term.

The NIRA, therefore, did invite some biting criticism. Some lawyers complained that in the name of emergency the Constitution was "set aside, relegated, abrogated, forgotten" and that the NRA functioned as a "virtual dictatorship." [20] The most direct and unequivocal critique came from James Beck, a prominent constitutional lawyer and a delegate in the House of Representatives, who dismissed the emergency doctrine altogether: "Of all constitutional heresies, the worst . . . is the theory that in case of emergency the Constitution is non-existent for the time being. The doctrine has been the wooden horse, under cover of which the citadel of the Constitution has been taken." [21] Beck argued that the NIRA offended "both the letter and the spirit of the entire Constitution" and described it as another "climax" in the "pernicious heresy of transferring the legislative power of the nation to executive officials, with little or no possibility of judicial review." [22]

Some lawyers, in short, did attack the NIRA as an unconstitutional law, and more intensely so as the New Deal itself seemed to have cured some of the "emergency conditions" of 1933. [23] Nevertheless, many lawyers were conspicuously prudent in attacking the constitutionality of the law. Committees of bar associations, in particular, tended to treat the NIRA as a law that raised "economic and social" issues and not necessarily legal ones. [24] The Report of the Committee on Federal Legislation of the Association of the Bar of the City of New York doubted the profession's competence to discuss the NIRA and other pending bills: "The Committee has in the main refrained from expressing any opinion upon the questions of social and economic policy involved in pending legislation and has confined itself to matters as to which it may be supposed that members of the legal profession have an especial competence. For this reason no action was taken as to many of the bills considered by the Committee."[25]

One prominent New York lawyer who was asked to discuss the NIRA declared that he preferred to speak only about the general "tendencies" of the administration's legislative agenda, explaining that "this is not my subject, nor is this the time or the occasion, for partisanship."[26] Orie Phillips adopted a similar tone: "I yield to no one in my admiration of the president for his courage, lofty idealism, humanitarianism, and his broad sympathy," Phillips said, adding, "I do not mean that, as an organization of lawyers, we should enter the field of partisan controversy. I mean that as lawyers we should stand as sentinels to guard against assaults . . . upon our free institutions."[27]

The profession's "especial competence" was felt to involve primarily a focus on the NIRA's administrative aspects. Holding firm to the argument that theirs was not a political but a professional perspective, lawyers developed their critique of the NIRA by distinguishing between the act's substantive provisions and its administrative features. The bar's leaders complained about the NRA's informal procedures, its disregard for judicial methods, and its general hostility to adversarial processes. One lawyer apparently spoke for many when he complained that the NRA's hearings were "far from being the character of hearings to which the American people are accustomed," while others lamented the "tyrannical" whims of the NRA's bureaucratic officers.[28] Others focused on the "legal uncertainty" that had been bred by the numerous regulations that the NRA issued: The New York State Bar Association's report on the NIRA, for example, contemptuously described an "apostolic succession" of "functionaries" who erected a "maze of administrative regulations."[29]

It seems that by separating the administrative features of the law from its political and *constitutional* aspects, many lawyers hoped to retain the distinction between law and politics. The ability to retain this separation was particularly important in the case of a law that had both popular support and the tacit approval of the nation's leading commercial groups. As we shall see, however, the focus on the administrative features of the law also reflected the pervasive sentiment among many lawyers that the rapidly expanding administrative field threatened their own professional prerogatives. In this sense, the NIRA created a dilemma: how to respond to a law that clients had little incentive to challenge but that elite lawyers had both ideological and practical reasons to resist? In what follows, I will try to systematically outline the pressures and forces to which lawyers had to respond in articulating their expert opinions on the law.

In general, in spite of all the mounting evidence that the NIRA threatened established legal principles and practices, the opposition of lawyers to the NIRA on grounds of its administrative and constitutional shortcomings had not been played wholeheartedly. Criticizing the NIRA involved a rather complex maneuvering among various conflicting considerations. Three major factors, in particular, have to be considered in evaluating the response of elite lawyers to the enactment of the NIRA: the wide support it enjoyed among leading commercial and industrial groups, the uncertainty concerning the way the Supreme Court would eventually treat this constitutionally doubtful law, and the administration's justification of the act in the name of national emergency. These factors, as we shall see, worked against the inclination to exhibit an outright hostility to the law and led many lawyers and bar associations to couple principled support for the substantive ideas embodied in the act with reservations about its legalistic shortcomings.

Lawyers Respond I: Coping with a Probusiness Measure

In contrast to many other New Deal laws, the NIRA enjoyed wide support among strong commercial and industrial groups. Not only did the NIRA relax antitrust legislation, but it also created favorable conditions for the more powerful and better-organized parties within each given industry or trade by providing them considerable leeway in shaping the codes of fair competition to their own advantage. In this regard, while the financial legislation of the New Deal was designed to curb the "curse of bigness," the NIRA had the opposite effect.[30] In fact, Gerald Swope, the general manager of General Electric, and Henry Harriman, who headed the United States Chamber of Commerce, were largely responsible for the NIRA's idea of "industrial self-government."[31] Swope and Harriman, backed by other influential business leaders, prepared the business community to recognize the bill's merits even before its final enactment. The U.S. Chamber of Commerce (COC) was swept by Harriman's advocacy of the act and expressed explicit support in favor of governmental intervention in the economy. Thus, after hearing an address by P. W. Litchfield, the president of Goodyear, who argued that traditional freedoms could only be maintained by the elimination of destructive competition and by concessions to what used to be regarded as a "radical school of thought," members of the COC responded by saying that the central administration was needed for "aid and guidance" in the crisis.[32] Similar preparations took place in numerous other business forums; for example, a day after Gerald Swope and J. S. Tritle, the general manager of Westinghouse, addressed the policies division of the National Electrical Manufacturers Association (NEMA) and praised the NIRA, NEMA became the first large industrial group to express its joint public support for the act.[33]

Trade groups all over the country were reported to hail the NIRA and to seek its rapid enactment.[34] Raymond L. Collier, the managing director of the Steel Founders Society of America, was quoted as saying that the NIRA represented "an advanced step in social evolution heralded by manufacturers, labor and the informed public as logical, workable and inevitable," and Axel J. Bayles, the president of the American Petroleum Institute, announced that NIRA "may save the country from a social revolution."[35] Even the influential National Association of Manufacturers (NAM), headed by Robert L. Lund, announced its principled support of the NIRA. Lund said that the measure required some revisions and specifically opposed the act's public-works program and its licensing and labor provisions. On the whole, however, he stated that the purpose of the NIRA enjoyed the support of the NAM's fifty-six thousand manufacturers.[36] Eventually, NAM was the only significant group to oppose the NIRA before the Senate House and Means Committee, which held hearings on the bill before it became law. James A. Emery, NAM's general counsel, attacked the bill's constitutionality and raised specific objections to some of its provisions. Yet even NAM's opposition was not played wholeheartedly. Emery assured the Senate committee that NAM agreed with the aim and tasks set forth by NIRA and simply qualified NAM's support for the bill by demanding that NIRA invoke the embargo as a means to curtail imports, and that the NRA be headed by an advisory board rather than a single administrator.[37] In any case, NAM's opposition represented the only significant voice against NIRA in the early days of the law.

True, support for NIRA tended to diminish throughout 1934, when many businesses regained their financial stability. Small industries and local manufacturers found it hard to cope with the codes, and some of the big industries had by that time turned against NIRA's labor provisions. Yet the struggle against these provisions should not be confused with a total resentment of the act.[38] In June 1934, a survey in *Fortune Magazine* still found that 70 percent of big-business leaders supported NIRA.[39] Jouett Shouse, the president of the American Liberty League, which was probably the strongest and certainly the most vocal group to oppose the administration's policies, was also careful in its critique of the NRA. On the one hand, he commented that "the NRA has indulged in unwarranted excesses of attempted regulation"; on the other, he added that "in many regards [the NRA] has served a useful purpose."[40] Further, there are no indications whatsoever that the corporate bar had been seriously mobilized by clients against NIRA. An analysis of NIRA-related litigation shows that the overwhelming burden of challenging the constitutionality of the act was assumed by solo practitioners and small law firms that represented small businesses, and that, in contrast, major law firms, with the notable exception of challenging the labor provisions of the law, were not involved in challenging the act in court.[41]

Given the support of many influential business leaders, it is not very surprising that many lawyers lent the act at least qualified support. The Trade and
Commerce Bar Association, a group that included a number of prominent
corporate lawyers, fully endorsed the idea of business self-government and the
relaxation of the antitrust laws. The trade and commerce group further suggested some amendments that would have allowed an even greater opportunity
to fully realize the relaxation of antitrust legislation; otherwise, a report of the
group stated, it was doubtful whether "the scope of the proposed bill [was]
broad enough to accomplish its purposes."[42]

Commercial and industrial interests in the relaxation of antitrust legislation
and in infusing some measure of industrial peace into the economy also seemed
to have shaped the attitude of the Commerce Committee of the American Bar
Association (ABA). The committee, chaired by Rush C. Butler, had its own
program of "economic recovery" prior to the passage of NIRA. In principle, if
not in detail, it included elements that were later incorporated into NIRA. The
Commerce Committee's proposals, which were hailed as "a new constitution
for industry," provided for collective agreements between labor and industry
that would be enforceable in courts, and for the establishment of a Federal
Industrial Council, which would consider "problems arising from the relationship of capital and labor."[43] In an attempt to catch up with events, Butler wrote
the executive secretary of the American Bar Association that since Roosevelt
was under pressure from strong groups of industrial leaders to relax the antitrust laws, "it is now quite apparent that substantive amendments [to the
antitrust laws] will undoubtedly be necessary if the President includes this
subject in his program of legislation for the present session of Congress. The
Committee has prepared a bill intended to be in effect only during the existence
of the present emergency, which by indirection permits fixing prices. Under
existing conditions this is a purely innocuous provision but is essential in the
carrying out of any emergency program."[44]

Consequently, the 1933 report of the ABA's Commerce Committee explained
that the NIRA "meets with the approval of substantial organizations of industry . . . and gives effect to every recommendation made during recent years by
the Commerce Committee." The report, however, also contained a few statements that revealed, in a subdued tone, a certain ambivalence. It greeted with
anticipation the new legal work and tasks that lawyers would assume under the
law: "It will be the duty as well as the privilege of lawyers," the report stated, "to
advise their clients as to how they may soundly proceed in the enjoyment of the
benefits the new statute confers." However, the report reminded lawyers that
"the complaint that government is in business cannot longer be heard to fall
from the lips of business men," and that "were it not for the existence of the

Sherman law this act in its entirety would be unnecessary." The sources of the ambivalence were stated in a very restrained manner: first, the report mentioned the "constitutional doubts" that surrounded the act and concluded that it could be sustained only on grounds of its being "an emergency measure"; second, and perhaps more important, the report anticipated what would become a cornerstone of concern for the bar's elite. Under the law, it warned, "it will be difficult for the administrative agency to deny to itself the exercise of the extreme powers conferred upon it."[45] The administrative features of the law, as mentioned earlier, were thus regarded with alarm and suspicion by the very same lawyers whose clients supported the act.[46]

Another indication of this ambivalence was apparent in the words of Francis E. Neagle, the legal counsel of the National Electrical Manufacturers Association. From the perspective of business, Neagle said, the law was "delightfully vague" and allowed business groups to do many things that might have been banned otherwise. Yet this vagueness, he warned, could be a double-edged sword: "The theory of the bill is to allow industry to govern itself . . . if industry fails to govern itself the government will not fail. If we do not regulate our own industry, government will regulate it for us . . . if we do not think for ourselves, maybe a dollar-a-year man or an $18000-dollar-a-year clerk will do the thinking for the electrical industry . . . here is an opportunity to do the things the lawyers said you could not do. You are now forced to do them."[47]

Worse still, he said, NIRA was a "revolutionary" act that was "absolutely unconstitutional"; the only way to uphold it, according to Neagle, was to treat it as an emergency measure enacted under the wartime powers of the government. This ambivalence reflected the understanding, shared by many elite lawyers, that the NIRA represented a mixed blessing. On the one hand, it provided their major corporate clients with long-sought relief from antitrust legislation and provided lawyers from all ranks with considerable new legal work. On the other hand, the NIRA was perceived as an unconstitutional measure and, worse still, as one law among many at the time that created a "lawyer-unfriendly" administrative mechanism.[48]

Lawyers Respond II: Coping with Emergency

Perhaps the most striking testimony to the effect of the administration's emergency rhetoric was the qualified support granted the NIRA by the American Liberty League.[49] Jouett Shouse, the president of the American Liberty League, wrote: "With [NIRA's] social objectives . . . I have deep sympathy. And while I feel very strongly that the prohibition of child labor, the maintenance of a minimum wage and the limitation of the hours of work belong under our form of government in the realm of the affairs of the different states, yet I am entirely willing to agree that in the case of an overwhelming national emergency the Federal Government for a limited period should be permitted to assume jurisdiction of them."[50] Bainbridge Colby, a former secretary of state who joined the American Liberty League, wrote that he agreed with Milton Handler: In times of emergency, in spite of constitutional difficulties, the duty of the lawyer was "to reveal once more the inherent flexibility of our Constitution."[51] Indeed, many lawyers and state bar associations enthusiastically responded to the patriotic duties called for by the emergency rationale of the NIRA. Not unlike the historical response of lawyers to patriotic defense of the nation in times of war, many lawyers eagerly adopted the attitude that the administration conveyed in regard to the depression, namely, that the American public should treat it as an economic war.[52] The link between the state of emergency and the patriotic duties of lawyers was clearly established by John Parker, a United States Circuit Court of Appeals judge. Parker, addressing the General Assembly of the American Bar Association at its 1933 annual meeting, explained that an "unprecedented situation" like the present state of emergency justified radical means:

> We must not forget that it is in times like these that the enemies of our institutions get in their most effective work. All true Americans, whether members of the dominant party or the opposition, find in any national danger or emergency an added cause for supporting our institutions with the utmost loyalty. Enemies of our institutions take advantage of such situations to make their most determined attacks. It is no mere coincidence that those who in the time of the world war were notorious for lack of patriotism are now loudest in proclaiming that the American government and the American civilization have failed and that the time has come for the adoption of socialism, communism, fascism or some other "isms" so dear to their hearts. It is against their efforts that we must be on guard; and the duty of guardianship rests with peculiar force upon the lawyers of America.[53]

Some lawyers took notice and responded with strong rhetoric. The Mississippi State Bar Association, for example, unanimously adopted a resolution promising "one hundred percent co-operation" with the new administration and its recovery laws:

> Being conscious of the national crisis and with a desire to serve our country at this time and without the purpose of retarding but rather the

humble purpose of serving the general welfare of the State of Mississippi and the nation; And whereas we are in full accord with the President's efforts to bring our country out of the present chaotic condition and to further his effort we hereby direct that the following telegram to be sent to the President of the United States: "To President Franklin D. Roosevelt: The Mississippi State Bar is now in session and we as a body and individually want you to know that the Members of the Mississippi State Bar are in full accord with your National Recovery Act."[54]

The annual address of Joseph Barksdale, the president of the Louisiana State Bar Association, contained unqualified support for Roosevelt's policies: "Let us as a profession do everything in our power to help the President put into effect and carry out the National Recovery Act, everything we can to sustain his stalwart faith in the American people." William Fitzgerald, the president of the Pennsylvania Bar Association, endorsed the self-regulatory philosophy of the NIRA as being in line with "much that is being attempted in that direction at Washington today." An editorial in the *Oklahoma State Bar Journal* called upon the members of the bar to be "ever ready to assist their country" and reminded them that "it is just as necessary to be patriotic in times of peace as in times of war." Peter Nyce cited a judicial opinion that argued that "it is thought that the Constitution and all other laws must be read in light of, and, to some extent, subject to, the primal and fundamental concept of the necessity of self preservation." James Cross argued that the purpose that NIRA set out to accomplish should be considered in light of the state of emergency which justified a departure from "ordinary" judicial interpretation: " 'A vital test is whether the statute under consideration has a reasonable relation to the mischief sought to be remedied. . . . The ultimate legal test is whether the end is legitimate and the means reasonably adapted to that end.' He concluded by saying that the courts 'should take a liberal view of constitutional power in this emergency.' "[55]

Other lawyers described the recovery legislation as a "war against the depression." Admitting that a judicial affirmation of NIRA required a reversal of previous decisions, one lawyer reviewed the history of court decisions in times of emergency and concluded that "if the Supreme Court accepts the declaration of Congress and the President that a national emergency exists, in view of previous decisions, sanction may be given to the Recovery Act on the ground that it is a measure upon which the prosperity of the nation in large measure depends."[56] And another lawyer said that "this is a time of war, a time when the fate of civilization hangs in the balance as much as it did when the cannons roared from the Alps to the Baltic . . . and the rights and property of the few must yield to the salvation of the millions."[57]

In sum, the tendency of many lawyers was to succumb to the rhetoric of emergency and to suspend, at least temporarily, whatever misgivings they might have had. Clarence Martin, the president of the American Bar Association, captured this spirit of compliance in the midst of a general apprehension about the nature and purpose of the recovery laws. Discussing the growing wave of New Deal legislation, he concluded that a state of emergency justified putting "ends before means": "In the absence of court decisions, which are probable, it would be unfair, as well as impolitic, at this moment, to argue or attempt a determination of the constitutional questions involved in, and the legal effect of, this legislation. Eliminating these matters, as a temporary expedient, it should have the support of this association."[58]

Many lawyers adopted the emergency rationale that government lawyers used to justify the enactment of the NIRA. The perceived state of emergency and its unavoidable link to the patriotic duties of the profession was another major factor that circumscribed the "professional" tendency to criticize the law. So great was this subservience to the emergency rhetoric of the times that Donald Richberg, the general counsel of the NRA, declared that "the response of the legal profession to this recovery effort has been most inspiring. The toast of the American bar today is quite properly: 'NIRA—My Code to thee!' "[59]

Lawyers Respond III: Coping with Judicial Uncertainty

One more major factor contributed to the unwillingness of many lawyers to criticize the NIRA: many prominent lawyers and potential challengers of the NIRA believed that the Supreme Court would uphold the act in spite of its constitutional flaws. Simply, many lawyers believed that the Supreme Court would succumb to the force of public opinion and to the sometimes aggressive rhetoric of the NIRA's supporters. Indeed, some of the administration's supporters in academia and a number of government lawyers indirectly and implicitly exerted some public pressure on the Court. Wesley Sturges of Yale, for example, admitted the NIRA's constitutional difficulties yet emphasized the wide support it enjoyed. On these grounds, he posed a challenging question: "Would the Supreme Court *dare* to hold so pervasive legislation invalid in any substantial respect?"[60] Patrick O'Brien, the attorney general of Michigan, responded: "No court," he declared, "will be allowed to stand in the path of progress . . . The NIRA offends against all of the cherished constitutional maxims." Yet he asked defiantly: "Where is the court that will attempt to mutiny? Where is the court that will attempt by injunction to scuttle the ship?"[61] Charles Clark, as previously mentioned, had an answer: the Supreme Court should not intervene in "economic" matters and would therefore decide in favor of the NIRA.[62]

The belief that the Supreme Court would uphold the NIRA was reinforced by some of the Court's recent decisions. The decision of the Court in the 1933 Appalachian Coal case signaled the readiness of the Court to relax antitrust legislation in times of "deplorable" industrial conditions. In the 1934 Nebbia case, the Court upheld state legislation that regulated and fixed the price of milk, resolving that "upon proper occasion and by appropriate measures the state may regulate a business in any of its aspects, including the prices to be charged for the products or commodities it sells." Finally, in the 1934 Minnesota Moratorium case, the Court upheld the constitutionality of a law that extended the period of exemption from foreclosure of mortgages on real estate on grounds of emergency conditions. This latter decision, in particular, was interpreted as foreshadowing the position the Supreme Court would adopt in passing on the validity of the NIRA.[63] The confidence that some government lawyers expressed, the belief that the Supreme Court would not dare to challenge the administration and disregard public opinion, and the recent decisions that had been interpreted as a sign that the Court would be responsive to the emergency rhetoric thus produced a pervasive sense of constitutional uncertainty among many lawyers. Esteemed jurists admitted that to predict the fate of the NIRA required guesswork. Guesswork was indeed the name of the game, as numerous articles in professional publications and the news media analyzed the personalities of the justices, surveyed past decisions, and counted the various political, psychological, and economic pressures to which the Court would have to respond.

However, the bar's leaders and various organs of the bar, even those who were openly critical of the NIRA, reluctantly agreed that extralegal considerations and the emergency rhetoric that had been effectively invoked by the administration's advisers would probably decide the case. The American Bar Association's Committee on Noteworthy Changes in Statute observed that "the legislatures which passed these acts, fearful of their constitutionality, have regularly provided them with the armor of emergency, and there is little doubt that the reality of emergency will be recognized."[64] And Maurice Finkelstein, of St. John's Law School, wrote that "many of the provisions of the legislation seem to go clearly against the weight of accumulated judicial precedents and policy—and yet such is the constellation of political forces that the Supreme Court will find itself powerless to arrest the disputed legislation," especially if "the New Deal continues to command its present popular support."[65]

Orville Rush, a practitioner writing for the *Mississippi Bar Law Journal,* complained that "recent decisions of the Supreme Court show that the Justices are ready to abandon, in some degree at least, traditional ways of doing business, and that ways of interpreting the constitution will be found, to make the change constitutional." Soberly discussing the "freedom of choice" that "a century and a half of discussion and decision have made available" to the Court, Rush concluded that "the trend of public opinion and the tremendous influence Mr. Roosevelt commands can cause the judicial process of the Supreme Court to become merely a form of submission to the current drift. Some of the present members of the Supreme Court are usually so attuned psychologically that they cannot see the hidden danger until it is too late to avert it."[66]

In his address to the California State Bar, Chester Rowell, a San Francisco lawyer, lamented the expected course that the Supreme Court was likely to take: "I do not need to cite articles and sections of the constitution, nor familiar decisions of the Supreme Court, to point out how at variance with a long line of precedents all these new federal powers appear on their face to be." Still, he admitted that "except in narrowly legalistic circles like this, the expectation is almost unanimous that the court will—indeed must—find a way to sustain these laws. . . . It is freely predicted that if the court should decide against them, *Congress would authorize an increase in the size of the court,* so that the president could pack it with enough members pledged to vote the other way to reverse the decision. . . . I have met almost no laymen, and comparatively few lawyers, who doubt that the Supreme Court will . . . 'follow the election returns' " (italics mine).[67] The Supreme Court, Rowell concluded, "confronted by a practical emergency in which any other course would be disastrous, should find it necessary to make some of these changes by a more elastic interpretation of the Constitution that has ever been made before."[68]

Henry Caulfield, who viewed the NIRA as part of a destructive unconstitutional legislative trend, nonetheless noted that the fate of the Constitution depended on "five men constituting a majority of the Supreme Court of the United States—five men and public opinion. Public opinion is the final arbiter of it all . . . the courts are themselves affected by that opinion."[69] And James Beck, who repeatedly expressed the opinion that the NIRA was flagrantly unconstitutional, seems to have thought that the Supreme Court would uphold the law. Having to pass judgment on this "clear violation of the Constitution," Beck argued, the Court would be "in a position of unparalleled embarrassment," especially if the economic results of the law could be shown to be "the salvation of the American people." The uncertainty surrounding the fate of the act, however, was reflected in Beck's hesitant conclusion that the Court "would approach this grave judicial inquiry with the resolute purpose of sustaining the statute, if it could in any reasonable way be reconciled with the Constitution—not only because such has been its uniform policy but because in the present matter the economic crisis which inspired this legislation would predispose the Court to sustain the declared will of Congress if it could be done without a clear violation of the Constitution. . . . The ways of the Supreme Court are . . . mysterious and past finding out . . . Why should we guess, when we may soon find out?"[70]

Thus, despite their independent judgment that the NIRA was unconstitutional by traditional standards or, to say the least, in some transcendental sense, the leaders of the bar were ambivalent and cautious because they also accepted the fact that in the final analysis, if the Court upheld it, the NIRA would *become* constitutional. Of course, the reluctance of clients to challenge the act and the emergency conditions that prevailed had also contributed their share. But it seems to me that the reluctance of lawyers to launch a frontal attack on the NIRA in various public forums also reflected their desire to avoid a situation whereby they would be embarrassed by a judicial decision to the contrary.[71] Moreover, in evaluating the chances that the Supreme Court would uphold the NIRA the bar's leaders displayed a remarkable degree of sober judgment. As practitioners, they accepted the penetration of extralegal consideration into the judicial calculus as a given that had to be considered among the purely constitutional considerations. Given these complexities, and independently of clients' concerns, the bar's leaders thus developed their own professional interest in clarifying the mist; they eagerly waited, in short, for a judicial decision that would settle the uncertainty one way or another.

The events that took place just weeks before the Supreme Court finally passed judgment on the NIRA revealed the eager expectation of lawyers in settling the case. The NIRA was originally enacted as a temporary measure that should have expired by mid-1935. Two proposals concerning the NIRA were pending in Congress shortly before its expiration date. One proposal provided for an extension of the act without any changes in its form and content, while another proposal, favored by the administration, included some important revisions of the act's original language. At the same time, in May 1935 it became clear that a determination of the NIRA's constitutionality was imminent, as the *Schechter* case was already pending in the Supreme Court. The administration's extension plan, therefore, reflected the hope that "the debatable issues of constitutional law arising out of the language and provisions of the Recovery Act might be eliminated by amendment to the law prior to a review by the Supreme Court."[72]

The NIRA was also high on the agenda of the American Bar Association and the American Liberty League. In March 1935 the ABA's Commerce Committee held a special meeting in which it decided to appoint a subcommittee, headed

by Raoul Desvernine, whose task was to produce a report stating the association's position on the NIRA's extension.[73] Earlier I argued that various retrospective accounts that claimed that the NIRA had lost its appeal to "big business" by mid-1934 were not entirely founded.[74] Desvernine's report and the
recommendations of the American Liberty League, which will be discussed
shortly, lend further support to this point. The report was submitted to the
ABA's Executive Committee and recommended that the NIRA be extended for
another two years. It reasoned that

> the NRA tends to promote and sustain a sound competitive system by
> permitting the establishment of fair competitive practices by industrial
> self-effort . . . Not only are the wasteful, uneconomic, and destructive
> business practices eliminated or controlled by means of the NRA, but the
> effects of destructive competition in forcing down wages to improper
> levels have been prevented or moderated with the result of largely remov-
> ing wages from the field of destructive competitive cost deflation. No other
> plan which holds promise of early adoption could be expected to accom-
> plish as much progress toward abolition of child labor and the sweat-
> shop . . . Trade and industry, after a period of considerable confusion, have
> adjusted themselves to the operation of the codes; to abruptly terminate
> the NRA without a reasonable period of readjustment would cause much
> confusion and uncertainty. . . . The committee concludes, therefore, that
> the present NRA should be continued substantially as at present.[75]

A report of the American Liberty League stated that "it will be agreed by all
that emergency conditions still prevail . . . A realistic view must be taken of the
present situation respecting the NRA. There are many who hold that it has been
a complete failure and that there should be no new legislation. It must be
recognized, however, that it is difficult to retrace our steps. We must start from
where we are now. Chaos might follow complete abandonment of this industrial experiment."[76]

The interesting point for present purposes, however, is that both the lawyers
of the American Bar Association and those of the American Liberty League, to
the degree that these two groups differed at all, voiced strong and uncompromising opposition to the administration's intention to amend the NIRA. The
report that Desvernine and his subcommittee submitted to the ABA's Executive
Committee urged that "some of the constitutional questions raised regarding
the powers sought to be exercised by this legislation be definitely answered by
the Supreme Court before attempting to enact permanent legislation."[77] The
report of the American Liberty League, apparently also prepared by Desver-

nine, took a less subdued tone and described the administration's bill as having "all the earmarks of a tricky attempt to avoid a definite determination of the constitutional validity of the Recovery Act through a decision by the Supreme Court. The shifting of the legal foundation for the NRA might permit its continuance, following an adverse decision, until new test cases could be advanced through successive steps to the highest court."[78]

The reports, in short, reflected the fear that the original act would be declared unconstitutional by the Court but an already revised NIRA would immediately replace it. It seems to me, therefore, that the reports also reflected the professional schizophrenia that the NIRA created among lawyers. Lawyers were highly aware of the act's doubtful constitutionality, but they were well aware of the support given the NIRA by some of their most powerful and influential clients. Under these circumstances, corporate lawyers were caught between their commitment to clients on the one hand and their own professional legalistic sentiments on the other. It is in this context that we should evaluate the bar's repeated calls for judicial review of the NIRA. The efforts to subject the NIRA to judicial review provided some relief of this schizophrenia. It allowed lawyers to strike a balance between their professional misgivings about the law and their reluctance to act publicly against the interests of their clients. By insisting on the urgency of judicial review, lawyers were sending a subtle message: they did not think the act was constitutional and yet could not fully disclose their belief in public; they thought that in order to uphold the law substantial constitutional acrobatics would be required and yet accepted the possibility that the Court would uphold the law; they resented the administrative features of the law and yet could not afford to fight them directly. The bar, unsurprisingly, looked to the Supreme Court. As long as the uncertainty continued, its members could but grind their teeth, complain, and support the law in public.

The NIRA, perhaps more than any other New Deal measure at the time, symbolized the arrival of an era in American law in which expediency and pragmatic considerations ushered in a spirit of relative disregard for strict legalistic practices and a rejection of what is known as "classical legal thought": the assertion that law is a comprehensive system of logical rules, immune to external interference and distinct from politics. Those who drafted the NIRA, those who administered it, and those who defended it were well aware that the law was unconstitutional by traditional legalistic standards. Nevertheless, the lawyers who sided with the administration tried to delay judicial review by avoiding confrontation with strong industries and, finally, by trying to amend the law in a way that would further postpone its constitutional determination by the Court. The NIRA, in this respect, was the first in a series of laws whose constitutionality had not been firmly situated within the body of existing judicial precedents; rather, it was based on an instrumental philosophy and on the belief that, if necessary, it would be possible to push the Supreme Court to uphold the law as an emergency measure, or, at best, to accommodate it within a new constitutional framework.

The story of the NIRA, however, raises some serious doubts about the accuracy of describing the legal battle of the times in terms of instrumentalists (i.e., New Dealers) versus formalists (e.g., corporate lawyers and the leaders of the bar). It is clear that lawyers who opposed the NIRA were not less realistic, in the commonsense meaning of the term, than were their adversaries in the administration and legal academia. Far from being captives of a strict legalistic rhetoric, these lawyers were acutely aware of the social context of the NIRA. Both in assessing the substantive merits of the act and, in particular, in trying to predict its fate in the Supreme Court, they reasoned that the law would be evaluated in light of the enormous popularity it enjoyed and of the surrounding spirit of emergency underlying its enactment. In fact, it was precisely this acute sense of the social, economic, and political implications of the NIRA that led many lawyers, and bar associations in particular, to avoid in-depth deliberations of the law, in spite of the fact that it also raised many strictly legal and constitutional questions. The apolitical image of the professional domain, these lawyers felt, would be impaired even if they limited themselves to such legalistic deliberations. It is fair to say that all parties involved—corporate lawyers, government lawyers, and legal academics—were taken by surprise when the Court finally invalidated the NIRA on strict and uncompromising constitutional grounds.[79]

The story of the New Deal in law has too often been written from a perspective that depicted New Dealers and their legal-realist allies in academia as enlightened jurists who had to overcome the reactionary opposition of Wall Street lawyers. But the reality of the struggle was more complex than that. Describing the leaders of the bar as detached jurists (the common, albeit contradictory, alternative to describing them as mere hired guns) risks the danger of falsely "recreating a naive formalist vision of law."[80] One element of legal realism, as Brigham and Harrington forcefully observe, is the portrayal of the legal consciousness of the bar's elite as if they blindly thought "in a way that is patently naive or mystified."[81] The story of the NIRA illustrates, however, that the bar's leaders responded to the act by framing it in instrumental and contextual terms—the very attributes of pragmatist legal thinking and realist consciousness. In fact, as Grey recently observed, "pragmatism is the implicit working theory of most good lawyers."[82] This is not to say that the leaders of the bar did not believe in the need to draw a line between law and politics. Yet they did so with the clear understanding that this was needed in order for them to pursue their own distinct interests in the best possible way, not because they naively thought that law and politics had nothing to do with one another. Richard Posner raised a similar point in writing that "although professional discourse has always been predominantly formalist, most American judges have been practicing pragmatists."[83] To the extent that the distinction between discourse and action is valid, the constitutional and legal debates of the times involved discursive struggles concerning appropriate modes of justification. This does not mean, however, that these struggles may be conceived of as nothing more than rhetorical differences, for the mode of justification that emerges as dominant within a given field is central to the actual formation that the field assumes. In other words, justification and persuasion are at the same time a cognitive foundation and a source for regulating the hierarchy of social relations within the field. The debate, in short, has to be cast in new terms if we are to go beyond the somewhat simplistic and idealistic description of the struggles of the times in terms of instrumentalists versus formalists.[84]

Further, unlike retrospective versions of history that portray the leaders of the bar as uncompromising enemies of New Deal measures, the case of the NIRA tells a more complex story. The NIRA created one of those rare instances in which corporate lawyers found themselves in an extremely uneasy position. Their clients backed the NIRA for practical reasons, and the administration invoked a strong rhetoric of emergency that was designed to equate opposition to the law with lack of patriotic zeal. Having to confront both the state and leading business elites thus put enormous pressure on those who were trying to criticize the law from a strictly professional perspective. The fact that some lawyers nonetheless managed, either privately or through the institutional organs of the bar, to voice their criticisms of the act has important theoretical implications. It is precisely in such rare instances that it is impossible to reduce lawyers' ideas and practices merely to the expectations of clients or to an extralegal commitment to laissez-faire ideology. Rather, the case of the NIRA allows us to identify the particular worldviews and distinct concerns that are bred by the structure of the legal field and the particular position of corporate lawyers within it.

This is not to say, of course, that lawyers simply pursued their own distinct concerns. Theirs was an incoherent attempt to do all at once: to criticize the act without offending clients' interests, to attack it while trying to avoid partisan politics, and to lament its features while still committing themselves to an emergency atmosphere. They did so by critiquing the NIRA indirectly, by channeling their misgivings about the act to the institutional organs of the bar, by invoking a rhetoric of legalism in the context of professional committees, and by insisting on the need to subject the law to judicial review. At the same time, they voiced principled support for the act, supported its extension, avoided learned discussions about its constitutionality, and succumbed to a spirit of emergency that allowed them to avoid facing their own professional schizophrenia.

The actual success of the bar's leaders in striking a balance between these conflicting pressures is doubtful. As we shall see, the ongoing effort of corporate lawyers to convincingly assert an autonomous professional aura is often fruitless. Nevertheless, we should not then assume that what lawyers say and do simply mirrors a reality that is construed outside the legal field. Rather, it should sensitize us to the complex way in which conformity to dominant politics, commitment to clients, and a vested interest in defending what lawyers perceive as their own jurisdiction and responsibility ultimately shape the rhetoric and practice of the bar's elite.

3 The Dilemma of Representation: Constructing the Aura of Benevolent Expertise

Introductory Note

In what follows I will identify some of the key players that composed the elite of the bar in the New Deal. Specifically, I consider the role that corporate lawyers played in congressional deliberations concerning the Securities Act of 1933, the Securities Exchange Act of 1934, the National Labor Relations Act of 1935, and the Public Utility Holding Company Act of 1935.[1] I also discuss a less dramatic case that nonetheless has special importance for present purposes: the reaction of lawyers to a proposed amendment in the judicial code that eliminated the jurisdiction of federal courts to restrain the enforcement of state administrative orders concerning public utility rates.

I also wish to further problematize a theme that surfaced in the previous chapter: the complex set of pressures that shaped the response of lawyers to various matters of legal relevance. Basically, the response of corporate lawyers and the bar's leaders to the New Deal cannot be unraveled and explained solely on grounds of their duties and commitments to powerful clients. All major New Deal laws created strong administrative commissions with sweeping discretionary powers, and elite lawyers, independent of their clients' concerns, feared and suspected them. This provides the foundation for the argument I develop later—namely, that the development of administrative law in the New Deal was a major source of tension between the bar's elite and the New Deal's administration.

I also follow the career of a special committee that the American Bar Association established in order to investigate the broader implications of the New Deal's legal agenda. I show that the reputation of the ABA as a relentless source of opposition to the New Deal assumes different proportions, if not meanings, when we look at this opposition from within. The story of the committee is a story of unintended consequences, lack of coordination, incoherence, confusion, bitter division of opinion, and high sensitivity to the political implications of the bar's activities.

All these narratives are considered in a specific framework of analysis. Accordingly, a substantial part of the discussion is organized around what I refer to as the "representation dilemma" of lawyers. By this I mean that in order to effectively serve clients, lawyers must objectify their arguments and invoke various distancing mechanisms that set them apart from the particular interests they represent. Indeed, as Larson notes, "legal representation is halfway between substitution and trusteeship: lawyers are neither mere proxies, substitutes subordinate to their clients, nor fully autonomous experts who enjoy free rein to exercise their superior knowledge and skill."[2] Haunted by this problematic position, the practices of lawyers involve a continuous effort to reach the "expert" end of the continuum and to escape their perceived function as mere hired guns. It is here that the dilemma of representation appears. Whenever lawyers advance a cause in the name of law their identification with clients becomes a burden. But when they try to transcend strict legalistic arguments, they immediately risk blurring the fragile line that separates law and politics, which at other times they are at pains to uphold. Two basic tactics were used through which lawyers tried to symbolically distance themselves from their clients' causes: their rhetorical attempt to frame arguments in the name of the public good and their attempt to mobilize the formal organs of the bar, presumably independent of client control, in order to articulate arguments in the language of value-free legal expertise. Both mechanisms, as we shall see, were ineffective.

This chapter is neither chronologically ordered nor systematic and comprehensive.[3] I single out a few selected themes in order to show that the discursive practices of lawyers reflect a complex and unstable relationship among their own structural position within the legal field,[4] their clients' expectations, and their sensitivity to the political culture and mood that happens to prevail at a given moment. Further, my analysis does not privilege issues of substance over issues of form or principled strategies over rhetorical tactics; rather, it assumes that the way lawyers frame their ideas is as revealing as the actual intent underlying them.

The Statutory Landscape

The Securities Act of 1933 was based on the idea that the well-established legal principle of "let the buyer beware" had to be supplemented by the principle of "let the seller also beware." Accordingly, the act made it unlawful to sell securities in interstate commerce without furnishing full publicity and information regarding them, and it provided that a purchaser of a security could sue to recover the consideration paid for securities, or for damages, in cases where a registration statement contained an untrue disclosure or failed to state a material fact. New securities had to be registered with the Federal Trade Commission (and later with the Securities and Exchange Commission) and required the approval of the commission prior to market distribution. The Securities and Exchange Commission (SEC) was given considerable powers to launch inquiries, hold hearings, and issue stop orders suspending the effectiveness of registration statements in cases where it appeared that they contained untrue or insufficient information.

The Securities Exchange Act of 1934 had three purposes: to prevent the excessive use of credit to finance speculation in securities; to ensure that the places in which securities were purchased and sold, such as the stock exchanges and the over-the-counter market, were purged of the abuses that had crept into them; and to make available to investors honest and reliable information sufficiently complete to acquaint them with the business conditions of the companies the securities of which they bought or sold. Again, the SEC was given broad discretionary powers to establish rules and regulations in regard to the prevention of manipulative practices and to hold hearings and inquiries concerning registration requirements.

The Public Utility Holding Company Act of 1935 prevented holding companies from financial pyramiding that harmed investors and consumers. The act required that holding companies register with the SEC and provided that unregistered companies could not engage in any form of business in interstate commerce. It provided for elaborate terms under which registered holding companies could sell securities and restricted their ability to acquire new businesses without the approval of the SEC. Most important, the act provided for a "death sentence" by stipulating that the SEC would examine the structure of holding companies and that those companies not approved by the SEC had to be dissolved within five years.

Finally, in 1935 Wagner's National Labor Relations Act came into effect. The act ensured the right of employees to freely organize and to select their own representatives for collective bargaining with employers. The Wagner act, and its earlier version, the labor disputes bill, replaced the labor provisions of the NIRA. The act also established a National Labor Relations Board, whose vast administrative powers promised that it would be able to effectively secure the rights of labor by settling controversies arising out of the implementation and interpretation of the act. The National Labor Relations Board replaced the former National Labor Disputes Board, which did not have any enforcement powers of its own and whose authority was effectively circumscribed by employers who resisted it.[5]

It is noteworthy that there was a marked difference between the response to the securities laws and that to the labor and utilities laws. The latter were enacted over the fierce and vocal opposition of most major employers and the vehement resistance of the financial community. The response of financial and business leaders to the securities laws, while not devoid of reservations, was remarkably less hostile. In fact, there is some evidence that the hostility of the bar's leaders to the securities laws exceeded that of their clients. The original securities exchange bill left its administration to the Federal Trade Commission, but it seems that it was the pressure of the financial lobby to allow greater discretion in the administration of securities matters that led to the creation of the SEC.[6] Benjamin Cohen, one of the principal drafters of the act, confirmed that the SEC was created at the urging of financial leaders, and that the drafters of the act did not favor the creation of such an independent body: "We fought against [the creation of an independent commission] because experience had indicated that commissions in time tend to be dominated by those they regulate and . . . a commission that had other tasks than stock exchange and security tasks might be less the prisoner of the financial community."[7]

All this, however, did not prevent the Commerce Committee of the ABA from consistently expressing its misgivings about the SEC. The 1934 report of the committee focused on the administrative powers of the Securities and Exchange Act and complained that it left the Securities and Exchange Commission with too much discretion and inefficient guiding principles for administering the regulation of securities: "Even if such broad delegation should be considered both legal and practical a further problem is presented by the trends that are likely to develop from centering so much discretionary control in a small federal body . . . [it] might be considered as contrary to the heretofore recognized principles of our government."[8]

To be sure, financial and business leaders did have some reservations about the securities laws and sought to restrict the liability provisions of the act. Nonetheless, the low-intensity litigation campaign that followed the enactment of the securities laws is another strong indication that they were not seriously resented by the leading forces of the financial community. In stark contrast to the litigation ordeal that followed the enactment of the labor and utility laws, only eight cases concerning the constitutionality of the two securities laws were brought before federal courts between 1933 and 1937. In most of these cases, again in stark contrast to those involving the labor and utility laws, constitutional challenges were not raised by the bar's leading corporate law firms.[9]

Trying to account for the lack of enthusiasm in challenging the Securities and Exchange Act, Thomas Gay argued that "the Securities and Exchange Act became law in June of 1934, and required all stock exchanges to be registered with the Securities and Exchange Commission . . . by October 15th. It seemed obvious, however, that no judicial determination of that controlling question could be had before the October 15th deadline. On the other hand . . . it seemed out of the question that the nation's largest stock exchange should be closed merely because of its desire to test the validity of the law."[10] Gay also added another explanation: "Litigation might antagonize the Commission, whose good will seemed essential to a cooperative administration of the Act, a consideration that undoubtedly influenced the decision of the Stock Exchange not to test its constitutionality."[11]

Indeed, there are good reasons to believe that stock exchanges, despite their misgivings, were not inclined to launch a frontal attack on the act. The only marked exception was the case of *Jones v. Securities and Exchange Commission*, in which the administrative powers of the SEC were challenged on constitutional grounds.[12] The decision of the Supreme Court in the Jones case was eagerly awaited by the leaders of the bar. In its decision, the Court did not pass on the constitutionality of the Securities Act, under whose provisions the case was tried, restricting itself to passing on the administrative powers of the SEC as they were exercised in this particular case. The majority opinion, delivered by Justice Sutherland, was framed in a language that clearly demonstrated the fundamental hostility of the court to the sweeping discretionary powers of the commission. The Court ruled that the SEC should have been prevented from carrying on an investigation in that particular case and described the commission's proceedings as resembling the "intolerable abuses of the Star Chamber."[13]

This spirit of hostility toward the administrative powers of the commission was promptly echoed in the 1936 report of the ABA's Committee on the Securities Act. The report stated that "we repeat and emphasize that the responsibility for matters of fundamental policy should be determined by the Congress and not put upon the shoulders of the Commission to be developed in the form of rules and regulations."[14] It seems, therefore, that at least some of the resentment that the leaders of the bar displayed toward the SEC could not be directly related to the concerns of interested clients.

The National Labor Relations Board, which had been invested with the task of administering Wagner's National Labor Relations Act, also enjoyed wide discretionary powers. Here again, lawyers had their own reasons to express reservations about an administrative agency—"which is itself investigator, prosecutor, and judge"—that used an "extraordinary procedure, going further than the Federal Trade Commission ever went."[15] The relationship of corporate lawyers to the expanding field of administrative practice will be dealt with at length below. For the present purposes, suffice it to note that the administrative problem was a major theme in the hostility of lawyers to the administration's legislative agenda. In their appearances before congressional committees, therefore, the bar's elite often expressed a blend of arguments designed to promote both the concerns of clients concerning issues of substance and their own misgivings concerning issues of form.

Another issue merits attention. The fierce hostility of clients to the labor and utilities laws seemed to have prompted lawyers to emphasize the constitutional difficulties these two laws would be likely to face in court. John MacLane and Justin Moore, two leading witnesses in the hearings on the public utility holding company bill, suggested that the bill was unconstitutional because of its attempt to regulate the production of electricity, a form of production they considered to be a purely local activity.[16] The Electric Bond and Share Company also supplemented its opposition with detailed legal briefs, prepared by leading utility lawyers William White, Charles Rosen, and Henry McCune, that argued against the constitutionality of the bill.[17] Similarly, a number of lawyers who appeared in the hearings on the labor bill suggested that Congress did not have the power to regulate local labor relations and therefore the bill as a whole failed to meet the test of the commerce clause of the Constitution. This view was vividly articulated by James Emery, counsel for the National Association of Manufacturers, who argued that the link between the bill and interstate commerce was like "the flea in the hair of the dog of the child of the wife of the wild man of Borneo."[18] Conversely, the relative absence of clients' opposition to the securities laws may have contributed to the fact that the questionable constitutionality of the securities laws had been played in a very low key. One prominent lawyer, Thomas Gay, did express some doubts concerning the constitutionality of the securities exchange bill. He argued that the activities of stock exchanges did not involve interstate commerce and therefore could not be regulated by Congress.[19] Two ABA committees also expressed some doubts. The committee that studied the Securities Act noted that it had some doubts about the constitutionality of the act but declared that this question *lay outside the scope of its mandate.* In 1934, a committee that discussed the Securities Exchange Act observed that the constitutionality of the law was a "much mooted question" but also refrained from further elaboration on this issue.[20]

Yet by and large, reading through the testimonies of lawyers before congressional committees on all of the above bills, one could hardly escape the impression that lawyers, in general, wasted relatively few words on constitutional issues. Apart from attacking the administrative features of the various bills, most lawyers engaged mainly in articulating social-policy arguments and challenging the general legislative wisdom of the bills. True, the reluctance to elaborate on constitutional considerations should also be understood in light of the fact that congressional committees, unlike courts, were prone to evaluate bills on the basis of general policy considerations. Yet it is noteworthy that avoidance of constitutional issues also characterized the "professional" reports of the ABA and, as we shall shortly see, directly affected the work of the ABA's New Deal Committee.[21] It seems to me that this phenomenon raises some important questions concerning the relationship between lawyers and the courts and the perceived ability of lawyers to invoke the Constitution as a conceptual link between their legal expertise and their asserted moral authority.

Dilemmas of Representation I: The Public-Interest Rhetoric

Most lawyers who appeared before the congressional committees that considered the New Deal's various legislative measures voiced their arguments in the name of the "public interest." The public-interest rhetoric, therefore, seems to have served lawyers who wished to distance themselves from the particularistic interests of their clients. Many lawyers insisted that their opposition was a constructive one, designed to enhance and improve the drive for economic recovery. Rush C. Butler, for example, a prominent corporate lawyer who also headed the ABA's Commerce Committee, told a congressional committee that his clients raised reservations about a certain bill "with the aim of promoting the aims and objectives of President Roosevelt's administration."[22] Similarly, many lawyers who appeared before congressional committees adopted a standard formula of opposition to New Deal legislation: they pledged allegiance to the administration's ideas of economic recovery, expressed principled support for proposed legislation, and only then proceeded to express doubts as to their legal, *economic,* or *social* wisdom. In most cases, the arguments of lawyers were a blend of general arguments against the wisdom and expediency of proposed bills and elaborate constitutional and legal doubts as to their validity and scope.

Such was the case, for example, when lawyers argued against the securities exchange bill in 1934.[23] While some reservations concerning the constitutional validity of the bill were voiced, the thrust of the opposition, shared by most lawyers, was that the bill worked against the desired economic recovery because it threatened to drive many security exchanges out of business.[24] The same type of reasoning characterized the opposition to the public utility holding company bill in 1935. Central to these hearings were the testimonies of Justin Moore and John MacLane. These two lawyers represented the Committee of Public Utility Executives, one of the most active organizations in its opposition to the proposed bill. While both lawyers challenged the constitutionality of the bill, they nonetheless joined forces with other lawyers who rested their opposition mainly on nonlegal arguments.[25] MacLane's lengthy testimony, for example, included detailed historical and statistical evidence designed to show that the holding companies were essential for the growth of the power industry, its stability, and its rate reduction policies. The thrust of the argument, therefore, was that the bill would bankrupt numerous operating companies and retard economic recovery, resulting in a financial disaster for millions of "widows and orphans" who held the securities of the power industry. The logic of the opposition, in short, was simple: the interests of the power industry coincided with those of the public in general.

Even the opposition to the national labor relations bill, which did involve some biting criticism of the bill's constitutionality and administrative features, was not put to rest on the basis of strict legal arguments.[26] In fact, most lawyers based their opposition to the labor bill on two overlapping general propositions: first, that the bill was based on a class-conflict philosophy that was entirely foreign to Americans; second, that the bill threatened to hinder recovery because it incited employees to strike and undermined the peaceful cooperation between employers and employees that existed in many plants and companies. Franklin Edmonds, who represented the Philadelphia Chamber of Commerce, argued, "This bill impresses me as having been written by a man who had been reading Marx on class war, and thought all employers and employees were standing in opposite corners making faces at each other, and it is unfair to American industry." Another lawyer, Roy Hall, described the bill as "a primer from Moscow, and I think this committee and the Senate . . . should turn their backs on it, pick up the American flag, and walk in the other direction."[27] Others argued along these lines that labor relations in many places were premised on personal and friendly terms, and that the bill would destroy "the human relationship factor" between employers and employees, thus undermining "any cooperation between an employer and his employees."[28] Walter Gordon Merritt, for example, arguing for the League of Industrial Rights (an employers' association that had been active since the beginning of the century), took pains to convince his listeners that he was "not out of sympathy with the purpose of the bill," that he supported the principle of collective bargaining, and that he should not be looked upon as a hired gun. The opposition to the bill, said Merritt, was inspired by the belief that it was inexpedient and unfair legislation that favored labor unions and threatened to destroy the peaceful cooperation that existed in many workplaces.[29]

Perhaps the most striking example of lawyers' attempts to frame their arguments in terms of the public's general good involved their opposition to the

Securities Act of 1933. In this case, legalistic arguments were almost nonexistent and were clearly secondary to those designed to appeal to the public's interest in economic recovery. Two prominent Wall Street lawyers, William C. Breed and Arthur H. Dean, led the opposition to the securities bill when it was pending in Congress in early 1933.[30] Breed argued that his clients were "heartily in accord" with the bill; at the same time, both lawyers declared that they were concerned that the bill in its present form would impede economic recovery. Their purpose in appearing before the congressional committee, they declared, was to offer amendments concerning some of the bill's imposed liabilities and the commission's powers to revoke registration statements.

Breed argued that the bill created unbearable business uncertainty because of the Federal Trade Commission's revocation powers and because the bill allowed purchasers to sue at any time after securities had been issued. This, he claimed, "would absolutely stop business." For the same reason, he also opposed those sections of the bill that made directors liable for issued securities. Breed argued that directors were in no position to know whether a statement was correct and were therefore not expected to bear responsibility for actions not under their control. He also argued that the clause with respect to directors' liability should be amended because directors would be afraid to sign and "guarantee . . . stock for all time to come." Similar arguments were made by Dean, who repeatedly claimed that the bill represented a "terrible" burden on commerce and industry and would therefore paralyze business.[31]

It seems that these "public good" arguments reflected a growing sentiment among lawyers that in order to be heard, both on behalf of clients and in their general ambition to shape public opinion, they had to prove their own commitment to the administration's plans for economic recovery. In a radio address in March 1935, while hearings on the labor bill were in progress, Donald Richberg described lawyers as "quibblers and evaders of the law" who were "simply dodging the law" on behalf of their clients under the guise of legalistic arguments.[32] A month later, in April 1935, O. R. McGuire, a member of the ABA's Committee on Administrative Law, responded to the challenge by publishing an article that based opposition to the proposed labor board on "non-legalistic" grounds. McGuire analyzed the Australian system of labor arbitration and argued that it tended to evoke a "spirit of antagonism inseparable from litigation" and "lessened the inducement to either side to resort to round table conferences for that frank and confidential discussion of difficulties in the light of mutual understanding and sympathy which is the best means of arriving at fair and workable industrial agreements."[33] Thus, while McGuire did not conceal his deep suspicion that the proposed labor bill was unconstitutional, he devoted all his efforts to show that it was also inexpedient from the standpoint of industrial recovery.

Here was a paradox that lawyers were not able to escape. When they raised legalistic arguments, they were exposed to the charge that they were irresponsibly oblivious to the social and economic realities of the day. When they tried to escape this charge by raising substantial arguments, however, they were immediately labeled the public-relations agents of their clients. Thus, for example, the fact that the thrust of the opposition to the Securities Act rested on its being a "hindrance to recovery," and not on distinct legal opinions, did not prevent opponents from depicting lawyers as mere hired guns. Bernard Flexner, writing for the *Atlantic*, accused Wall Street lawyers of participating in an "ugly campaign of propaganda" in order to discredit the act, and Fred Rodell wrote about the "financial leaders and the lawyers who work for them who have blown the meaning of the Act to impossible proportions."[34] The irony, therefore, is that rather than being an effective mechanism for distancing themselves from particularistic interests, the attempt of lawyers to frame their opposition to various laws in terms of a concern for economic recovery was regarded as trivial and empty rhetoric. The representation functions of these lawyers, in short, turned them into social suspects regardless of their distancing efforts.

Dilemmas of Representation II: The Rhetoric of Impartial Expertise

Another mechanism that promised to distance lawyers from the particular interests of their clients involved the mobilization of the ABA as a nonpartisan body of legal experts. The ABA made a considerable effort to present itself as an authoritative, impartial speaker on New Deal issues. This was not an easy task. First, as hard as the ABA tried to dissociate its position from that of identifiable interested parties, there was a substantial personal overlap between lawyers who represented industry and finance and lawyers who shaped the policies and reports of the ABA. Second, even when there was no such personal overlap, it was often extremely hard to draw a clear distinction between the objectives and positions of lawyers who acted in the capacity of private legal counsel and those who acted in the capacity of impartial experts.

Thus, for example, the failure of lawyers to persuade the public that their reservations about the Securities Act were based on genuine concerns for the public good may be easily understood when we consider the circumstances that preceded the ABA's decision to establish a special committee whose purpose was to study the act. In August 1933, John O'Connor, the financial manager of the United States Chamber of Commerce, wrote Silas Strawn, an influential member of the ABA, "I mentioned to you that a number of investment bankers and others whom I have consulted are hopeful that at the meeting of the ABA plans will be laid for careful scrutiny of the Federal Securities Act. . . . if no formal committee report is there presented, proposing reasonable modification of the statute, it is hoped that such a report might be published before or soon after Congress meets."[35]

The ABA's Executive Committee promptly responded by creating a Special Committee, whose goal was to suggest amendments to the Securities Act. The 1934 report of the committee practically echoed the arguments of Arthur Dean and William Breed in Congress. The report attacked the act for being "extraordinarily complex" and "very vague and uncertain." It criticized the act for imposing "drastic liabilities" and proposed a complete revision of the act in order to curtail the *in terrorem* liability provisions of the act. Further, although the report contained no concrete evidence to that effect, it stated that "the Act is a definite brake on recovery."[36] Given the similarity between the ABA's arguments and the opposition of lawyers who were acting on behalf of clients, it was not surprising that Merrick Dodd, Jr., of Harvard responded to the ABA's amendment proposals by politely asserting that its committee approached "the problem primarily from the standpoint of persons engaged in the business of security distribution."[37] The American Bar Association, therefore, as an organization that aspired to represent the collective position of the bar, had to present more than a ritualistic commitment to the idea of economic recovery if it wished to have an impact on policymaking.

The ABA had a vital interest in convincing its relevant audiences that its actions did not simply reflect the opinions of influential capitalist groups, especially when it defended what it considered to be its own distinct interests. The problems that the ABA faced when it wished to act upon its own "professional concerns" became evident in 1934, when Congress considered the Johnson bill (Act to Amend Section 24 of the Judicial Code). This bill provided that the jurisdiction of federal courts to restrain the enforcement of state administrative orders concerning public utility rates would be eliminated, and that local state courts would be invested with authority to pass on such orders in cases of dispute. Federal jurisdiction in such cases was traditionally invoked on grounds of "diversity of citizenship" or on grounds that the case raised a constitutional question. The diversity rule applied to disputes between citizens of different states; its historic rationale has been to overcome possible biases of local courts against out-of-state litigants. Corporations who had business in one state but were incorporated in another were thus able to invoke the diversity principle in order to transfer litigation to federal courts.

Apparently, the ability of corporations to remove controversies from their local setting had many advantages. First, federal courts were generally assumed to offer procedural protections that were not available in local courts. Second, litigation in federal courts was more expensive and time consuming, a fact that often resulted in commissions' exhausting their budget in the course of litigation. Third, and most important, federal determination of disputes allowed for a trial *de novo*: the factual determinations of the regulatory commissions were not admitted as conclusive evidence, so federal courts were willing to hear new evidence that could further circumscribe the implementation of rate orders. Further, federal judges, unlike judges in most state courts, had lifetime appointments and were thus regarded as more insulated from the political pressures that were likely to affect utility rates. Finally, the corporate law firms that were often involved in the representation of utilities wanted to avoid practicing before local state courts, whose procedures tended to change from one locality to another. Appearing before federal judges, therefore, made more sense in terms of both quality and uniformity.[38]

The interest of utility companies in opposing the Johnson bill was quite clear: the removal of federal jurisdiction constrained their ability to resist dispute rate orders. Some leaders of the ABA, however, believed that they had their own legitimate reasons to oppose the Johnson bill, because it was perceived as part of a larger scheme to expand the power of administrative bodies at the expense of the centrality and authority of federal courts. The ABA's 1933 Report of the Standing Committee on Jurisprudence and Law Reform stated the underlying theme and purpose of the ABA's opposition to the Johnson bill: "It was believed by a majority of this committee that this bill was the beginning of an effort to limit the federal jurisdiction step by step, and that it would be followed by others of the same character."[39]

Congressional hearings on the bill were held in May 1933 before the Senate Committee on the Judiciary and in February and March 1934 before the House Committee on the Judiciary.[40] The ABA sent three of its most distinguished members to the hearings: Clarence Martin, the president of the ABA; Harry Covington, the chairperson of the ABA's Committee on Jurisprudence and Law Reform; and Edward Everett, a member of this committee.[41] Opposition to the bill was also handled by prominent utility lawyers, most notable among them Rush C. Butler, Harry J. Dunbaugh, George Lee, Robert Coulson, and George LePine.[42]

One of the major concerns of the ABA's representatives, therefore, was to convince the congressional committees that their opposition to the bill reflected genuine professional concerns, independent of the particular interests of the utilities. Everett opened his testimony by reminding the committee that he personally was not representing utilities "in any capacity whatsoever," and that the opposition of the ABA was based on its regard for the integrity of the judicial system. He also emphasized that the position he and his friends represented was shared by "the most able and unbiased leaders of the American bar."[43]

Substantively, the ABA's position revealed deeply held reservations about the growing powers of administrative bodies and the ability of state courts to restrain them. Martin described the administrative process as a "cancerous growth" and cited the arbitrariness and systematic avoidance of judicial rules of evidence by administrative commissions that regulated utility rates, which violated the democratic principle of the separation of powers. There was a dire need to ensure the subjection of these commissions to federal judicial review, he argued, and the ability of state courts to assume these review functions was questionable; their review power was limited to questions of "fact," and, further, they were prone to be biased against the utilities because of popular pressure and the politically charged nature of utility rate orders.[44]

Yet the efforts of the ABA to appear as unbiased professionals were complicated on several grounds. First, many of the utility lawyers that spoke on behalf of interested clients were also distinguished members of the ABA. Butler, for example, was also the chairperson of the ABA's Committee on Commerce; Dunbaugh was a member of the ABA's Utility Section; and Coulson was a law partner of Charles Whitman, a former president of the ABA, and William Ransom, a member of the ABA's Executive Committee and a future ABA president. Second, it was extremely difficult to separate the "unbiased" expert opinion of the ABA from the opinions voiced by the utility lawyers. Not only was Everett charged with the overall task of orchestrating the opposition to the bill, but utility lawyers and ABA representatives could not avoid using each other's arguments. The representatives of the ABA, in other words, found themselves advocating a position that enhanced the arguments of utility lawyers who were fighting the bill on behalf of their clients.

Utility lawyers, on their part, enthusiastically adopted the position of the ABA and emphasized the arbitrary nature of the administrative process in order to justify their position. Most of the lawyers that represented the utilities raised arguments concerning the fate of federal courts. Justin R. Whiting, for example, speaking for Commonwealth & Southern Group, warned that the bill "would be a serious step in the lessening of the power of what has been the backbone of our form of constitutional government." Dunbaugh explicitly aligned himself with the position of the ABA; George Lee warned that the bill was part of a plan to destroy federal courts and to establish a "super government here, with a super constitution'ism [*sic*] of administrative agencies and quasi legislative tribunals"; and Coulson, on behalf of Consolidated Gas Company of New York, went so far as to claim that he was more concerned with protecting federal courts than with the interests of his clients.[45]

The representatives of the ABA, on their part, invoked arguments that resembled those of the utility lawyers. Everett, for example, practically echoed the argument of many utility lawyers in asserting that the bill would depreciate the value of utility securities. The bar "did not care" for the utilities, he said, but for the millions of helpless widows and orphans who held their securities. The depreciation of these securities, said Everett, "could hinder the development of the country. . . . At this particular point of the depression it would be disastrous to pass legislation that would have a tendency to depreciate the value of the securities of public utilities. Public utilities have become one of the most important businesses and their securities are widely purchased and held for investment."[46] The depreciation argument was the backbone of the utility lawyers' opposition to the bill; most of the dozen lawyers who represented the utilities made it part of their own standard way of embedding their arguments in the context of the public good.

In short, the arguments of the utility lawyers could hardly be distinguished from those of the ABA's representatives. The ABA may have tried to articulate its own "expert" opinion, but its views were warmly embraced by utility lawyers who had no less an interest in cloaking their arguments in such terms. Nonetheless, the leaders of the bar naively believed in their ability to prevent the passage of the bill. Covington thus wrote Earle Evans, who by then had replaced Martin as the association's president, about "the successful outcome of our efforts": "It is my hope that the influence that the Association exerts will be recognized by the various Congressional Committees, to the end that our association will be recognized as an impartial body, who advocate only opposition to unwise and undesirable legislation and who support proper and necessary legislation."[47]

A month later, the Johnson bill became law. Senator Norris, recommending the enactment of the bill, referred in his report to the role that the ABA played in the hearings. Norris blamed the representatives of the ABA for holding a position that had been identical to that of the utilities, and for using unfair tactics in their attempt to stall passage of the bill.[48] The passage of the Johnson bill, in short, served as an unpleasant reminder that the ABA had little influence over issues it truly considered part of its expertise, and that its efforts to speak in the name of impartial professionalism were deeply suspect.

In sum, the various attempts of lawyers to convey an image of impartial professional experts who cared for the public good were far from effective. Unable to distance themselves from particularistic interests, both individual lawyers and the ABA were labeled servants of corporate power throughout the New Deal. The inability to convey an impartial image may have contributed to the reluctance of the ABA to create other special committees and to further articulate opinions in public about various New Deal laws. Apart from its committee on the Securities Act and the New Deal Committee, the ABA consciously avoided open deliberations of highly contentious laws such as the National Labor Relations Act and the Public Utility Holding Company Act. The inherent strain created by the representation functions of lawyers therefore became a serious impediment to the ability of the organized bar to defend even what it perceived as its own distinct interests and its own version of the "rule of law."

Dilemmas of Representation III: The ABA's New Deal Committee

The most glaring example of the ABA's difficulties in articulating and presenting a coherent position on the New Deal's legislative agenda is the story of a committee that at the time of its inception was described as "the most important committee in the history of this association."[49] In 1934, the ABA's General Assembly resolved to create a committee whose task was to study the legal effects of the New Deal:

> Whereas the rapid development in recent months of novel legislation and governmental trends in the federal government, affecting the rights and liberties of American citizens and our constitutional form of government, have resulted in a great diversity of opinion throughout the United States as to the effect of these theories; and the questions involved hold a deep and peculiar interest for the bar of this country; And Whereas, The people of this country at all such times, look to the Bar for advice and guidance in such a crisis;
> Now, therefore, be it resolved, that the general council recommends that the executive committee create a special committee to study the effect of recent developments in national legislation and governmental policies, as affecting the rights and liberties of American citizens and the maintenance of the guarantees furnished by the United States Constitution; and that such committee report its findings to the executive committee, and that the executive committee report the same, together with its comments thereon, at the next meeting of the American Bar Association.[50]

The mandate of the committee, in other words, combined the two mechanisms discussed above: speaking in the name of the public good, while voicing such speech through the formal organs of the bar.

The language of the resolution and the scope of the task were uncommon; the ABA traditionally assigned much narrower and more precise tasks to its committees. The New Deal Committee was given an extremely broad mandate.[51] A year earlier, the ABA's president, Clarence Martin had explicitly rejected a proposal to create such a committee. Responding to a letter from a member of the ABA to that effect, Martin replied that the Committee on American Citizenship and the Committee on Jurisprudence and Law Reform already had a mandate to cover the broader constitutional aspects of the New Deal.[52]

It is noteworthy, however, that the New Deal Committee was not born of a deliberate collective strategy designed by the association's top leadership. The initiative came from George L. Buist, a member of the General Council, who managed to pass the resolution by an overwhelming majority of the General Council's members. Some members of the ABA's Executive Committee, on the other hand, thought that the mandate of the new committee was too broad, and that the language of the resolution held little promise for a truly comprehensive study. Harry Lawther, a member of the Executive Committee, observed that the scope of the work was too loosely defined and the task of the committee too demanding: "If there is any member of this committee who has to spend his time making his own living, I don't know how he is going to work on that." Glenn Fairbrook, in a like manner, said: "I think it is an endless job and I don't think it will ever get anywhere."[53] Some members wanted to pass the responsibility of creating the committee to the incoming Executive Committee, but most members argued that it would be a political mistake and suggested that the time was politically ripe for articulating the ABA's position on the New Deal: "Next year [when the report would be published] will be an off year, so far as national elections are concerned, and we ought to be in a position to handle that in an intelligent manner at that time. If we don't do it next year, it will come up the year following, which will be the presidential election year, and we will find ourselves in a position where the American Bar isn't speaking out as it should."[54]

The advocates of the idea among the members of the Executive Committee reminded the more prudent members that adopting the recommendation involved no risks. Ransom said that it was not the Executive Committee's responsibility to ensure that a report would eventually be produced, and another member explained that the Executive Committee would retain its control over the final product: "[W]e will be in a position where we may reserve our fire now until we see the report, probably a year from now, and then we can make any comment that we see fit on the basis of the report that we have before us," and another assured the Executive Committee that the report could always be rejected by it.[55]

Further, many members of the Executive Committee also felt that they had to respond in a positive way to a resolution that came from "below," from the less prominent members of the bar who sat in the association's General Assembly. Glenn Fairbrook, for example, stated that his sole reason for supporting the creation of the New Deal committee had to do with his opinion that the Executive Committee "should recognize the General Council by granting this request."[56] The Executive Committee was well aware of the sentiment among many members that the ABA played down the significance of the New Deal and concentrated instead on relatively "marginal" issues.[57] The members of the Executive Committee, therefore, tended to adopt the resolution not because they favored the idea of publicly voicing their attitude toward the New Deal but because they felt that in creating a committee with a "hopeless job" they were simply displaying smart internal politics. The Executive Committee, therefore, resolved to create a subcommittee consisting of three Executive Committee members whose responsibility was to receive the report from the New Deal Committee and to control its final form. In November 1934, the new president of the ABA, Scott Loftin, appointed seven members to serve on the New Deal Committee: the former ABA president, Clarence E. Martin, who chaired the committee; George L. Buist of Charleston, South Carolina, who sponsored the initiative; John D. Clark of Cheyenne, Wyoming; Senator George Pepper of Philadelphia; former Attorney General William Mitchell; Owen D. Young, and Charles Taft.

The composition of the committee seemed to ensure a very critical stance toward the New Deal. At least five members of the committee had already established reputations as critics of the New Deal. Martin was a strong advocate of states' rights. In a series of speeches in 1933 he condemned federal attempts to abolish child labor and warned against a governmental trend that would destroy the republic.[58] Martin's position on matters of administrative law also seemed clear, for he was one of the representatives who had attacked the Johnson bill in congressional hearings a few months earlier.[59] Buist was a member of the National Lawyers Committee of the American Liberty League. Pepper was a declared enemy of the New Deal. He headed one of the most active anti–New Deal law firms; among other things, it later handled the Butler case, in which the Supreme Court invalidated the Agricultural Adjustment Act.[60] Clark carried the flag of resistance to administrative practices and later attacked the New

Deal in his lectures about administrative law to the ABA's Judicial Section in 1935. And Mitchell, who ran a prominent Wall Street firm, had been attorney general under the Hoover administration. The "most important committee in the history" of the ABA was ready to set sail.[61]

The first interim report of the committee was submitted to the Executive Committee in January 1935. It was surprisingly restrained. The committee backed away from its mandate and decided to *stay away from constitutional questions* and to focus on "the philosophical side of the recent legislation." It explained that the Supreme Court was "inches" away from passing on the constitutionality of the NIRA, and that under these circumstances any constitutional opinions it might have expressed would "lead to political discussion."[62] In other words, the committee realized that it was politically hazardous to commit the ABA to a constitutional position that might prove wrong within days.[63] The Executive Committee, however, rejected this self-imposed restriction and advised the New Deal Committee to deal with constitutional issues in its final report.[64] The New Deal Committee, on its part, promised a full report in May 1935, a few months before the scheduled annual meeting of the ABA in Los Angeles. Yet no such report was submitted to the Executive Committee in its May meeting either. By that time, the only indication that a New Deal Committee existed was the decision of the Executive Committee to appoint three of its members, Arthur Vanderbilt, Harry Lawther, and Charles Beardsley, to serve as the subcommittee that would pass on the expected report. This subcommittee had very little to report to the Executive Committee in July 1935, when the annual meeting was already in session. On July 18, after four days of last-minute efforts to produce a report, the General Assembly was informed that no report has been received from the New Deal Committee. Consequently, the Executive Committee resolved to extend the mandate of the New Deal Committee and required it to submit a report "not later than November 1st" to a joint meeting of the Executive Committee and the General Council that would convene especially for this purpose.[65] The failure of the committee to produce a report was all the more embarrassing in light of the fact that a few weeks earlier the Supreme Court had invalidated the NIRA. Precisely at a moment of crisis, when jurists hotly debated the significance of the decision for the future of the New Deal's legislative program, the ABA committee that was supposed to convey the organized bar's position remained silent. Yet the reasons behind the committee's failure to produce a report had to do less with substantive differences of opinion among its members and more with personal animosities.

The committee's work progressed through the individual initiatives of the members, who drafted reports and circulated them among the other members of the committee. Four such partial reports were drafted between January and July 1935 by Buist, Pepper, Mitchell, and Martin. Pepper prepared his report in May 1935; it followed the committee's decision not to deal with constitutional issues in spite of the Executive Committee's instruction to the contrary. Pepper sent a draft to Mitchell, who by then had completed his own draft. The two reports, by all accounts, were not at odds over substantive issues. Mitchell wrote Martin what he thought of Pepper's report and made a somewhat tactless remark about Pepper's draftsmanship. Pepper was offended and sent Martin a letter in which he asked him "to chuck my draft into the discard and to sign Mitchell's with a few modifications. I have written [Mitchell] to that effect, but I have added that I doubt the value of such a report, as it contains little except restrained restatements of a sort not likely to stimulate thought."[66] In another letter, addressed to Charles Taft, Pepper again stated that he was reluctantly ready to sign Mitchell's report and to abandon his own "piece of patchwork."[67] Buist, on his part, complained that Mitchell's report was never sent to him or to any other member of the committee before the Los Angeles meeting. He claimed that Mitchell's report "was sent to Martin who put in his files and never turned it over to any member of the committee." Buist further argued that he also had a draft, parts of which were inserted into Pepper's report. According to Buist, Martin suppressed Pepper's report and instead composed his own, which he sent to the members of the committee. Buist claimed that under those circumstances he and the rest of the committee's members would refuse to sign it.[68]

In any event, it is clear that emotions were running high among the members of the committee. Buist felt that Martin tried to suppress some reports. Pepper was dissatisfied with his own report, but also with Mitchell's, and Martin could get no one to sign his own report. Just before the association convened, Martin came to New York in the hope of meeting Mitchell and Pepper, whom he evidently considered to be the more important members of the committee. He hoped that by inserting elements of Mitchell's and Pepper's reports into his own "neutral" one he would be able to convince them to sign it. Yet Pepper was busy with out-of-town litigation and wired Martin that "unless such unanimity [on Martin's version] is obtainable I should think that the discharge of the committee from further consideration of the matter would be more desirable."[69] In short, Martin and Mitchell could agree on one report, Pepper suppressed his own report, but Buist, Clark and Taft wanted to sign Pepper's report.

Such was the situation when ABA president Loftin asked the subcommittee to meet those members of the New Deal Committee who came to the Los Angeles meeting in a last effort to publish a report. Only three members of the New Deal Committee were present: Martin, Buist, and Clark. On July 15, the subcommittee met Martin. The next day the subcommittee met with all three members and heard Buist's report, which, in the opinion of one member of the subcommittee, "was an excellent document meant to provoke the thinking of the committee, but it was not a report." The subcommittee also heard the reports of Mitchell and Pepper.[70] It was unanimous in its opinion that Martin's draft was the only report that would "meet the Executive Committee approval." Buist's report, by his own admission, was only a working paper. Mitchell's report came to light on the third day, on July 17, and was no more than a three-page memorandum. Pepper would not sign his own report and did not want the committee to adopt it. The subcommittee did try to exert some pressure. First, they tried to persuade Pepper to change his mind because Buist, Taft, and Clark were ready to sign his report. With Pepper's own signature, his report could be presented as the majority report. Martin and Vanderbilt held some long-distance phone talks with Pepper, but he did not change his mind. The eagerness to get a report, according to Lawther, was due to the fact that no one wanted a delay that would carry the work of the committee into 1936, a presidential election year. Yet "it was perfectly apparent . . . that the committee originally appointed couldn't agree then and couldn't agree further if you were to continue them for a thousand years."[71]

The main obstacle was the difference between the reports of Pepper and Mitchell on the one hand and that of Martin on the other hand. At their joint meetings with the subcommittee, Buist openly told Martin that he would never sign his report. Martin, on his side, told Buist that he would never sign his. Martin claimed that Buist's report criticized the attorney general and the Department of Justice for intentionally avoiding the constitutional determination of New Deal–related legislation, and that Mitchell told Martin that he would never sign such a report "because one Attorney General never criticizes the acts of another Attorney General."[72] Arthur Vanderbilt confirmed the course of events: "It turned out that the main objection to the Martin report was a provision or a sentence to the effect that while there was a blocking of constitutional determination in the Department of Justice, the Attorney General was not responsible for them because he did not approve of what was being done. Buist and Clark came back to this sentence every half hour. That was the thing Martin would not take out of the report. This produced the deadlock."[73]

On July 17 the subcommittee presented the Executive Committee with a "progress report." It mentioned the different drafts and surveyed possible courses of action that the Executive Committee might wish to take. It ruled out an extension of the committee's mandate to summer 1936, because that meant that the report would be announced "in the midst of a political campaign." It also ruled out extensions to midyear, because the subcommittee was of the opinion that the report had to be accepted and approved by the "entire membership of the ABA." Finally, the subcommittee offered to accept Martin's report, to present it to the General Assembly as a minority report, and to discharge the committee. The Executive Committee did not accept the opinion of its subcommittee. It decided to extend the committee's mandate to November 1, 1935, and resolved to consider the report in a special joint meeting of the Executive Committee and the General Council.[74] It was in this joint meeting, held in Chicago in January 1936, that most of the details concerning the Los Angeles events were revealed in the statements of Buist, Vanderbilt, Lawther, Beardsley, and Ransom. The joint meeting was called in spite of the fact that no report had been provided. Further, in the fall of 1935, four members of the committee—Pepper, Young, Martin, and Mitchell—resigned, and the committee became inactive. The joint meeting, therefore, was called in order to decide upon the future of the New Deal Committee.

By that time it had become apparent that the three remaining members of the committee, Buist, Taft, and Clark, were open critics of the New Deal. When Pepper resigned, he circulated a letter explaining his motives; he argued that because he was involved in anti–New Deal litigation, his membership tainted the professional integrity of the committee. Worse still, in September 1935, at about the same time that the members of the committee resigned, the American Liberty League's National Lawyers Committee published a controversial report about the Wagner Labor Act, which was regarded by many observers as proof of the hostility of the bar's leaders to the New Deal. Under these circumstances, Ransom did not want to assume the responsibility of filling the vacancies in the committee without the formal consent of the joint meeting.

The discussion in the joint meeting exposed a divided bar. Some members, led by Buist (who was also one of the drafters of the American Liberty League's report), complained about the timidity of the ABA. Buist lamented the successful blocking of previous reports by Martin and blamed him for trying to dissolve the committee because "he had political allegiance with the New Deal, because his son, who was his law partner, had a job with the Department of Justice." The fear of some ABA leaders of being accused of partisanship, claimed Buist, crippled the association's ability to act: "If we become so weak and flabby that we cannot dare to speak because, forsooth, it might offend somebody, well then perhaps we don't deserve to have the system of government that we have." He bitterly criticized the ABA's reluctance to deal with constitutional issues, its hands-off attitude, and its tendency to shift the responsibility to the Supreme Court: "It is easy enough to say: 'Let the Supreme Court do it.' The executive department has suggested that to Congress. It is easy for us to say here: 'We will do nothing, and let the Supreme Court do it.' The result is that we, as a national association, have succumbed to the pressure and challenge imposed by New Dealers and shut our mouths. In short, it is now agreed that the Bar Association hasn't got the guts to speak."[75]

Martin responded to these charges by asserting Buist's "very bad character."[76] Other members of the Executive Committee, led by Lawther, tended to give up on the whole affair. Lawther advised his listeners to "bid this committee good-bye" and reminded them that if Buist's, Clark's, or Pepper's report was adopted by the ABA, "the only appearance in the world it would have to the country at large is that the ABA was simply an aid society to the Republican party." Lawther appealed to the members' sense of professional neutrality and cited Ransom's speech in Atlanta some months earlier, in which the latter argued that the ABA should be kept "out of the politics of the country." Other members expressed similar sentiments, and even Charles Beardsley, one of the drafters of the American Liberty League's report, joined Lawther in his complaint.[77] Beardsley argued that it was too late for the committee to resume its work because it would now collide with the political campaign. In their attempts to separate law from politics, most lawyers could find a common ground.[78]

Ransom disagreed. He argued that he had no authority to discharge the committee. He expressed his interest in its continuance and searched for the safest way to ensure that it would be difficult to pin it down as a partisan group. He discussed Pepper's resignation not as a sign of despair but as an authorization that cleared the way for new members who could not be identified with particular clients. Ransom therefore requested the approval of the joint body for the creation of a "client-proof" committee. Eventually, Ransom had it his way. In a close vote that exposed the divided opinions among the leaders of the bar, the joint meeting approved the nomination of four new members to the committee and ordered them to produce a report for the 1936 summer meeting in Boston.[79] The joint meeting ended with Ransom's request that the participants not inform the press about their discussion: "It would be very regrettable if any of you, or myself, talked with the newspapers about this matter, or let them get the idea there had been some great division of sentiment here with respect to filling vacancies in the committee."[80]

Ransom's choice in filling the vacancies were in line with the eager efforts of the association to escape political labeling. He selected members who could not be identified "with litigation or controversy as to the matters to be surveyed by the committee."[81] Ransom appointed judges rather than practicing lawyers: James G. McGowen, of the Supreme Court of Mississippi; Fred H. Davis, of the

Supreme Court of Florida; Kenneth Wynne, of the Superior Court of Connecticut; and Fred L. Williams, formerly of the Supreme Court of Missouri.

The final report of the New Deal Committee revealed that Ransom's attempts were only partially successful. The Advance Program of the ABA for the Boston Annual Meeting of 1936 contained a majority report, a minority report, and an additional "concurring memorandum with majority report." The majority report was signed by the three members of the original committee, who were joined by Justice Davis. Buist was not wholly satisfied with this report and added his own memorandum. The minority report was signed by the chairperson of the committee and the two remaining newly appointed members—all three of them from the bench.[82] Thus, although the new committee finally generated reports, the idea of having a committee that could speak authoritatively and in one voice about the New Deal was disappointed. When Ransom opened the August meeting of the Executive Committee, he asked Arthur Vanderbilt to report upon the recommendations of the subcommittee in regard to these reports. "You can take either the Republican or the Democratic ticket and vote it, whichever you prefer," replied Vanderbilt, "they are both there."[83]

The minority report briefly stated that the purpose for which the New Deal Committee was established had become obsolete because the Supreme Court had already reviewed and decided the fate of various New Deal laws: "[T]he effects of said legislation upon the constitutional rights and liberties of the citizens [have] been carefully set forth in the many opinions of the judges of said court, and the text of said opinions (both majority and minority opinions) have been published in full and given very wide circulation by most of the metropolitan press of the country."[84] The minority were therefore of the opinion that a report at this stage could serve no useful purpose and, given the political context, would only result in "embroiling the Bar Association . . . in bitter partisan political discussion."[85] In fact, the implication of the report was that the bar faced an insoluble dilemma when sensitive political and constitutional issues were involved. Articulating constitutional opinions before the Supreme Court ruled upon them involved too many risks. Citing constitutional opinions after they had been passed by the court sounded like empty rhetoric.

This dilemma largely explains the structure and content of the majority report as well. The majority report stated that the fact that the Supreme Court invalidated major New Deal laws did not exhaust the committee's scope of inquiry, because its task was to inquire into the more personal aspects of the American citizen's rights in his relationship with the government. Accordingly, it set out to examine a few of these areas. The central part of the report dealt with "economic rights." This was a thinly disguised version of the outdated earlier drafts that Clark had obtained from Pepper, Buist, and Martin. The report analyzed the machinery and the codemaking process of the NRA and warned that the NRA's abusive administrative practices should remain in the public mind as "a lesson."[86] Another part of the majority report contained bold statements in favor of judicial review along the lines advocated earlier by Mitchell and Buist. This part of the report contained the statement that created the deadlock a year earlier: "One of the most disturbing features of administration policy *in its first year* was the studied effort to close to the citizen all opportunity to secure the declaration and vindication of his constitutional rights" (italics mine). By 1936, however, when the Supreme Court had already reviewed and invalidated both the Agriculture Administration Act and the National Industrial Recovery Act, this statement was simply outdated.

The decisions of the Supreme Court, however, encouraged the majority of the committee to praise the merits of the court as a final arbiter of constitutional questions, to call for the unification of the bar under the banner of "judicial protection," and ultimately to criticize President Roosevelt in straightforward language: "One who would preserve our constitutional system must deplore the action of President Roosevelt in recommending that members of Congress set aside any doubts they might have about the validity of proposed legislation." This last statement was borrowed from Buist's attack on the New Deal in January 1936.[87]

Even those who sympathized with the idea that the ABA should not have refrained from criticizing New Deal practices were embarrassed by the generality of the report, its discussion of irrelevant issues, and, most troublesome, its use of political rhetoric. Not only did the report opt to discuss past events, not only did it bypass constitutional questions, not only did it avoid discussing aspects which belonged with other committee's jurisdictions, but it also completely ignored at least two issues that were still unresolved and had direct relevance to the mandate of the committee: it did not comment on the National Labor Relations Act and the Social Security Act, with their own respective administrative apparatuses and constitutional problems. This avoidance should be understood in light of the uproar that accompanied the American Liberty League's attack on the constitutionality of the Labor Act in the fall of 1935. Nevertheless, the report was interpreted by all observers as a direct attack on the New Deal at the height of the election campaign. President Ransom spent some moments reading to the members of the Executive Committee press commentaries and editorials that treated the report as a direct attack on Roosevelt and admitted, "I think the impression is around the country pretty generally that the Bar has made a whale of an attack on the administration."[88] Consequently, the Executive Committee made no attempt to discuss the merits of the reports; the only issue on the agenda was how to bury them. Hours of discussion were spent in an attempt to find a formula that would guarantee that no further debate and controversy would follow the formal presentation of the Executive Committee's "report on the report" to the General Assembly. The consensus in the Executive Committee was that the committee should simply inform the General Assembly that it had received the reports and filed them, without further comment.[89]

In spite of the attempts to ignore the need to discuss the reports in a joint session, effective complaints from some members, headed by Jacob Lashly, eventually convinced the Executive Committee that such discussion was unavoidable and that the committee had "to stand up here and face the issue." The ABA's state delegates (formerly the General Assembly) and the Board of Governors (formerly the Executive Committee) met for a joint meeting. Ransom assumed the task of informing the audience about the response of the Executive Committee. He justified the decision to "receive and file" the reports by arguing that it was a common practice with regard to reports that carried no practical recommendations:

> Usually we have each year a great variety of reports which contain no recommendations; they are reports which review and study particular matters. This report is of such a character. Usually these reports which are mere studies are not acted upon by the association in the sense of being adopted . . . On the present situation, the report having been made, having been transmitted to the membership, each and every citizen having his own angle with respect to the matters reviewed and even those who hold with either majority or minority being of a mood and mind to pick at least their own language about it, there is an inclination on the part of many members of the Executive Committee to recommend to the association that instead of the language and the phraseology and the full text of these reports being adopted, the reports, the study that has been made of this mattter in so comprehensive a way, be received and filed without endeavoring to commit the meeting to a detailed consideration of particular phraseology in these reports.[90]

Two days later the General Assembly was also informed about the decision to receive and file the reports, and a motion to that effect was carried with no further complications. Only one person, John D. Clark, the author of the majority report, stood to speak against the burial of the report. Frustrated and angry, he reminded the audience that the committee had been established by the ABA because it had been assumed that the public looked up to the bar as a source of guidance, especially in times of crisis; by burying the report, he said, the ABA implied that it had given up on this presumption. His remarks, however, were brushed aside by Ransom, who had formerly described the committee as the most important one in the history of the New Deal.

In sum, the career of the New Deal Committee exposed some of the fundamental difficulties lawyers had in mobilizing the formal organs of the bar in order to shape public opinion and confirmed the fears that some leaders of the bar expressed at the time of the committee's creation. The report itself was of little substantive value, it was made public at a time the ABA was determined to avoid, and, perhaps worst of all, it demonstrated the inability of the ABA to speak authoritatively on matters of national concern. Rather, a successful maneuver by one legal entrepreneur, Buist, produced a chain of events that no one seemed to want. Very few members of the Executive Committee were genuinely interested in carrying out this task, and still fewer believed in the ability of the committee to embrace such a broad subject. The decisive factor in the eventual decision to execute the General Council's recommendation had been the desire of the Executive Committee to demonstrate its receptiveness to "popular demands" coming from the bar's rank and file. However, it was greatly mistaken in its belief that it would be able to control the final product. The greatest miscalculation was the belief that the Executive Committee would still be able to protect the ABA from being labeled a partisan body. Not unlike the attempt of lawyers to invoke a public-good rhetoric while representing clients, and not unlike the fruitless attempt of the ABA to directly influence Congress through its most distinguished representatives, the attempt of the association to speak in broad terms about the New Deal damaged, rather than enhanced, the impartial image of the bar.

Lawyers are, to use Gordon's words, "double agents."[91] Their primary and most visible commitment is to clients whose demands they must satisfy. But lawyers' ability to do so depends on the degree to which they are able to appear as guardians of law and as experts who are responsible for ensuring the ordered functioning of the legal system as a whole. This does not mean, however, that lawyers defend the rule of law *only* in order to serve their clients in the best possible way. They are indeed double agents insofar as they do develop their own vested interests in shaping and drawing the boundaries of a distinct legal field. In other words, in order to command the authority of the expert and to extract the material and nonmaterial benefits that accord the position of the knowledgeable expert in modern society, lawyers must constantly persuade relevant audiences—clients, legislators, state authorities, and the public at large—that they own a distinct form of symbolic capital.

Throughout this chapter, however, we have seen that the project of lawyers *qua* professionals had been inherently strained. Practitioners were suspected of voicing the interests of clients even when they articulated their own distinct professional concerns. This suspicion was not unfounded. Indeed, clients' expectations largely determined the agenda, if not the tone, of the response of the bar's elite to the various legislative measures of the New Deal. Yet at the same time, the representation functions of lawyers also frustrated their ability to defend their own vision of law. We have seen the attempts of lawyers to frame arguments in the name of the public good and to channel their grievances through the works of professional committees of the ABA. These distancing mechanisms did not seem to have a significant effect. To the degree that distance—achieved through language, time, space, intermediaries, and other non-discursive symbols—was a measure of power and autonomy, and to the extent that lawyers indeed engaged in an ongoing effort to distance themselves from the image of mere proxies, the political atmosphere that prevailed in the New Deal and the proximity of elite lawyers to the powerful financial interests that were pilloried at the time doomed the efforts of lawyers to appear as impartial experts.

The story of the ABA's opposition to the Johnson bill, and in particular the story of the ABA's New Deal Committee, also cast serious doubts on the ability of lawyers to invoke their professional expertise in order to command moral authority and to shape public opinion in general. Terrance Halliday argues that "the varying capacity of professions to make such a transition rests significantly on their epistemological foundations. It can be posited that, the more normative (or syncretic) the epistemological core of professional knowledge, the more readily that profession will be able to exercise moral authority in the name of expertise."[92] However, the failed attempt to invoke the objective language of legal expertise as means of discussing politically sensitive issues failed. In contrast to Halliday's assertion, it was precisely the all too obvious relationship between legal issues and normative questions that circumscribed the ability of lawyers to speak authoritatively in the name of legal science. Presumably, constitutional rhetoric provides a particularly advantageous conceptual link between the language of public discourse and that of legal expertise. Yet the reluctance of various committees of the ABA to discuss constitutional matters may have reflected the subtle yet unacknowledged understanding that constitutional arguments could not ensure professional immunity from politics, and that in their public utterances (in contrast to the form of legal briefs in the judicial arena) lawyers had to defer to the Court the "right" of discussing issues of constitutionality. The New Deal Committee, for example, thus balked at the idea of a constitutional discussion, and the Executive Committee of the ABA, which in early 1935 still insisted that the committee should have discussed constitutional issues, backed away from its demand. "Professional influence *can* be extensive," writes Brint, "when professionals are able to assert a central cultural value in the absence of a strong counter ideology."[93] Yet in the New Deal *there* was a strong counter-ideology at work. The administration's emphasis on the urgent need to experiment with new social and economic programs offered a powerful antidote to the values associated with the sacredness of the Constitution, the separation of powers, and, ultimately, the rule of law. Consequently, the ability of the bar to shape public opinion in the first years of the New Deal was very limited.

The story of the New Deal Committee also demonstrates the intellectual dependency of the organized bar on courts in general and on the Supreme Court in particular. The decision of the New Deal Committee to avoid constitutional issues rested in part on the expectation that the Supreme Court would soon pass on the constitutionality of various New Deal laws. Following the resignation of four members of the committee, moreover, the ABA appointed judges, rather than practicing lawyers, as new committee members. In an attempt to convey an aura of expertise, in other words, the ABA had to rely on judges to speak for the profession as a whole.

Responding to Schechter

It is hard to exaggerate the sense of professional jubilation with which the leaders of the bar welcomed the decision of the Supreme Court in *Schechter Poultry Corporation v. United States*.[1] The decision, in which the NIRA was held to be unconstitutional, was perceived as an assuring message that clarified much of the uncertainty surrounding the New Deal's legislative agenda.[2] John Davis, for example, declared that "we have . . . lived to rejoice that in the courts of the country the law has found its champions and defenders," and James Beck, to the applause of the ABA's members, ridiculed a recent book entitled *The Twilight of the Supreme Court* by saying that "the twilight proves to be the most glorious sunrise of the Supreme Court."[3]

Of special significance was the fact that the Court's decision had been unanimous, thus undermining the often politically convenient division between liberals and conservatives on the bench.[4] The *United States Law Review*, for example, wrote: "In all the discussions as to what the Supreme Court would do with NIRA, the speculation has been as to how the Court would be divided. That the Court would be unanimous was apparently as little anticipated by those who were moved by the decision to 'thank god for the Supreme Court' as it was by those to whom the decision brought chagrin and dismay."[5] The *ABA Journal*, for its part, snapped at the "unfounded assumptions" of those experts who anticipated a divided Court and treated the decision as proof of the scientific nature of legal reasoning:

> Where nine able men, frequently different in their view on many subjects, are agreed, it is vain to look for partisanship, social, political, or economic, in the decision. The reasons for it must be sought elsewhere. The interpreters of the Constitution have found their meeting point in a common view of the strictly legal principles involved and their application to the facts presented by the case under consideration. Whatever the public may

think of the policy involved in a particular piece of legislation, it is hardly likely to question a unanimous decision based on what it recognizes as *purely legal grounds* [italics mine].[6]

Indeed, *Schechter* provided the leaders of the bar with enhanced confidence in the logic and consistency of the law. Some lawyers were quick to analyze the decision in light of past precedents and concluded that the decision had been inevitable.[7] The remarks of George Farnum, a former U.S. assistant attorney general, illustrate this retrospective self-assurance. Writing on the NIRA just a few months earlier, Farnum had been at great pains to avoid decisive predictions. He analyzed the political convictions of the Court's justices and vaguely concluded that as to the "manner in which the great constitutional questions which are arising under the New Deal will be ultimately dealt with by the Supreme Court . . . I make the confident prediction that, in the hands of this wise tribunal, these questions will be solved for the best interest and welfare of the American people." Shortly after the *Schechter* decision, however, Farnum wrote, "[A]fter all, [the *Schechter* decision] announced no new principle. It simply applied old fundamental ideas to a radical departure in legislation . . . Reading the two opinions which constituted the unanimous decision dispassionately, *it is difficult to see how the draftsmen of the act could have believed that it could be squared with American political ideals and familiar legal theory*" (italics mine).[8]

Having at their disposal the authoritative statement of the court in *Schechter*, many lawyers freely and publicly offered their opinions concerning the constitutionality of other New Deal laws as well. Illustrative of this new daring spirit was an article published in *Fortune Magazine* by Edwin Blair, a New York corporate lawyer. Blair listed a number of key New Deal laws and commented authoritatively on their constitutionality. He concluded that the Agriculture Adjustment Act, the Guffey Coal Bill, the Public Utility Holding Company bill, the Wagner Labor Relations bill, the Bankhead Cotton Control Act, the Tobacco Industry Act, the Thomas Disney bill for petroleum control, and the alcohol control bill were unconstitutional. He stated that the social security bill "in the main is constitutional," the Tennessee Valley Authority legislation "is constitutional except in regard to the retailing of its power," and that the Securities Exchange Act "is constitutional in its control of exchanges but unconstitutional in many of its ancillary provisions."[9] Such free constitutional opinions were seldom given prior to *Schechter*.

To be sure, doubts concerning the constitutionality of various New Deal laws were voiced by lawyers before *Schechter* as well.[10] *Schechter*, however, seems to have enhanced the belief of many lawyers that future constitutional challenges to other New Deal laws would also succeed. To emphasize once more: in referring to the importance of *Schechter* I by no means wish to suggest that it *caused* lawyers, in any positivist manner, to launch a frontal attack on the New Deal. Rather, I suggest that *Schechter* supplied lawyers with ammunition—both in the sense of providing them with the urgently needed constitutional foundation for representing clients in an era of uncertainty and in the more diffuse sense of allowing them to rely on this judicial utterance as a source of legitimation for their own project of resisting the expansive tendencies of the administrative process. Thus, the assuring message from the Court, combined with the strong opposition of business leaders to Wagner's National Labor Relations Act and the Public Utility Holding Company Act, encouraged lawyers to advise their clients to actively avoid compliance with various new measures.

Some corporate lawyers, in fact, preached a kind of "capitalist civil disobedience." John Foster Dulles, for example, gathered the executives of leading holding companies in his Wall Street office and declared that the Public Utility Holding Company Act could not survive a constitutional challenge: "The men who drafted and promoted this law obviously do not know the law or the Constitution. I can assure you that it violates basic constitutional guarantees and that the Supreme Court will strike it down. My strong advice to you gentlemen is to do nothing. Do not comply; resist the law with all your might, and soon everything will be alright."[11]

It seems that *Schechter* also "bolstered belief in [Wagner's Labor] Act's unconstitutionality and encouraged resistance to its enforcement."[12] The *American Bar Association Journal*, for example, published an article by Henry Chandler, a Chicago lawyer, who wrote that "it is difficult to see how the Schechter decision can be reconciled with any other view than that the National Labor Relations Act is unconstitutional."[13] The legal department of the National Association of Manufacturers circulated twelve thousand copies of a report stating that in the wake of *Schechter* there could be no doubt about the unconstitutionality of the Labor Act. And Elisha Hanson, the general counsel of the American Newspaper Publishers Association, described the Labor Act as "unconstitutional beyond question or doubt" and advised employers to "flatly refuse to have anything to do with the National Labor Relations Board, other than to notify it is without power under the Constitution to interfere with their business."[14]

The most dramatic response to the Labor Act came from the National Lawyers Committee of the American Liberty League. Backed by strong corporate interests and encouraged by the *Schechter* decision, the committee published a special report on the constitutionality of the Labor Act. Unlike previous reports that expressed doubts about the constitutionality of various New Deal measures in a relatively restrained manner, the Labor Act report invoked unambiguous language.[15] Prepared by eight lawyers and signed by fifty-eight, the report was written in the form of a legal brief. It provided an elaborate review of *Schechter* and opined that on the basis of the principles announced in that case there could be "no hesitancy in concluding that [the act] is unconstitutional and that it constitutes a complete departure from our constitutional and traditional theories of government."[16]

It is difficult to assess the impact of the lawyers' report on the litigation ordeal that followed the enactment of the Labor Act. The National Labor Relations Board, however, believed that the report did have a significant impact and that it incited both employers and lawyers to disobey the law. The board's first annual report reviewed some eighty injunction suits brought by employers who did not wish to submit to the authority of the board. The Labor Board's report maintained that these cases were based on a "sample brief," namely the report of the National Lawyers Committee, which provided the pretext for "a deliberate and concerted effort by a large group of well known lawyers to undermine public confidence in the statute, to discourage compliance with it, to assist attorneys generally in attacks on the statute, and perhaps to influence the courts." Based on this "sample brief," the board argued, the litigation campaign looked like "a rolling snowball. The allegations in a pleading filed by an employer in Georgia, for example, would show up in precisely the same wording in a pleading filed in Seattle."[17]

The litigation campaign notwithstanding, the publication of the lawyers' report damaged the ability of the organized bar to convey a nonpartisan professional image. The report was countered by critics who described the National Lawyers Committee as the servant and the public relations agent of powerful clients, questioned the ethical standards of the committee, mocked the professional value of the report, and condemned the "ugly spirit" of those who attempted to constitute themselves as a "super Supreme Court."[18] Not only New Dealers and their academic allies but also some members of the Lawyers Committee were embarrassed by the self-assured tone of the report. Consequently, the committee decided not to publish two planned reports about the constitutionality of the Holding Company Act and the Social Security Act.[19] The activities of the league's Lawyers Committee apparently embarrassed the ABA. Earlier I noted the reluctance of various committees of the ABA, realizing that a "constitutional discourse" could not provide immunity from partisanship, to generate public deliberations of various New Deal laws. The lawyers' report proved this point with a vengeance. It drew vigorous criticism, tainted the bar as a whole as politically biased, and, perhaps worst of all, unintentionally exposed the inherent uncertainty of the Constitution. Offering conflicting constitutional interpretations in court was one thing; exposing them to the broad daylight of the public arena was another. At least that was what Felix Frankfurter thought. It was Frankfurter who reminded the lawyers of the league that the report turned "the Constitution into that most dangerous of all things, *a political instead of a legal document*" (italics mine). He illustrated his point by implying that other legal experts could, with the same spirit of conviction, "prove" the constitutionality of the New Deal's legislative measures:

> What would those very leaders have said if, not fifty-eight but fifteen deans of law schools, Dean Pound and Dean Clark and Dean Young Smith and Dean Arant and Dean Harris and Dean Burdick and the rest of them had come out with a measured statement some two months ago that, in their judgment, the TVA and AAA and all the other combinations of letters were constitutional? Suppose they had written precisely the same kind of a document that the fifty-eight lawyers signed but had come to the opposite conclusion . . . Is there any doubt that there would have been a furor throughout the whole legal profession against the impudence, the arrogance of the attempt of dragoon, I think is the word that would have been used, on the part of law deans, to influence illegitimately the judgment of the Supreme Court of the United States?[20]

The affiliation of so many prominent leaders of the ABA with the fifty-eight members of the league's Lawyers Committee became a serious liability. As an obvious voice for the economically privileged, the more openly hostile the league became, the less able the American Bar Association was to appear as an impartial body when it wished to articulate its own position on various issues of relevance. Worse still, the association's Committee on Professional Ethics and Grievances had to consider a complaint against the Lawyers Committee and to determine whether its offers for free legal counsel to those who wished to resist New Deal laws violated the profession's code of ethics. The finding that the practices of the league were not unethical further contributed to the impression that the National Lawyers Committee enjoyed the protection, if not the silent approval, of the American Bar Association.[21]

In other words, while *Schechter* may have clarified constitutional uncertainties, the growing resistance of employers and corporations to the New Deal and the public activities of lawyers who represented them further constrained the ability of the ABA to appear as an impartial body of legal experts. It is probably for this reason that the ABA remained conspicuously silent on labor issues and avoided any discussions of the Public Utility Act. In fact, it was only in 1936 that the ABA approved the creation of a committee on labor, and it was only in 1937, after the Supreme Court had already upheld the constitutionality of the Labor Act in *Jones & Laughlin*, that this committee published its first report.[22] Similar avoidance followed the enactment of the Holding Company Act, in spite of the fact that the ABA had an active and powerful Utility Section controlled by leading utility lawyers who, throughout the 1920s, published reports that were unabashedly hostile to local and federal regulatory attempts. After the enactment of the Holding Company Act, however, the Utility Section largely refrained from expressing any concrete opinion concerning its merits, expediency, or constitutionality.

A certain strategic division of labor between "private" and "public" professional functions thus characterized the aftermath of *Schechter*. While the bar's corporate elite and many leaders of the ABA vigorously challenged the new measures in their individual representation functions, in fact often inciting clients to launch an aggressive litigation campaign, the formal institutional organs of the bar, in an apparent effort to preserve an image of professional impartiality, abstained from critiquing specific laws and legislative programs.

As we shall see, however, *Schechter* did create a new opening for lawyers who were alarmed by the New Deal and sought ways to collectively mobilize against it. The reaction of the administration's legal advisers and supporters to *Schechter* persuaded the bar's leaders that the administration was determined to undermine judicial authority and to rearrange the legal field around new ideas and new hierarchical principles. A campaign to "save" the Court and "unify" the bar, on which the ABA's leaders enthusiastically embarked, could not be directly attributed to the demands of clients and allowed elite lawyers to reassert their role as the defenders of the rule of law. In the name of protecting judicial prerogatives, therefore, the ABA did become a site of opposition to the New Deal's legal agenda.

New Dealers and the Horse-and-Buggy Court

Schechter brought to the surface the heretofore subtle debate concerning the legitimate role of the Supreme Court in shaping national policies. New Dealers responded to the decision with new attempts to alter the structure of authority in the legal field. The leaders of the practicing bar, on the other hand, summoned lawyers to an Armageddon in defense of an autonomous judicial system and an autonomous legal profession.

It was President Roosevelt who set the tone of the attack on the Supreme Court. Four days after *Schechter* was announced, Roosevelt faced reporters and declared, "The implications of this decision are much more important than almost certainly any decision of my lifetime or yours. . . . We have forty-eight nations from now on under a strict interpretation of this decision . . . we have been relegated to the horse-and-buggy definition of interstate commerce."[23] Twenty months later, in February 1937, Roosevelt sent Congress a bill that sought to pack the Court with justices who would be more sympathetic to the administration's recovery plans.

The story of the brief period that the court-packing plan dominated the American legal-political landscape is a well-documented one.[24] Yet instead of focusing on the 168 days that elapsed between the time the plan was publicly announced and its final burial, I suggest that a court-packing era in fact began immediately after *Schechter*. The second half of 1935 saw a multitude of proposals and ideas as to how to overcome what one observer described as a "government by judiciary."[25] Some suggested constitutional amendments that would have granted Congress explicit power to regulate commerce and industry on a federal basis; others entertained various means to curb the power of the Court, either by revoking or limiting its judicial review powers or by increasing the number of justices on the bench.

Charles Clark, the dean of Yale Law School, chaired a symposium on "The Constitution and Social Change" and argued that constitutional amendments were the preferred solution to the problem of the Court.[26] Lloyd Garrison, the dean of Wisconsin Law School, addressed the same panel and argued that "business today, in its larger aspects, has ceased to be of purely local significance . . . the Constitution does not contain, as it is now interpreted and as it is likely to be interpreted, sufficient power for these purposes. . . . I think we have reached a point where the Constitution should be amended, and the federal power broadened."[27] Garrison argued that the prevailing "constitutional consciousness" prevented pragmatic thinking and resulted in an ever-widening discrepancy between national exigencies and constitutional limitations. This, he argued, brought about "bad legislation" and a constant state of "legal uncertainty": "In the case of much of our legislation, neither Congress nor the President nor the Attorney General nor all of our constitutional oracles put together can prophesy in advance, with the least assurance, whether the legislation will survive or not." Furthermore, constitutional amendments were necessary in order to save the Court "from itself," from "currents of opposition" by those who grew increasingly impatient with the power of the Court to invalidate publicly desirable statutes.[28]

It seems that a constitutional amendment was also the solution favored by Felix Frankfurter. Throughout 1936 Frankfurter looked for people who would join in an effort to formally amend the Constitution.[29] Thomas Reed Powell of Harvard was also one who did not shudder at the thought of a constitutional amendment. Powell criticized *Schechter* for offering a restrictive interpretation of the Constitution and asserted that he had no principled objection to the idea of constitutional amendments. Cynically referring to the Court's conservative bloc, Powell said, "I feel safe enough in saying the Constitution should be amended to make us as much of a nation as four justices of the Supreme Court think that we already are, but I am not confident enough to say much more . . . If the Supreme Court continues to expand its self-directed censorship, I think that the time will come when something will have to be done about it."[30] Still, probably aware of the political difficulties involved in an attempt to amend the Constitution, Powell held that it was better for the time being to wait for future decisions of the Court. Referring to two other major New Deal laws, he said that they had

> possibilities of legitimacy under the commerce power not foreclosed by the Schechter case. To the secret of the constitutionality of many of these statutes, two men hold the key, and the secret is in a joint safety deposit box which it takes two concurring keys to open . . . If one of them says "No," the "No" will not be to me the voice of a god that should not be overridden by the Lucifer of a constitutional amendment. If nine say "No," it will give me great pause; but even then the "No" may come from legitimate considerations of the past which may be outweighed by considerations of the future.[31]

Powell, in short, warned the Court that a constitutional amendment would be headed its way unless it mended its ways.

The calls for constitutional amendments, however, were somewhat at odds with the frequent emphasis of many of the New Deal's legal minds on the "uncertainty" of law and the "flexibility" of the Constitution.[32] The implicit, perhaps unintentional, message of people like Clark, Frankfurter, and Garrison was that *Schechter* had been based on some essential properties of the Constitution rather than on the voluntary decision of the Court to adopt a restrictive line of constitutional interpretation. Even Powell, who clearly saw the problem as being grounded in the out-of-touch "bad politics" of the Court, eventually came to consider constitutional amendments the most effective way to deprive the Court of the constitutional foundation for its detached politics. This was a position that resonated with the "emergency" reasoning that many New Dealers adopted in defending NIRA prior to *Schechter*.[33] In both cases, the message was that constitutional "difficulties" inhered in the text, not in its readers, thereby implicitly affirming the autonomous and scientific character of legal reasoning.

The contradiction between the recommendation to amend the Constitution and the legal-realist spirit of uncertainty that permeated the New Deal's legal politics did not go unnoticed by some interested observers.[34] Thurman Arnold, for example, insisted on the importance of treating the Constitution as a flexible text and regarded the amendment proposals as a blow to the idea of legal uncertainty. The cultivation of the idea of legal uncertainty, and constitutional uncertainty for that matter, allowed Arnold to focus on dissenting opinions in the Court as an opening for a potentially new interpretive space. Addressing the New York State Bar Association shortly after the Supreme Court invalidated the Agriculture Adjustment Act, Arnold thus focused on the dissenting opinions of Chief Justice Hughes and Justice Stone as omens of future possibilities:

> The Supreme Court is sometimes full of surprises. It surprised me in the recent decision. There is always a possibility that it may surprise some of you in the future. At any rate, it is easy to find within the four walls of the Constitution, traditions and doctrines on which we may hope for a reversal in the future of present judicial trends. These hopes are based in the two great dissenting opinions of Mr. Justice Hughes and Mr. Justice Stone . . . and, therefore, I would insist that dissenting opinions are the great safety valve of the Constitution.[35]

John Dickinson, addressing the Illinois State Bar Association, also turned to Chief Justice Hughes in order to make an authoritative point about the uncertainty of law. Dickinson quoted Hughes:

> How amazing it is, that in the midst of controversies on every conceivable subject, one would expect unanimity of opinion upon difficult legal questions. In the highest ranges of thought, in theology, philosophy and science, we find differences of view on the part of the most distinguished experts . . . The history of scholarship is a record of disagreements. And when we deal with questions relating to principles of law and their application, we do not suddenly rise to a stratosphere of icy certainty.[36]

Dickinson, however, also objected to constitutional amendments and reminded listeners that

> [t]here is one problem which amendment will not solve and will not eliminate and which will remain no matter what amendments to the Constitution should be adopted. I refer, of course, to the problem of

interpretation. Amendments themselves will have to be interpreted by lawyers and by courts, and their meaning and effect, like the meaning and effect of the Constitution as it now stands, will be at the mercy of the interpreters . . . There is no substitute for wise and enlightened interpretation; without it, the possibility of amendment is but a barren hope.[37]

Not unlike other New Dealers, Dickinson flavored this observation with a warning:

What is needed today is nothing more nor less than for the bar and the courts today and in the future, as in the past, to recognize and apply canons of interpretation based on Story's conception of the Constitution as permitting a continuous evolutionary growth within its own provisions. If this is not recognized, if interpretation is applied from a purely restrictive standpoint and with no sense of responsibility for making progress possible under the Constitution . . . but one result can follow—increasing dissatisfaction with the Constitution, increasing disrespect for constitutional government itself, and *ultimate resort to some form of extra constitutional action* [italics mine].[38]

Louis Boudin, a sharp critic of the Court, argued that "the talk about amending the Constitution is on a par with the talk about liberal judges. It assumes that there is something in the present Constitution which says that the NIRA is unconstitutional. . . . The assumption that there is something in the Constitution which the judges have 'interpreted illiberally,' and that the difficulty is to be overcome by getting either some different provisions into the Constitution for the judges to 'interpret' or a different set of judges, more liberal than the present ones is nonsense based on ignorance."[39]

One important implication of such views was the public restatement of the idea that law and the Constitution were not much more than what the Court said they were. In fact, it was one of the members of the Executive Committee of the American Bar Association, Harry Lawther, who stated in those days that "the truth of the business is we don't know what is constitutional or unconstitutional until the Supreme Court says it is or it isn't."[40] This deference to the Court's constitutional interpretation, either approving or disapproving, explains the outrage people like Frankfurter and Powell expressed when the fifty-eight lawyers of the American Liberty League publicly announced their "verdict" on the constitutionality of the National Labor Relations Act.[41] At the same time, it also exposes the contradiction in the positions of Frankfurter and Powell, who advocated constitutional amendments instead of emphasizing the Court's interpretative capacities.[42]

Another important implication flowing from the emphasis on the uncertainty of law, and far more consequential, was the at least tacit understanding that questions of law were to a large extent questions of will rather than reason, or, to put it even more bluntly, questions of power. Boudin, accordingly, was among those who favored a direct assault on the authority of the Supreme Court. The only way to overcome judicial tyranny, Boudin argued, was to abolish the Court's judicial review powers, thus "depriving it of the power to declare acts of Congress unconstitutional."[43] Morris Cohen, a distinguished philosopher of law, also argued that because the Supreme Court was in effect constantly reinventing the Constitution, constitutional amendments could not provide a guarantee against judicial tyranny. Because the power of judicial review was born of judicial usurpation of power and was nowhere to be found in the Constitution itself, Cohen argued, there was no reason Congress should not escape its subordination to the Court by abolishing its review powers.[44] Edward Corwin argued that the power of judicial review should belong not less with the President than with the Supreme Court, whose judicial review power he described as "purely derivative, a corollary of the judicial duty to decide cases in accordance with the law of which the Constitution is a part,"[45] and Charles Clark reasoned that the power of judicial review was deficient because the Court assumed no responsibility for the consequences of its actions; it was "only saying 'No' to some other political agency." The review power of the Court, therefore, encouraged the executive and legislative branches of government to practice the "good old American game of passing the buck" and had to be reconsidered.[46]

Accordingly, various proposals explicitly designed to curb the powers of the Supreme Court were introduced in Congress in the second half of 1935. One proposal provided that any law held by the Supreme Court to be unconstitutional should nonetheless be held valid if approved by the electorate or reenacted by Congress; another provided for the submission of certain judgments of the Supreme Court to the people; another proposed the concurrence of a specified number of justices to declare a statute unconstitutional; and others provided for an increase in the number of justices on the bench in order to pack it with jurists who were more sympathetic to the New Deal's legislative agenda.[47]

In the summer of 1936 the solicitor general, Stanley Reed, and the attorney general, Hommer Cummings, began to secretly prepare the court-packing plan. Publicly, they spoke highly of the Court's prerogatives, defended the review powers of the Court, and pledged allegiance to its rulings. At the same time, both also emphasized the "uncertainty" of law as a "very real cause for hope in the future."[48] By combining supportive declarations of the Court's authority, statements about the uncertainty of law, and hopes for a future "enlightened" Court, these lawyers prepared the ideological foundation for the court-packing plan of 1937. The plan, from this perspective, was a logical extension of the idea that majority and minority opinions on the bench should enjoy equal normative footing. Thus, one could legitimately claim that a given majority opinion at a given moment was no more than a politically contingent reflection of a state of affairs that might well be out of tune with the necessity of the times. Packing the Court, according to this logic, could be legitimately viewed as an attempt to preserve the Court's role in providing the necessary legitimation of new constitutional doctrines by simply "correcting" a contingent, if not accidental, unfortunate "imbalance" on the bench. The court-packing plan, in this respect, was indeed the epitome of an approach that embedded law in the realm of will.[49]

In sum, it was immediately after *Schechter* that various ideas about how to curb the power of the Court began to float around in academic, congressional, and governmental circles. None were seriously considered by Congress prior to the official announcement of Roosevelt's court-packing plan in early 1937. Nonetheless, the plan, which is often referred to as a single event that lasted for a few months, may be better described as the court-packing era—a period of two years during which the administration's lawyers and academic supporters systematically questioned the authority of the Supreme Court and publicly reconsidered the relationship of law and politics and the internal structure of the legal field. By the time the various proposals to curb the power of the Supreme Court began to float around, it should be recalled, the administration had already eliminated the jurisdiction of federal courts to restrain enforcement of state administrative orders concerning public utility rates. In a letter to Frankfurter dated February 1936, Justice Brandeis wrote that "not only should the diversity jurisdiction be abolished . . . but most . . . other jurisdiction[s] added in 1875 & later should be abrogated and in no case practically should the appellate federal courts have to pass on the construction of state statutes."[50] Thus, the suspicion of the bar's leaders that all these various voices were part of a general effort to limit the jurisdiction of federal courts had not been unfounded. Consequently, it was to this daring spirit of defiance towards judicial authority that many of the bar's leaders responded with accusations against those who "refuse allegiance to our Constitution and form of government."[51]

The Bar Responds: In Defense of Judicial Authority

Differences of opinion between many of the bar's leaders and the supporters of the New Deal were evident even prior to *Schechter*. Reform-minded jurists emphasized the flexible nature of the Constitution and the uncertainty inherent in judicial decisionmaking. According to this view, which had a profound influence on government lawyers, the Constitution had to be treated as a kind of a working hypothesis, as a text of truth to be constructed and as a source for future creative interpretations in the service of desired social ends. In line with these ideas of legal construction, therefore, New Dealers spoke against "maintaining the deadly letter of the law" and in favor of its "life-giving spirit."[52] The treatment of the Constitution as a "working hypothesis" met with fierce opposition from some prominent members of the bar. One of the most vocal speakers was James M. Beck, an eminent constitutional lawyer with an established reputation both as a scholar and as an active politician.[53] Beck, like some other lawyers who shared his views, turned to the principles of natural justice in order to counter the view that the Constitution was only a source for "practical interpretation." For Beck, the Constitution was a Gibraltar, a fundamentally unaltered text that defined the boundaries of legal discourse.[54] Similarly, Jouett Shouse, the president of the American Liberty League, compared the Constitution's sacredness to that of the Ten Commandments; Raoul Desvernine argued that constitutional rights were a "divine endowment" that existed prior to "any human institution or government"; and Nathan Miller, a former governor of New York and a law partner of Desvernine, argued that the Constitution "provided a scheme of government based on fundamental principles as unchanging as human nature itself."[55]

Beck saw the New Deal as a *coup d'état*, a revolutionary attempt to transform the United States into a "totalitarian socialistic state" and to deliver a death blow to the Constitution using methods that resembled those of "Stalin over the unhappy peasants of Russia": "The Constitution for the last fifty years has been in process of slow demolition. Here an arch has fallen; there a pillar; and now it is the foundations themselves that are fast sinking, and if the present process of destruction proceeds, it is not unlikely that within the next fifty years the whole structure will fall into cureless ruin."[56]

The warnings of lawyers like Beck, Davis, Miller, and Desvernine fell on truly receptive ears only after *Schechter*. Combined with the expansion of the administrative process, it was the open attack on the Court in the aftermath of *Schechter* that finally persuaded heretofore prudent lawyers that they were indeed experiencing a real crisis—a systematic undermining of the autonomy of law as they knew it, of the prerogatives of the judicial system, and, by extension, of the power and autonomy of the practicing bar as a whole. More and more lawyers perceived the events of the times in terms of a political usurpation of their own jurisdiction and criticized the attempts to "abolish the Supreme Court, to 'control or to do away with the influence of the Judicial Department,' and to establish a 'government by men.'"[57]

The court-packing spirit that had been set in motion after *Schechter* also provided an excellent opportunity to unite the bar behind a common cause.[58] Here, for the first time since the beginning of the New Deal, the representatives of the American Bar Association could publicly speak about what was perceived as a nonpartisan issue. Scott Loftin, the outgoing president of the association, thus dedicated his 1935 farewell address to the importance of an independent judicial system, in stark contrast to the previous year's address by Evans, who avoided any reference to the New Deal. Another lawyer, in an emotional appeal, asserted the professional duty of lawyers to unite under the banner of "defending the courts":

> We as lawyers have a duty right here and now to meet the more or less popular clamor about the courts . . . I don't care one iota whether you think the Supreme Court was right or wrong in its decision in the Schechter case. What I am tremendously concerned about is that lawyers, and whether we are political partisans—republicans and democrats, and new dealers and what not—we as lawyers owe it to our oath—for we took oaths to support the Constitution of the United States, to see to it that in our communities, insofar as within us lies, we stand up for the integrity of the courts and their right to prevent usurpation of power by anyone.[59]

Applauding Faville's speech, the president of the Nebraska State Bar Association directly linked the urgent duty of lawyers to defend the courts with the efforts to unite the bar of the country under the leadership of the ABA.[60] Indeed, the attack on the Court provided an excellent opportunity to advance the call for a stronger and coordinated national lawyers' association that would truly be able to speak in one voice for the profession as a whole. William Ransom, the ABA's newly elected president, promoted a National Bar Program project by emphasizing the potential effectiveness of lawyers in preserving the independence of the judiciary. Ransom, an enthusiastic believer in the potential influence of an organized bar and a staunch critic of the New Deal, traveled extensively across the country, addressed numerous bar associations, and championed the cause of a coordinated bar.[61]

To Ransom's mind, there was an inherent connection between the status of courts and the social influence and prestige of the legal profession. Addressing the Alabama State Bar Association, he outlined the purpose of the National Bar Program:

> When we survey what is taking place today as to the courts, we find directed against them the same trends, the same forces, which seek to

discredit the Bar. . . . At the recent session, there were pending in the Congress of the United States many bills to limit or take away the powers of the Courts to declare and enforce the fundamental law of the land, and to take away the powers of the Courts to protect the citizen against laws and executive acts which violate the Constitution. . . . All of these proposals, and others, seem to me to indicate an increasing disposition and desire, on the part of government, to take the law into its own hands and to exercise powers untrammeled by constitutional limitations. . . . Irrespectively of party, I believe it to be the highest duty of lawyers, along with all good citizens, to stand firmly against all forms of disrespect for the Constitution and for law, and against all efforts to seize and exercise arbitrary, lawless powers, whether attempted by those in public office or by those in the ranks of private citizens.[62]

In another address Ransom directly tied the attempts to "take away the powers of the courts" to the attack on the legal profession: "As to lawyers, both in pending legislation and in administrative regulations and departmental rules, there is a manifest tendency and purpose to circumscribe and limit the activities of lawyers in behalf of clients [and] to limit or deny the right of citizens to be represented by counsel."[63] All this, Ransom concluded, indicated that "there goes forward the effort to force the doctrines of Karl Marx into legislation."[64]

Such unprecedented statements from a president of the American Bar Association reflected a deep sense of suspicion toward the rhetoric and practice of the administration's legal advisers and an acute sense of insecurity in dealing with the new developments. Bar associations all over the country braced themselves for the defense of the judiciary. The New York State Bar Association and the Association of the Bar of the City of New York compiled and placed on file various "court-curbing" measures and promised to resist the "agitation for such amendments."[65] The Committee on Federal Legislation of the Chicago Bar Association also documented various proposals to curb the review power of courts and resolved to oppose "any legislation limiting the jurisdiction of the Federal Courts . . . beyond the present limits now provided in the Constitution and by Acts of Congress." Further, in an attempt to demonstrate the degree of consensus among lawyers from all professional ranks, the Chicago Bar Association conducted a referendum showing that an overwhelming majority of Chicago's lawyers disapproved of such measures.[66]

Finally, the ABA's Committee on Jurisprudence and Law Reform, which also compiled various court-curbing measures, bitterly criticized them as "absolutely subversive."[67] Walter P. Armstrong, the chairperson of the committee,

addressed the association's General Assembly and declared that the unconstitutionality of these "dangerous" proposals was "so glaring as to be fantastic." The
role of the united bar, said Armstrong, was to educate the public: "We feel that
in view of the reorganization of the American Bar Association, *now finally
become truly representative of the American bar,* this is the organization to take
the lead in informing and guiding public opinion in order that the courts may
be protected" (italics mine).[68]

In sum, two major developments took place in the legal field in the aftermath
of *Schechter.* Many of the nation's most prominent lawyers challenged New
Deal laws with enhanced vigor and self-assurance, encouraged recalcitrant clients to disobey various laws, and publicly conveyed their misgivings about the
administration's legislative policies. Bar associations, on the other hand, organized a campaign against what was perceived as the administration's calculated
subversion of judicial authority. The protection of the judicial system, instead
of concentrating on the content of specific laws, allowed the organized bar to
assert its public responsibilities and to promote the unification of the bar under
the authoritative umbrella of the American Bar Association.

A recurrent theme and focus of this book so far has been the effort of lawyers to
draw a clear line between law and politics. This effort was not based on a naive
formalist vision of law as a separate universe of discourse. Rather, it was generated by the *political* understanding that the ability to retain the *symbolic* separation between these two discursive fields was a crucial element in maintaining
the aura of professionalism and in cultivating and protecting the profession's
social and economic privileges.

What I have previously termed the "intellectual dependency" of the bar on
the federal judiciary was derived directly from the desire to constantly reconstruct the apolitical nature of legal reason. The relative independence of the
federal judiciary from direct political interference and the historic function of
appellate courts as the primary producers of legal doctrines and juristic knowledge were paramount in curating the metaphorical neutral space within which
lawyers could also appropriate the position of the impartial expert. Like a secret
chamber that could be approached and entered only by those who had de-
ciphered hidden codes, the legal field in the United States was established
around the centrality of courts in producing and announcing legal truths and a
surrounding ring of legal practitioners as their most entrusted officers and
gatekeepers. The historic centrality of courts in the development of law in the
United States was the foundation upon which lawyers, as a professional group
in "civil society," acquired prestige, influence, and wealth. Thus, underlying

the asserted connection between the duty of the lawyer to defend the integrity of courts and the autonomy of the legal profession in private practice was the much-feared imagery and prospect of a newly structured legal field. The prospect of a strengthened federal state relying upon a strong executive and administrative apparatuses and backed by a new breed of government lawyers and academic legal scholars committed to public service (i.e., state service) threatened the established hierarchy of authority and prestige within the legal field.

In other words, a significant group of elite lawyers, willing to devote time and energy to activities that transcended the immediate concerns of their daily practice, had their own distinct reasons to dread the New Deal, independent of their ongoing complicity with clients and of political and economic worldviews generated *outside* the legal field. This shift toward an analysis of an analytically decontextualized legal field within which the positions of actors who are pulling and pushing at conflicting directions dictate, but do not always determine, discursive and practical moves is the main project of the next part of the book.

Excursus I

The Professional Network

It is now possible to look more closely at the individuals whom I designated as the leaders of the bar. In designating these individuals as an "elite," as "prominent lawyers," and as "leaders," I did not mean to suggest that all or even most lawyers in private practice looked to them for professional and moral guidance. In fact, it is more likely that most lawyers were not very interested in the abstract jurisprudential and theoretical implications of the New Deal or in the politics of the bar. Most lawyers in private practice, after all, are more concerned with attending, representing, and getting clients than in the broader implications of their collective professional lives. Moreover, among those lawyers who were involved with the broader aspects of the New Deal there were many who were evidently disenchanted with those whom I called "the leaders of the bar." Thus, for example, a group of disenchanted lawyers broke ranks with the American Bar Association in December 1936 and established the National Lawyers Guild as a counter–national organization that they hoped could undermine the hegemony of the conservative corporate lawyers who dominated the ABA.[1] I invoked these terms, however, as a convenient way of expressing, first of all, these individuals' own belief that they were speaking for the profession as a whole and were devoting time and energy to matters and concerns that transcended their obligations to clients. At least some of these corporate lawyers, in other words, were truly acting as if they had professional and moral duties to fulfill. Second, the designation of these lawyers as an elite may be justified on objective grounds. They enjoyed and shared privileged positions: financial security, professional prestige, considerable political influence, and access to decision makers in the market and the state apparatuses. Most of these lawyers were partners in big (by the standards of the day) law firms who had strong connections to the major business circles of the nation. Many of them were involved in the important legal and judicial struggles of the times and at the same time dominated the major bar associations and shaped their policies and agenda. Finally, in talking about "leaders" and about an "elite" of corporate lawyers, I also have in mind a network of lawyers who maintained strong social, professional, ideological, and institutional ties among themselves. Many of these lawyers, in short, knew each other and coordinated their responses to various matters of professional relevance.

In order to reconstruct this network of lawyers, I first look at some of the major firms that fought New Deal laws in legislative and judicial arenas, and particularly at the activities taken in connection with the National Industrial Recovery Act, the Securities Act, the Securities Exchange Act, the National Labor Relations Act, and the Public Utility Holding Company Act. For reasons of space, I have in each case singled out only those who were also involved in other types of challenges to the New Deal, either challenging other laws in courts and congressional settings, actively participating in bar committees and projects, or publicly discussing the New Deal legislative agenda in noteworthy addresses and articles. To be sure, this method suffers from some unavoidable shortcomings. First, many lawyers and firms were probably left out of the sample. Second, the attempt to talk about "opposition" to the New Deal necessarily involves as a series of arbitrary choices regarding what is and is not relevant to the New Deal. Third, I do not discuss at length some key New Deal measures: the Agricultural Adjustment Act, the Social Security Act, the Bituminous Coal Conservation Act, and important aspects of the Public Works Administration and the Tennessee Valley Authority, to mention but a few.[2] Still, I believe that this method of singling out allows me to identify a core group of lawyers who challenged the New Deal in the double capacity of representing clients on the one hand and speaking in the name of law for the profession of whole on the other hand. The emerging picture also happens to provide another way of looking at those New Deal laws that attracted the most vehement opposition from the leading business and financial circles of the nation.

The National Industrial Recovery Act

Elite lawyers played a minor role in congressional hearings on the National Industrial Recovery Act. The strongest opposition to the bill came from the corporate executives and the lawyers of the oil industry who focused their criticism on those provisions of the NIRA that dealt with the regulation of oil production.[3] The only marked exception was the testimony of James Emery, the legal counsel of the National Association of Manufacturers, who raised doubts concerning the overall constitutionality of the proposed bill.[4]

Ninety-one NIRA-related cases were decided by United States federal courts between the enactment of the NIRA in June 1933 and March 1935, shortly before the Supreme Court invalidated the act in *Schechter.*[5] The NIRA was challenged on constitutional grounds in thirty-eight of these cases.[6] Major corporations, and consequently major corporate practice law firms, took little part in this litigation campaign.[7] Of a total of seventy-two lawyers who appeared in those cases, forty-six were solo practitioners and partners in two-lawyer partnerships (70 percent), fourteen worked for firms who had three to five members (19 percent), seven for firms of six to nine members (10 percent), and five for firms with more than ten members (7 percent).[8] Further, the burden of challenging the NIRA was disproportionally carried by lawyers who represented small businesses in small towns and rural areas. Of the seventy-two lawyers, three were from Chicago (two solo practitioners and one firm lawyer), six from New York (five solo practitioners and one firm lawyer), one from Pittsburgh, and one from Detroit.[9] Out of this list of challengers, I isolated only those lawyers and firms that were also involved in other forms of opposition to the New Deal. This short list appears in table 1.[10]

The Securities Act

A considerable number of lawyers appeared before congressional committees when the securities bill was pending in Congress.[11] Leading the opposition were senior partners in two prominent firms: William Breed of Breed, Abbott & Morgan and Arthur H. Dean of Sullivan & Cromwell. The constitutionality of the Securities Act was challenged on eight occasions in the course of enforcement efforts by the Securities and Exchange Commission (SEC).[12] Analysis of these eight cases shows that major law firms were not heavily involved in the attempts to kill the act. Twenty-eight lawyers and law firms appeared in these eight cases: twenty solo practitioners and members of two-member firms (71 percent), seven lawyers of small to medium-sized firms, and one from a firm

Table 1

Name of Lawyer/Firm	Size	Case/Activity Involved
Cravath, DeGersdorff, Swaine & Wood	17	*Schechter Poultry Co. v. United States*
Beaumont, Smith & Harris	13 + 5	*United States v. Houde Engineering*
Thorp, Bostwick, Reed & Armstrong	5 + 3	*United States v. Weirton Steel*
Cabannis & Johnston	5 + 3	*Ashwander v. TVA*
Norman, Quirk & Graham	3	*Sparks v. Hart Coal Corp.*
Saye, Smead & Saye	3	*Panama Refining Corp. v. Ryan*
		Amazon Refining Corp. v. Ryan
Davis, Polk, Gardiner & Reed	20	amicus curiae (*Schechter*)
James Beck		amicus curiae (*Schechter*)
James Emery		in Congress

with more than ten members.[13] In table 2 I again identify only those legal actors who were involved in other forms of challenges to the New Deal.

The Securities Exchange Act

A considerable number of lawyers challenged the expediency, wisdom, and constitutionality of the bill when it was pending in Congress.[14] The only constitutional challenge to the act following its enactment was in the case of *Securities and Exchange Commission v. Torr*, in which the constitutionality of the Securities Act had also been challenged.[15] Consequently, the number of lawyers who directly challenged the act was extremely limited, as table 3 demonstrates. Again, table 3 singles out only lawyers whose role in challenging the Securities Exchange Act combined with other forms of activity.

Table 2

Name of Lawyer/Firm	Size	Case/Activity Involved
Gleason, McLanahan, Merritt & Ingraham	11	*SEC v. Torr*
Saye, Smead & Saye	3	*Jones v. SEC*
James Beck		*Jones v. SEC*
Breed, Abbott & Morgan	14	W. Breed (in Congress)
Sullivan & Cromwell	28	A. Dean (in Congress)
R. V. Fletcher		in Congress

Table 3

Name of Lawyer/Firm	Size	Case/Activity Involved
Gleason, McLanahan, Merritt & Ingraham	11	*SEC v. Torr*
Hunton, Williams, Anderson, Gay & Moore	9 + 3	T. B. Gay (in Congress)
R. V. Fletcher		in Congress
Covington, Burling, Rublee, Acheson & Shorb	8 + 7	H. Covington (in Congress)

The National Labor Relations Act

From its inception opposition to the Labor Act was fierce. An impressive number of lawyers opposed the labor bill, in its various forms, in congressional
hearings.[16] A sample of labor-related litigation that followed the enactment
of the law also reveals a heavy involvement of prominent lawyers and firms.
Eighty-six labor-related cases were decided by federal courts in the first year of
the act's life. Of this number, I was able to retrieve the identity of legal counsel
in forty cases.[17] Fifty-four lawyers and firms appeared in these forty cases:
twenty-five solo practitioners and lawyers from two-member partnerships (46
percent), eight lawyers from firms with three to five members (15 percent),
eight lawyers from firms with six to ten members (15 percent), and thirteen
lawyers from firms with eleven or more members (24 percent). In other words,
in contrast to the NIRA and the securities legislation, big law firms clearly
played a greater role in challenging the Labor Relations Act. Table 4 below
lists some of the major firms that were involved in challenging the Labor
Relations Act. As may be observed, this list is significantly longer than the
ones concerning the securities laws and serves as a quantitative reminder that
the bar's elite had been fully recruited to the battle against the act. It must
be said, however, that table 4 provides a very limited and narrow picture of
the scope and intensity of the legal struggle against the Labor Act. Thus, some
of the biggest firms in the nation were involved in the litigation campaign
but do not appear on the list.[18] Further, one of the unique features of the
litigation campaign against the act was the impressive degree of cooperation
among various lawyers and firms who represented interested clients. For example, the representation of Bethlehem Steel Corporation was carried out not
only by the Cravath firm (listed below) but also by the Boston firm of Choate,
Hall & Stewart (14 members) and the Los Angeles firm of O'Melveny, Tuller
& Myers (34 members). These complexities, regrettably, do not show up on
table 4.

Table 4

Name of Lawyer/Firm	Size	Case/Activity Involved
Thorp, Bostwick, Reed & Armstrong	5 + 3	*NLRB v. Jones & Laughlin*
Davis, Polk, Gardiner & Reed	20	*Associated Press v. NLRB*
Butler, Pope & Ballard	17 + 5	*NLRB v. Clayton*
Cravath, DeGersdorff, Swaine & Wood	17	*NLRB v. Bethlehem Corp.*
Pepper, Bodine & Stokes	9 + 6	*NLRB v. Blood*
James Emery		in Congress
Gleason, McLanahan, Merritt & Ingaraham	11	in Congress
Elisha Hanson		in Congress
Beaumont, Smith & Harris	13 + 5	in Congress

The Public Utility Holding Company Act

A number of prominent lawyers appeared before congressional committees on behalf of major utility and holding companies, while others were involved in intense lobbying efforts.[19] A compilation of cases by the Securities and Exchange Commission revealed that eight well-coordinated cases challenged the constitutionality of the act in its first two years. The degree to which these cases were part of a coordinated effort is demonstrated by the fact that the firm of Davis, Polk, Gardiner & Reed took part in five of these eight cases. In two of these five cases, the firm cooperated with the law firm of Whitman, Ransom, Coulson & Goetz. Other firms were also involved in some of these cases: Re American States was also handled by the Baltimore, Maryland, firm of Piper, Carey & Hall; the case of Consolidated Gas also engaged the New York City firm of Frueauff, Burns, O'Brien & Ruch (formerly Frueauff, Robinson & Sloan) and the New York firm of LeBoeuf & Winston (later LeBoeuf, Winston, Machold & Lamb). The case of Cities Service also involved Frueauff, Burns, O'Brien & Ruch. The case of Burco was also handled by Piper, Carey & Hall and by the Baltimore, Maryland, firm of Niles, Barton, Morrow & Yost. These additions to table 5 below may provide further insights into the degree of intensity and cooperation that accompanied the attack on the Utility Act. In this table, however, I again list only those lawyers who opposed the New Deal in other capacities as well.

As previously mentioned, the above lists by no means exhaust the number of lawyers who actively opposed, by various means, an unspecified number of New Deal measures. There is hardly any doubt that there were many other lawyers who escaped the above compilations. A notable example is Newton D.

Table 5

Name of Lawyer/Firm	Size	Case/Activity Involved
Davis, Polk, Gardiner & Reed	20	*Re American States Public Service Co.*; *Consolidated Gas v. Hardy*; *Cities Service v. Hardy*; *United Corporation v. Hardy*; *Burco Inc. v. Whitworth et al.*
Whitman, Ransom, Coulson & Goetz	7	*Consolidated Gas v. Hardy*; *Cities Service v. Hardy*
Sullivan & Cromwell	28	*Electric Bond & Share Co. v. SEC*; *North American Co.*
Simpson, Thatcher & Bartlett	12	*Electric Bond & Share Co. v. SEC*; in Congress
Covington, Burling, Rublee, Acheson & Shorb	8 + 7	*North American Co.*
R. V. Fletcher		in Congress
Hunton, Williams, Anderson, Gay & Moore	9 + 3	in Congress

Baker, who was recruited by the Edison Electric Institute to challenge the Utilities Law and was also involved in litigation challenging the Public Works Administration. Further, Baker, probably like many other lawyers of his stature, acted behind the scenes in coordinating some activities against various New Deal measures and had a considerable although subtle influence in the American Bar Association.[20] Yet there are also good reasons to believe that the lawyers listed above by and large comprised the core of the legal profession's opposition to the New Deal. When we look, for example, at a number of cases that reached the Supreme Court in connection with other New Deal laws, we again find the same challengers. Thus, for example, the case of *Carter v. Carter Coal* of 1936, in which the Supreme Court invalidated the Guffey Bituminous Coal Act, was handled by the firm of Cravath, DeGersdorff, Swaine & Moore, which was also involved in cases concerning the NIRA and the Labor Act. Amici curiae briefs in this case were submitted by three other firms that appeared on some of the above lists: Davis, Polk, Gardiner & Reed; Norman, Quirk & Graham; and Cabannis & Johnston.[21] Similarly, *United States v. Butler*, in which the Supreme Court invalidated the Agricultural Adjustment Act, was handled by the firm of Pepper, Bodine & Stokes, which was also involved in labor-related litigation. Amici curiae in this case were submitted by firms that also show up on the

Table 6

Name of Lawyer/Firm	Size	Challenged Laws	Bar Activity
Beaumont, Smith & Harris*	13 + 5	NIRA; NLRA	X
Beck James*		NIRA; SA	X
Breed, Abbott & Morgan	14	SA; SEC	X
Butler, Pope & Ballard*	17 + 5	NLRA; FJ	X
Cabannis & Johnston*	5 + 3	NIRA; BC	X
Covington, Burling, Rublee, Acheson & Shorb	8 + 7	PU; FJ	X
Cravath, DeGersdorff, Swaine & Wood*	17	NIRA; NLRA; BC	X
Davis, Polk, Gardiner & Reed	20	NIRA; NLRA; PU; BC	X
Emery James		NIRA; NLRA	
Fletcher, R. V.		SEA; SA; PU	
Gleason, McLanahan, Merritt & Ingaraham	11	SA; SEA; NLRA	X
Hornblower, Miller, Miller & Boston*	12	NLRA; AAA	X
Hunton, Williams, Anderson, Gay & Moore*	9 + 3	SEA; PU	X
Norman, Quirk & Graham*	3	NIRA; BC	
Pepper, Bodine & Stokes*	9 + 6	NLRA; AAA	X
Saye, Smead & Saye	3	NIRA; SA	
Simpson, Thatcher & Bartlett	12	PU; FJ	X
Sullivan & Cromwell	28	SA; PU	
Thorp, Bostwick, Reed & Armstrong	5 + 3	NIRA; NLRA	
Whitman, Ransom, Coulson & Goetz	7	PU; FJ	X

Note: Abbreviations used: NIRA: National Industrial Recovery Act; NLRA: National Labor Relations Act; SA: Securities Act; SEC: Securities Exchange Act; PU: Public Utilities Holding Company Act; AAA: Agricultural Adjustment Act; BC: Bituminous Coal Conservation Act; FJ: Federal Jurisdiction over Utility Rates.
*Firms with ties to the American Liberty League (see also table 7).

above lists: Hornblower, Miller, Miller & Boston, and Davis, Polk, Gardiner & Reed. When we add to this emerging picture some of the lawyers who fought the administration's attempt to abolish the jurisdiction of federal courts in matters of utility orders, we again find considerable overlap with the existing network. Thus, for example, Robert Coulson, who appeared in the congressional hearings on behalf of Consolidated Gas Company, was a partner in Whitman, Ransom, Coulson & Goetz, which was involved in utility-related litigation; and Rush C. Butler, who represented the Council for the American Federation of Utility Investors, was a partner in Butler, Pope & Ballard, a firm that was involved in labor-related litigation.

In table 6, therefore, I have collapsed the above five tables into a more comprehensive list of firms and lawyers who were most actively involved in opposition to various of the New Deal's legislative measures analyzed in this work. In the fourth column of this table I specify whether the firm or one of its members had been significantly involved in activities of the American Bar Association.

Table 6 provides us with a group of seventeen major law firms and three solo practitioners who were especially active in opposing New Deal legislation in congressional hearings and in the courts. Naturally, this small group handled only a minor part of the overall burden of litigation that followed the enactment of the labor and financial laws. The distinguishing characteristics of most of the lawyers in the above group, however, become clearer when we look at other activities in which they took part. The overwhelming majority of the above-mentioned lawyers engaged in all sorts of public activities that far transcended the relatively narrow horizons that mere service to clients dictated. All in all, out of the above list of twenty lawyers and firms, fourteen had in one way or another been active in the American Bar Association. Eleven firms on this list had partners who held key positions in the ABA and other important state bar associations. Thus, for example, the firm of Whitman, Ransom, Coulson & Goetz featured William Ransom, the 1935 president of the ABA, and Thomas D. Thatcher, of Simpson, Thatcher & Bartlett, was the president of the Association of the Bar of the City of New York. Some of the firms that did not have direct and active involvement in the ABA were nonetheless closely associated with other public activities. Gordon W. Merritt, for example, a partner in Gleason, McLanahan, Merritt & Ingraham, was one of the more visible leaders of the League for Industrial Rights, an employers' organization that fought the labor policies of the New Deal. And two lawyers from Sullivan & Cromwell, Arthur Dean and John Foster Dulles, were active in opposing the Securities Act and the Public Utility Holding Company Act. Of the three solo practitioners on the list, James Beck has to be singled out. Beck was a lawyer-politician, a Pennsylvania representative in Congress, and a leading figure in the American Bar Association, the League for Industrial Rights, and the American Liberty League. In 1935 he came close to being elected as the president of the ABA, losing to William Ransom by a narrow margin. Beck launched a one-man campaign against the New Deal that far exceeded in importance his relatively limited role in litigation.

Particularly important for present purposes is the fact that eleven of the above-mentioned list of lawyers and firms had ties to the American Liberty League. The American Liberty League was joined by fifty-eight lawyers who created the league's National Lawyers Committee. Other prominent lawyers were members of the National Executive Committee of the League, and two

Table 7

American Liberty League	Firm	Role in the ABA
Beardsley, Charles	Fitzgerald, Abbott & Bear	Executive Committee
Beck, James		Com. on Citizenship, Chair
Benson, Lewis	Churchill & Benson	GC, Insurance Section
Buist, George	Buist & Buist	GC, Com. on New Deal
Butler, C. Rush	Butler, Pope & Ballard	Com. on Commerce, Chair
Caldwell, G. Louis	Kirkland, Fleming, Green & Martin	Com. on Administrative Law, Chair
Collins, C. James	Tillinghast & Collins	GC, Public Relations Com.
Coudert, Frederick	Coudert & Coudert	Int'l Relations Com., Chair
Davis, John	Davis, Polk, Gardiner & Reed	former president
Desvernine, Raoul	Hornblower, Miller, Miller & Boston	Commerce Committee
Dodge, G. Robert	Palmer, Dodge, Barstow, Wilkins & Davis	State Council, Mass.
Evans, W. Earle	Vermillion, Evans, Carey & Lilleston	former president
Fleming, P. Francis	Fleming, Hamilton, Diver & Lichliter	General Council
Fowler, R. Charles	Fowler, Carlson, Furber & Johnson	Commerce Committee
Gallagher, Harold	Hornblower, Miller, Miller & Boston	Com. on Commerce, Chair Utilities Section
Green, W. Garner	Green, Green & Jackson	Com. on Membership; Insurance Section
Guthrie, J. Thomas	Parrish, Cohen, Guthrie & Watters	General Council; Insurance Section
Hogan, J. Frank	Hogan, Donovan, Jones, Hartson & Guider	Executive Committee
Johnston, Forney	Cabannis & Johnston	ABA vice president
Newlin, E. Gurney	Newlin & Ashburn	Executive Committee
Norman, J. Van Dyke	Norman, Quirk & Graham	Com. on Commerce
Patterson, J. Giles		Sect. on Municipal Law; Public Relations Com.
Robinson, F. Lucius	Robinson, Robinson & Cole	State Legislation Com.
Root, Elihu	Root, Clark, Buckner & Ballantine	former president reorganization of the bar

Table 7 Continued

American Liberty League	Firm	Role in the ABA
Stinchfield, Frederick	Stinchfield, Mackall, Crounse, McNally & Moore	Executive Committee 1937 president
Taylor, Tazewell	Taylor & Taylor	State Council, Virginia
Wickersham, W. George	Cadwalader, Wickersham & Taft	Resolutions Committee

Note: Abbreviations are: GC: General Council; Com.: Committee; Sect.: Section.

thousand others joined as members. Some of the most prominent lawyers who joined the American Liberty League not only were active in resisting the New Deal's legislative agenda through the various means outlined above but also had a considerable ability to shape the policies of the ABA. An analysis of the fifty-eight members of the league's National Lawyers Committee reveals that twenty-seven of them held key positions within the ABA. Table 7 illustrates this point.

Other lawyer-members of the American Liberty League also enjoyed considerable influence in the American Bar Association. William H. Rogers, for example, was a member of the League's National Advisory Council, a member of the ABA's Committee on Judicial Selection, and the representative of the state of Florida in the ABA's State Council. Another member of the National Advisory Council, Fred Gause, was also a member of the ABA's influential Resolutions Committee. Other firms had some of their partners in the American Liberty League and still others in influential positions in the ABA. One such example concerned the firm of Winston, Strawn & Shaw. Harold Beacom and Ralph Shaw, two partners in the firm, were members of the league's National Lawyers Committee. Two other partners in the firm were influential members of the ABA: Silas Strawn, who had an important role in the creation of the ABA's Committee on the Securities Act, and Edward Everett, who was a member of the ABA's Committee on Jurisprudence and Law Reform. Similarly, Randolph Williams, of the prominent firm of Hunton, Williams, Gay & Moore, was a member of the National Lawyers Committee. Thomas B. Gay, a partner in the firm, represented the state of Virginia in the ABA's State Council and at one time was a member of the ABA's Committee on Administrative Law. The firm of Hornblower, Miller, Miller & Boston also had its own internal division of political-professional labor. Two partners in the firm were members of the

League's National Lawyers Committee: Raoul Desvernine and Harold Galla-gher, who were also active members of the ABA. Another partner, Nathan Miller, a former governor of New York, was one of the league's directors and an active member of the Association of the Bar of the City of New York. In general, the New York State Bar Association and the Association of the Bar of the City of New York had among their more influential members some prominent leaders of the American Liberty League: George Wickersham, William Breed, Frederick Coudert, and John Davis, to mention a few.

In sum, the overall picture that emerges out of tables 6 and 7 above is that the opposition to the New Deal's legislative policies was handled by a rather limited circle of law firms that were tightly related to each other through an extensive system of mutual activities in the American Bar Association and the American Liberty League. Earlier we saw the sometimes desperate attempts of the ABA to retain an impartial image. To this end, various committees on keeping a narrow legalistic focus, carefully measured the timing according to which reports were released, and often avoided constitutional issues. Yet the considerable overlap that existed between lawyers who joined the American Liberty League and officers and active members of the ABA damaged the ability of the organized bar to convincingly convey an aura of impartial expertise. Those who joined the American Liberty League contributed to the inability of lawyers in general, and the ABA in particular, to transform their professional expertise into normative and moral authority. It is no wonder, therefore, that New Dealers labeled the ABA a "second" Liberty League and effectively blocked the attempts of the ABA to have a voice in national policymaking.

As previously mentioned, many lawyers were dissatisfied with the fact that the ABA was controlled by such a limited inner court of elite corporate lawyers who shaped the association's policies in light of their own interests and convic-tions. The creation of the National Lawyers Guild in 1936 was the most provocative expression of the growing disillusionment with the ABA that some lawyers felt. Their project, therefore, was to provide "the first national answer to the Liberty League and the American Bar Association."[22] Still, the guild, for various reasons, never established itself as a real alternative to the American Bar Association. Throughout the New Deal, a rather limited group of corporate firms spoke for the legal profession as a whole. In this respect, it may be a good reminder to cite Larson: "A profession is always defined by its elites . . . it is always an elite that speaks to relevant outsiders for the 'whole profession,' maintaining the image of a unified and solitary community."[23] In the New Deal era, it was this elite that defined the image of lawyers as the servants of power and wealth.

5 Administrative Law: Negotiating a New Professional Space

The Plight of the Forgotten Lawyer

The attorney-at-law—the urban solo practitioner who in the 1930s was still the overwhelmingly typical representative of the American legal profession—suffered financial drawbacks during the depression. Auerbach portrayed a profession whose upper echelons flourished while its lower echelons barely survived: "Nearly half the members of the metropolitan bar earned less than the minimum subsistence level for American families"; in 1934, "1500 lawyers in New York City were prepared to take the pauper's oath to qualify for work relief."[1] A New York lawyer probably exaggerated when he said that "in this city [where] 30,000 retail grocers employed 30,000 lawyers, there is now one lawyer representing the entire 30,000 in the chain," yet an acute sense of overcrowding—too many lawyers and too little work—was prevalent among solo practitioners and small firms in urban areas.[2]

Yet the New Deal's aggressive legalization of economic life carried a promise of relief. The establishment of numerous administrative agencies with rule-making and adjudicative powers pulled an ever-growing number of consumers into the domain of law, and the consequent proliferation of various legal and quasi-legal proceedings created new opportunities for legal practice. Some lawyers spread the word that administrative agencies created new professional opportunities that would "relieve unemployment among lawyers," and others invited lawyers to "guide bewildered clients" through the administrative regulatory maze.[3]

The promise of new professional opportunities, however, was yet to be realized. The new opening was a door with no keys. In this newly expanded space of administrative practice, lawyers had to compete over clients not only among themselves but also with "lay practitioners"—persons fulfilling representation functions without legal education and formal certification. The members of the New York State Bar Association, for example, listened to the complaint that "many more lawyers are beginning to feel, that there is more unlawful practice of law by laymen before governmental and administrative bureaus than all the title companies and insurance companies and all the other people that we claim are taking away a lot of business from the lawyers . . . whatever little business there possibly could be in the proper representation of the public before governmental administrative bureaus, to allow the conditions to continue as they are, I think we are doing ourselves great harm and the public a great injustice."[4]

Worse still, some administrative agencies discouraged the participation of lawyers and triggered the accusation that lawyers were deliberately excluded and prevented from exploiting the new professional opportunities. In chapter 2, I described the exclusionary practices of the National Recovery Administration as an example of an anti-lawyers law.[5] Similarly, the administrative provisions of the Home Owners' Loan Act of 1933, as one alarmed lawyer wrote to the president of the American Bar Association, deprived clients of the "right of legal counsel and legal aid" and was explicitly "directed against lawyers."[6] The Chenoweth & Whitehead brief, on its part, analyzed the practices of the Veterans' Administration, which handled about 600,000 insurance policies that had been issued to soldiers during World War I. The detailed brief was signed by fifty-eight lawyers, many of them solo practitioners, and was widely circulated among members of the ABA and state bar associations.[7] The brief joined a chorus of complaints when it described the practices of the Veterans' Administration as another step in the administration's plan to destroy the federal system of courts and to discourage lawyers from representing those who sought veterans' benefits.[8]

Recruiting to their aid arguments from the rhetorical arsenal of professionalism, concerned lawyers asserted that laypersons who practiced before administrative bodies could not provide high-quality service to the public. William Robinson, writing for the *American Bar Association Journal*, described lay practitioners as persons who lacked lawyers' "moral and intellectual fitness," and a report of the ABA's Committee on Unauthorized Practice of Law stated that it was "distinctly detrimental to the general welfare for persons and agencies to perform the functions of a lawyer when they have not met the qualifications required for a lawyer's license and are not subject to the control by the bar and are not responsible for the observance of its ethics."[9] This sense of unwarranted exclusion, coupled with the prevailing feeling that the profession was overcrowded and that lawyers already faced competition from banks, accountants, real estate agents, insurance companies, and other persons and firms who performed what lawyers saw as the "unlawful practice of law," nourished a drive to eliminate lay competition in the administrative arena.[10]

The main group of lawyers who advocated this course of action consisted of members of the Federal Bar Association of New York, New Jersey, and Connecticut (FBA). Like many of the other lawyers who complained about having to compete with lay practitioners, the active members of the FBA were solo practitioners, and their small organization, as the ABA's president, William Ransom, put it, was "not affiliated with any other organization of the legal profession."[11] It was this group that sponsored the bill Senator Wagner introduced in Congress in 1935, which provided for the exclusion of lay practitioners from practicing in administrative tribunals, thereby transforming the administrative arena to the lawyers' exclusive domain.[12] Members of the FBA urged the American Bar Association and the New York State Bar Association to endorse the bill. Their initial efforts seem to have had some effect. Benjamin Miller, a New York solo practitioner and one of the leading advocates of the bill, persuaded the New York State Bar Association as early as 1934 to create a special committee on administrative law that would consider the proposed measure; and William Ransom, preparing for the ABA's upcoming annual meeting, sent the Executive Committee a memorandum in which he urged a serious consideration of future measures: "I recommend that consideration be given to the question as to what, if anything, should be done by the ABA to organize and make effective the resistance of the legal profession to legislative acts and administrative regulations affecting lawyers, their relations and duties to clients, their admission to practice before various boards and bodies, their bases of compensation, and the like, which tend seriously to impair the independence of the legal profession and indeed are a challenge of its status as a profession owing personal and confidential relations to clients."[13] Consequently, a resolution was prepared for approval at the ABA's annual meeting in 1936:

> Resolved, that we favor the restriction of practice before departments, bureaus, commissions or other executive or administrative agency of the United States to attorneys at law, and Further Resolved, That to bring about such restriction we favor the passage of the bill proposed by Senator Wagner, known as S. 2944, of the 74th Congress.[14]

Wagner's exclusionary bill itself, by the time it was considered by the ABA , had already been adversely reported on and "indefinitely postponed" by the Senate Committee on the Judiciary. Ransom nonetheless assured the association's General Assembly that the bill would be before Congress upon its reintroduction in the new Congress. Consequently, the resolution was unanimously adopted by the General Assembly.[15]

Yet this unanimous resolution was significantly circumscribed on the following day. John W. Davis, one of the leaders of the bar and an avowed enemy of the New Deal, expressed his opposition to the bill: "I should hesitate myself to put the profession in the attitude of endeavoring to achieve a monopoly in the transactions with the Government of the United States," and Ransom, who had seemed to endorse the bill, backed away and advised the ABA's House of Delegates, which considered the resolution, to be aware of the insignificance of the bill's sponsoring group.[16] Finally, upon the recommendation of two corporate lawyers, the House of Delegates decided to refer the resolution to the Committee on Unauthorized Practice of Law for "further study."[17]

The solo practitioners who sponsored the resolution tried to prevent this turn of events. G. W. Reed, an attorney from Ohio, appealed to the profession's sense of responsibility: "If this proposition were simply a matter to procure or secure additional business to members of the bar I should not be interested and I shall not address myself to that matter, but that the practice before the departments of the Federal Government by Tom, Dick and Harry in a matter that he is not at all familiar with, as is the ordinary practitioner in law, I am sure results in unfortunate methods in the departments in Washington."[18] Henry Weinberger, a solo practitioner from New York, criticized Davis for "distorting" the purpose of the bill and argued that "by lawyers only being permitted to practice before these departments can the liberties and rights of individuals and of the people can be best protected." Responding to Davis's accusation that lawyers were merely trying to monopolize the market, Weinberger asserted that "it is a monopoly approved by the common law[;] it is a monopoly approved by the American people."[19] As a last resort, the bill's advocates invoked the association's by-laws, which stipulated that when the House of Delegates disapproved or modified a resolution of the General Assembly, members could ask the assembly to vote on whether to conduct a general referendum on the issue.[20] The efforts to save the resolution from being buried in a committee, however, were unsuccessful. The General Assembly voted against the referendum proposal and approved the decision to refer the matter to the Committee on Unauthorized Practice.[21]

Similar developments took place in the New York State Bar Association. The 1934 decision to create a committee that would study means of regulating administrative practice was never implemented. Benjamin Miller, who initiated the early drive to eliminate lay competition, raised the matter again in late 1935. The New York State Bar, however, also referred the proposal to endorse Wagner's bill to its Committee on Unlawful Practice of the Law.[22] Again, it was the coordinated pressure of the leaders of the New York bar that frustrated the efforts of the distressed solo practitioners. Meyer Kraushaar, a solo practitioner and a member of both the FBA and the New York State Bar Associaton, revealed that Henry Saxe, the president of the association, and Julius Henry Cohen, the influential chairperson of the Committee on the Unlawful Practice of the Law, pressured him to support the idea of referring the issue to Cohen's committee. Kraushaar nonetheless joined forces with Miller in asserting that the referral was designed as a tactical move the purpose of which was to deliberately misplace the issue.[23]

Indeed, the referral of Wagner's bill to the committees on unlawful practice proved fatal for those who sought to mobilize the organized bar in an effort to eliminate lay competition. The New York State Bar Association's Committee on Unlawful Practice failed to mention the subject in its annual report for 1936. When Abner C. Surplus, a solo practitioner from Brooklyn, asked Henry Cohen to account for this omission, Cohen replied that the committee had decided not to support the Wagner bill and had reported its decision directly to the association's Executive Committee. Cohen ended his reply in saying that, at any rate, the New York bar should have rejected the attempt of the FBA to "swamp" it with views that it did not share.[24] The ABA's Committee on Unauthorized Practice of Law issued a report that was in perfect harmony with the views of the New York committee: it refused to endorse Wagner's bill and reversed the ABA's earlier approval of the measure.[25]

The attempt to directly monopolize the space of administrative practice, then, was mainly the project of solo practitioners. Their failure to mobilize the organized bar in this direction in turn reflected the uneven distribution of power and influence between the upper and lower echelons of the bar. Some of the leaders of the American Bar Association and the New York State Bar Association, most likely in coordination and with the assured cooperation of the inner-circle committees on unlawful practice, managed to marginalize the issue of market control in the administrative field and eventually to suppress it. This episode fits well with Heinz and Laumann's argument that the American legal profession is in fact composed of two "hemispheres": lawyers who cater mainly to corporate clients and lawyers who cater mainly to individuals and small businesses. Corporate lawyers typically work in different organizational settings, often as partners in big law firms, while "personal client" lawyers are typically solo practitioners. These two groups differ so much in values, education, social background, prestige, influence, and wealth that Heinz and Laumann argue that "only in the most formal of senses . . . do the two types of lawyers constitute one profession."[26] As the story of the Wagner bill indicates, elite corporate lawyers were able to disappoint a "drive from below" by channeling an issue with which they did not want to deal to unsympathetic committees.

The crucial question, of course, concerns the reasons elite lawyers had for rejecting the project of exclusive market control in the administrative field. The decision to allow committees on unlawful practice to consider the matter may have been a result of a general sentiment among elite lawyers that administrative practice by laypersons had not been more than a marginal problem. The results of a 1934 survey by the American Bar Association's Committee on Unauthorized Practice of the Law could lend support to such a view. The survey addressed to lawyers some fifty-odd questions asking them to identify those areas of work in which they felt most threatened by unlawful competition. Among these fifty questions, which concerned the activities of private corporations, government bureaus, title companies, banks, collection agencies, real estate firms, and credit associations, only one question could be read to address the issue of administrative practice. It asked lawyers whether they faced a problem of laymen's "conducting legal proceedings before justices of the peace, bankruptcy courts, administrative commissions, etc." Nearly 90 percent of the 128 respondents to this question did not think of the issue as a grave "problem."[27] One way of interpreting these results, therefore, was to conclude that administrative practice by laypersons had been only a marginal problem. This interpretation seems to have matched the viewpoint of elite lawyers. After all, elite lawyers in general were hardly disturbed by various forms of competition from below to which the weaker segments of the bar were exposed. In the case of administrative practice, in particular, elite lawyers encountered little competition from lay practitioners because the nature of their practice often involved complex matters over which they enjoyed a *de facto* control of practice. For elite lawyers, in short, administrative practice by laypersons was not a question of economic survival. Combined with the recognition that Wagner's bill had little chance to survive, the incentive to endorse it had not been great.

But the findings of the survey could be interpreted in a different way as well. The fact that the questions barely touched on the subject of administrative practice and the fact that many lawyers did not consider it a problem may have reflected a prevailing sentiment that administrative practice by laypersons was not a form of unlawful practice. After all, administrative practice by lay practitioners was lawful in an area lawyers had yet to define as their own exclusive domain. Indeed, that was precisely the argument that Benjamin Miller used in a last effort to persuade the members of the New York bar to endorse Wagner's bill. Administrative practice by laypersons, he argued, was not "a question of unlawful practice of the law at all. It is definitely legal practice for [laypersons] to appear before any of these governmental administrative bureaus."[28] To the extent that Miller did have a point, the framing of administrative practice by laypersons in terms of "unlawful practice" had been a deliberate distortion.

Whether a misplacement, a calculated marginalization, or both, one still needs to go a step further in order to understand why the bar's leaders not only remained indifferent to the idea of direct market control but actively resisted and undermined the efforts to secure that monopoly. An insightful comment by Julius H. Cohen should be considered: "It is a grave blunder to have the practice of law defined by the legislature," Cohen argued, because "what constitutes the practice of law is for the courts to determine."[29] Excluding lay practitioners by means of statutory provisions might have relieved the plight of solo practitioners, but it threatened to undermine the paradigmatic conception of law as an autonomous space of activity whose boundaries were defined by lawyers and judges. The enactment of the Wagner bill, from this perspective, would have brought about an abrupt and externally imposed incorporation of a whole spatial universe of practice and discourse into the domain of law. The meaning, scope, and nature of the law that was generated in the course of the administrative process, however, was in itself the subject of an intense discursive struggle and, not less important, one that carried visible seeds of threat to established patterns of lawmaking and legal thought in America. The bar's leaders were quick in grasping this point. Indicative of the recognition that the administrative arena was bound to have far-reaching implications for legal practice was the creation of an American Bar Association Committee on Administrative Law. As early as May 1933, the Executive Committee of the association authorized the creation of the committee and named Louis G. Caldwell, a partner in one of Chicago's leading corporate law firms, as its chairperson.[30] This committee became one of the ABA's busiest in the early years of the New Deal. It was mainly through the committee's sponsored reports and discussions that elite lawyers tried to shape and mold the future development of administrative law, a struggle that took place on a plane far removed from the mundane concerns of economically and politically weak solo practitioners.

Administrative Law as an Earthquake

Elite lawyers did not think of the expanding administrative process as a field of opportunities but as a minefield full of threats; it held out a prospect of a transformed legal field in which they were expected to have a lesser say. New Dealers left no doubts as to their intentions. "The story of the rise of administration," declared Robert Jackson, "is also a story of the eclipse of the courts."[31] Whole classes of controversy were to be shifted from the judicial system to the administrative arena. There, free from constraining methods and operating outside the established hierarchy of the judicial system, a new form of law would be created, one that would be informed by a cause and not by the occasional case. Courts, according to the newly emergent view, were slow, congested, and inefficient forums that did not have the substantive expertise and procedural flexibility necessary for handling from a broad social and economic perspective the complex affairs of a society in flux. "The judicial process," argued Milton Handler, "cannot keep pace with the far-reaching and rapid changes occurring in the world today."[32] Thurman Arnold elaborated that courts were operating on the basis of an archaic legal theory based on the idea that "only the particular and narrow issues brought before courts by contesting parties may be the basis of judge-made law." Judicial creation was based on the assumption that rules and regulations could only emerge in the context of contests, in a theatrical arena that was based on a "catch-as-catch can philosophy." The very idea of a "trial by combat," he argued, was part of the mystifying symbolic elements of jurisprudence. The insistence on the combat and contest as a way of finding out the truth was irrational, fragmentary, inconsistent, nonsensical, and socially irresponsible; society needed the drama of combat, and courts willingly took part in this mystifying arrangement.[33]

The development of administrative methods, said Arnold, was an inevitable response to the inability of courts to provide a basis for friendly cooperation and to serve as a source of enlightened social control. Given this inadequacy of the common law, "regulatory functions escaped into another system of courts, called commissions," where a technique of conference replaced the judicial combat. The envisioned administrative tribunal was to become a body of experts, a forum for cooperation that disregarded legalistic procedures and judicial rules of evidence and above all was free from routine judicial review. The inability to cope with the administrative method of deciding issues from a broad social and economic perspective, coupled with having a stake in asserting judicial supremacy over decisions arrived at by this method, turned courts into socially irresponsible forums: "To the two story structure of law and equity was added a third story of administrative law, and the whole structure was equipped with noiseless elevators and secret stairways, by means of which the choice was always open either to take a bold judicial stand or make a dignified escape." Arnold, realistically, understood that it was the latter option that had been routinely taken by courts, meeting the former "with an air of shocked surprise."[34]

The leaders of the bar, in short, had solid reasons to believe that the rapid development of the administrative process and the transfer of classes of controversy from the judicial to the administrative arena were the ultimate manifestation of a draconian plan to destroy the federal judicial system. All across this perceived spectrum of subversion—from modest attempts to restrict the jurisdiction of federal courts over public utility commissions to proposals to limit the review powers of the Supreme Court[35]—the prospect of an independent administrative machinery lingered like a constant threat over the horizon of the traditional legal mind. As fiercely as they could, concerned lawyers warned against the "cancerous growth" of administrative powers not subjected to judicial review and against boards that violated "elementary principles of justice and fair play" in their multiple roles as investigators, prosecutors, and judges.[36] Nathan Miller, commenting on the powers of the National Labor Relations Board, argued that they did not "even approximate due process" and that the board's judicial review procedures were "a farce."[37] The ABA's Committee on Commerce, for its part, attacked the vast discretionary powers of the Securities and Exchange Commission as "contrary to the heretofore recognized principles of our government," a critique that intensified after Supreme Court Justice Sutherland opined that the powers of the commission were as arbitrary as the "intolerable abuses of the Star Chamber."[38]

The report of the ABA's Special Committee on Administrative Law, in accordance with these catastrophic visions, sent a highly pessimistic message:

> Having in mind these tendencies to attempt to remove large fields of legal controversy from the jurisdiction of the courts and to place them under administrative machinery, to deprive administrative tribunals of safeguards necessary to the exercise of judicial functions, to reduce and so far as possible to eliminate effective judicial or independent review, and to employ indirect methods of adjudication, the committee believes it is not going too far to state that the judicial branch of the federal government is being rapidly and seriously undermined and, if the tendencies are permitted to develop unchecked, is in danger of meeting a measure of the fate of the Merovingian kings.[39]

The bar's leaders were determined, therefore, to "block the invasion of judicial powers."[40] Underlying this firm defense of judicial powers were yet unsettled negotiations over the very meaning of "administrative law"—that body of knowledge which claimed authoritative status in regard to the form and content of the administrative process. Carl McFarland won an award from the ABA for articulating the two images of administrative law that collided head-on in the early New Deal: "There seem to be two theories of the relations of courts to administrative agencies in Anglo-American law—the one treats the justice dispensed by courts and the social control exercised by administrative tribunals as parts of a single system of law in which the courts wield ultimate authority ... [while] the other recognizes a dual system of public administration of justice and seeks a division of function."[41] These two "theories," or imagined structures of authority, correspond to what Arthurs describes as two competing paradigms—two ways of thinking about law in general. One is a "centralist paradigm" that postulates law as a *singular*, objective, and hierarchical formal system that exists as a thing apart from society, politics, or economics; the other is a "pluralist paradigm" that conceives of law as stemming from a multitude of sources that may be diverse in methods, "content, causes, and effects."[42]

The crucial point about the centralist paradigm—the "single system of law" theory—was that it subjected administrative practices to the centralist hierarchy of comprehensive judicial scrutiny. Successful enforcement of a centralist paradigm thus involved a movement toward the universe of the judicial system, where established hierarchies and methods conditioned administrative practice. The question of administrative law, in other words, was first of all a question of production: who wielded power to say what administrative law was, and who was the producer who could legitimately shape the product? "For most lawyers," writes Arthurs, "administrative law is not the law *of* the administration; it is the law directed *against* the administration, the law by which reviewing judges ensure that the administration does not overreach."[43] The leaders of the American bar in the 1930s, McFarland insightfully observed, were predominantly disposed to prefer the single system theory and to resist the not-so-humble growing legitimacy of an alternative vision of law.[44]

The preference of the bar's leaders for the centralist paradigm expressed more than a principled ideal. The defense of judicial authority as the primary, if not the exclusive, source of law production was rooted in the intimate perceived connection between judicial powers and the practicing bar's own professional status. The judicial system, to the established legal mind, was not only the pinnacle of an autonomous law, a singular source of authority, a symbol for the coherence and self-consistency of law, but also, ultimately, a fountain from which lawyers derived their own assertions of autonomy. The umbilical cord that tied the practicing bar to the judicial system stretched back to a time when the American state was hardly a state at all. In the mid-nineteenth century, writes Skowronek, America was a state of parties and courts—the only institutions that provided some measure of coherence to the national system. Federal courts were the ultimate producers of law, a primary source of authority "binding the legal apparatus of government," shaping the boundaries of "intergovernmental relations," defining relations between state and society, and, in general, filling "a governmental vacuum left by abortive experiments in the administrative promotion of economic development."[45] The unique feature of this court-centered legal system was that it allowed judges to speak and act as if they were operating outside, if not above, the domain of the state; theirs, in contrast to the language of politics, was a domain of informed reason. Judges applied strict rules of legal reasoning that decontextualized the cases on which they were to pass judgment, thereby creating an autonomous system whose "closedness" was daily demonstrated in the application of legal rules to particular cases. Not will (i.e., political power) but reason (i.e., truth) determined the development of law. This imaginary distinction, which compelled the assumption that there was "a separate faculty of the human mind called 'reason' and another separate faculty called 'will,' " was crucial for the distinction between law and politics.[46]

This distinction, in fact, crystallized precisely at the point where law came to be seen as a matter of will. The codification movement of the 1820s and 1830s, operating on the basis of this premise, sought to replace the court-centered common law with formal statutory legislation that would reflect the will of the popularly elected sovereign.[47] Lawyers reacted with outright hostility. Under threat here were not only courts but also lawyers in private practice. The image of the judge at the center, surrounded by a ring of practicing lawyers who operated as officers of the court, played an important role in distancing lawyers from the particular demands of clients and in distinguishing their doings from mere politics. Leaning on this concentric image, the professionalization of the legal profession gained momentum in mid-nineteenth-century America. The idea of judgeship as a symbol, says Botein, "loomed large in the process by which lawyers articulated ideology to establish their professional authority in modern American society" and allowed them to derive a whole set of "economic and psychic rewards."[48] It was the distinctive and monopolistic character of judicial reasoning that allowed lawyers to assert and secure their own professional jurisdiction. Law as reason justified exclusive rights of access to the judicial arena and allowed lawyers to construct their own craft as a unique form of expertise. Moreover, these exclusive rights of access allowed lawyers to actively control and shape the pace and direction of legal development. The prospect of statutory legislation, in contrast, undermined "any special claims of the profession to determine the nature and scope of legal development." Hence the "underlying conviction held by all nineteenth century legal thinkers that the course of American legal change should, if possible, be developed by courts and not by legislatures."[49] Statutory legislation as an alternative source of law was viewed by lawyers as a flow of arbitrary acts of power that exposed the law to uneven development and to unpredictable and abrupt changes. Statutory law was the law of strangers who had not "eaten and prayed" with lawyers and had to be countered with an "upsurge in judicial review of legislation."[50] In short, it threatened to blur the fragile line that separated law from politics and to thereby expose the unstable cognitive basis of law and its vulnerability to external interference.[51]

The flood of statutory law in the 1930s brought echoes from the past. It was during the New Deal, writes Calabresi, that America became "a nation governed by written laws": "[U]nlike earlier codifications of law, which were so general that common law courts could continue to act pretty much as they always had, the new breed of statutes were specific, detailed, and 'well drafted.' Again, unlike the codes, which were compilations of the common law, the new statutes were frequently meant to be *the primary source of law*" (italics mine).[52] An American legal profession that had been molded in the image of the judicial system, explained Robert Jackson, was simply "afraid of legislation. Laymen often influence it too much. . . . The law in a statute we fear, the law in a leading case we revere."[53] George Wickersham, however, had a different view on the matter. The duty of lawyers was to resist this legislative frenzy because "[t]he Jurisprudence of a nation is not made by acts of legislature or decrees of administrative bodies. The Jurisprudence of a nation is something which reflects the morals, the conceptions, and the ideals of the people . . . *Laws come and go, but the jurisprudence of a people moves on from precedent to precedent*" (italics mine).[54] Worse still, many of these newly introduced statutes created an amalgam of administrative tribunals which carved out a space that escaped both judicial methods and review.

Nowhere was the dissolution of law and politics, of reason and will, more obvious than in the administrative arena. Administrative lawmaking functions were compared by Wickersham to the activities of the Roman emperor Caligula, "who wrote his laws in small letters, and placed them at the top of high columns, the better to ensnare his subjects."[55] The phenomenon that solo practitioners conceptualized as lay competition created a profound crisis of identity for elite lawyers. Surrounded by lay administrators and having to cope with loose methods, observed Max Radin, damaged the professional aura of exclusive expertise: "What the lawyer doubtless misses is the air of the cock-pit, the *chaude-melee* of the tournament, the *strepitus judicili* which in all reformatory efforts, popes and emperors, philosophers and publicists, have always attempted to eliminate. It cannot be wholly eliminated because lawyers love it, as all craftsmen enjoy opportunities to exhibit their skill, as musicians love virtuosity, as aviators love stunts when they can do them."[56] Above and beyond lost "love," however, administrative practice undermined the carefully construed distance between lawyers and clients. The informal nature of administrative negotiations, the lobbying activities that accompanied the administrative process, and a maze of unpublished and unclear procedural and substantive rules compromised the "scientific" nature of a legal practice that had been based on "differential knowledge of normative codes, conventional procedures, and interpretive techniques."[57] The form and character of the administrative process were simply "startling" in that they blurred the difference between law as a profession and law as a mere trade or business.[58] Charles Whitman, a former president of the ABA, spoke with alarm about the trend that "removed the disposition of many problems and controversies from the judicial forum and placed them under the control of administrative agencies."[59] Consequently, he said, the lawyer was compelled to "seek other outlets for his talents," to become involved in the economic, social, and political aspects of the client's business, to commercialize and become subject to the domination of trade: "To make the lawyer a commercial consultant rather than a legal adviser, is to create an alliance which in the end must lessen the usefulness of the profession to the public as a whole and *destroy its noblest attributes*" (italics mine).[60]

Furthermore, the dissolution of law and politics directly affected the ability of lawyers to preserve their control over the pace and direction of legal change. In a space that escaped judicial review, law was indeed perceived as a "cancerous growth." The adversary system, with its elaborate procedural protections, meant less control by the decision maker over the process and, further, lessened the ability of lawyers to control the nature, substance, and destiny of contested issues.[61] At stake was more than a problem of "fear" and inability to adjust.[62] The analyses and observations of critics, along with the visibly growing powers of numerous administrative bodies (of which the Securities and Exchange Commission, the National Recovery Administration, the National Labor Relations Board, and the Social Security Administration were only the most politically visible), persuaded many leaders of the bar that they were witnessing an irreversible process, yet one that nonetheless had to be controlled. In this they followed the advice of Elihu Root, who had observed as early as 1916 that lawyers had to ensure that "these agencies of regulation must themselves be regulated."[63] Thus, when the ABA's Committee on Administrative Law promised to "bring controversies back into the judicial system," it had in mind a struggle that would end with a reintroduced centralist paradigm: the reformulation of administrative law as a judicial domain and a successful incorporation of the administrative space as yet another story in the hierarchical structure of a court-centered law.

The Story of the Committee on Administrative Law

The first and most urgent task of the ABA's Committee on Administrative Law was to build its reputation as an independent body of experts. Aware of the strong connection between the growth of administrative law and New Deal policies, the first report of the committee made public its intention to study administrative law without "any spirit of criticism or disapproval."[64] By explicitly distancing themselves from issues of constitutionality and general legislative policy, the members of the committee hoped to become a truly professional body—detached from New Deal politics, rooted in impartial expertise, invested in the formal aspects of its subject matter, and informed by a variety of scholars—which would concretize the contribution of the legal profession to a progressive legal order for the public good.[65]

Louis Caldwell, the committee's chairperson, declared:

> Let me hasten at this point to prevent any misunderstanding of our committee's attitude toward this new legislation. We believe that it is not our province to express any opinion as to the constitutionality or as to the legislative wisdom of the fundamental purposes and the substantive provisions of these statutes. We are not going to discuss whether the *laissez faire* philosophy and Adam Smith should or should not give way to the industrial discipline and planned national economy. We regard ourselves at least for the present as concerned with *adjective* law, so to speak—with the adequacy and the efficiency of the machinery employed and not with the purposes for which it is employed.[66]

Declarations of nonpartisanship notwithstanding, the Committee on Administrative Law soon became one of the primary vehicles through which lawyers could snap at New Deal policies on what they perceived to be purely professional grounds: the duty of lawyers to defend the fundamental maxims of the rule of law and the separation of powers in democratic society. The trouble with administrative agencies, according to the committee, was that they functioned as rulemaking bodies, which were permitted to adjudicate controversies arising out of the regulations they themselves issued. This fusion of legislative and judicial powers resulted in the disregard of "a maxim fundamental to the administration of justice . . . , that a man should not be permitted to adjudge his own case."[67] The implied message of the report was that administrative bodies were prone to be biased and partial adjudicators, and these in turn were a menace to healthy democracy. Thus, in language that could not be interpreted as criticism of the administration's policies, the report remarked that "enthusiasm for attractive experiments in the substantive field of law should not be permitted to carry . . . disastrous and futile experiments in the machinery for making laws or for administering justice."[68]

In an apparent effort to preserve its promise of nonpartisanship, the committee tried to enlist the support of Felix Frankfurter of Harvard. Frankfurter, one of Roosevelt's trusted and influential advisers, had indeed agreed to join the committee soon after its creation but had not signed the report.[69] The committee explained that "because of absence in Europe during the year, Dr. Felix Frankfurter . . . has been unable to participate actively in the committee's work and has not had an opportunity to examine the report. He has suggested, therefore, that his name be not included among those signing."[70] It is unclear whether Frankfurter's visit to England during 1934 genuinely prevented him from adding his name to the report. Upon his return to the United States he did attend the November 1934 meeting of the committee, but he resigned shortly afterward "due to the pressure of other duties." At any rate, the January 1935 interim report of the committee asserted that "during the period in which Mr. Frankfurter was a member of the committee he expressed himself as being in complete agreement with the substance of all three undertakings [including the Administrative Court plan]."[71]

The committee also wished to convey the impression that its report enjoyed the unqualified support of the bar. Louis Caldwell worried that the presentation of the report to the ABA's General Assembly would result in an open discussion that would expose a divided bar. William Ransom, accordingly, opined that "it would be a good break for [Caldwell] if he didn't have time to explain the report and if the report went through more as a formal practice. That the most dangerous thing he could do is try to explain it."[72] This attempt, however, was unsuccessful. Two members of the General Assembly who listened to Caldwell's brief presentation were quick to articulate their oral response: they accused the drafters of the report of entering the "realm of political controversy" and described it as "nothing more nor less than an essay of political propaganda."[73] Theirs, however, was a minority opinion. The report was voted upon favorably by the General Assembly and consequently was cited by New Dealers as proof of the ABA's hostility to the administration's plans.[74]

The fact was, however, that the committee could boast some degree of success in influencing administrative law policies. First was the issue of certainty. "The lawyer," the committee's first report complained, "must look to the President's executive orders and to the releases and announcements of the several administrative agencies for accurate and up-to-date knowledge of the existing state of the law."[75] Rush C. Butler, of the ABA's Committee on Commerce, was more outspoken: "In these days of legislative frenzy . . . it is impossible under most favorable circumstances for men of affairs to keep themselves advised as to the law applicable to their respective business. Even lawyers who are supposed either to know the law, or to know where to find it, are in constant confusion."[76] Both the Committee on Commerce and the Committee on Administrative Law, therefore, urged Congress to require the publication of every "rule, regulation, or order entered by any executive officer or administrative board."[77] Unlike any other proposal in regard to administrative law in the New Deal, the call for certainty met with the approval of the Association of American Law Schools (AALS) and apparently gained the support of some of the administration's senior legal advisers.[78] Harold Stephens, a justice of the U.S. Court of Appeals for the District of Columbia; John Dickinson, an assistant to the attorney general; and Erwin Griswold, of Harvard, advocated the need for orderly publication of administrative regulations when hearings on the Federal Register Act took place in Congress in 1935.[79]

A second success that the committee could credit to its influence concerned Roosevelt's decision in September 1934 to divorce the National Recovery Administration's judicial functions from its legislative ones. The committee's 1934 report indeed argued that there was a desperate need to segregate the judicial functions of administrative bodies from their legislative and executive ones. The *United States Law Review* suggested that the president acted on the advice of the ABA's committee, although it further added that this policy had also been urged by Felix Frankfurter, "who is at once a leading authority in the field of administrative law and an intimate adviser of President Roosevelt."[80] At any rate, the *Review* announced that "the country indeed owes the committee a debt of gratitude" and described the committee's work as complementary to that of Frankfurter.[81]

Yet these successes were marginal compared to the inability of the committee to advance its main goal. The committee's primary goal, reflecting a widely held sentiment among the bar's leaders, was to "bring controversies back into the judicial system" by subjecting administrative tribunals to strict judicial review. Newton D. Baker, an influential member of the bar, argued that the main shortcoming of the administrative process was that "there has been a constantly increasing tendency on the parts of legislatures to deny to the acts of administrative tribunals the scrutiny of a judicial review," and O. R. McGuire, a member of the ABA's Committee on Administrative Law, argued that "there is unquestionably need for the most efficient and expeditious procedure for review of Federal administrative action that may be devised."[82]

In the New York State Bar Association, the call for judicial review was made by Thomas Thatcher, who argued that it was essential "to strip from every board, commission, executive or otherwise, every judicial power and permit it to remain in the courts, where it belongs, should have been, and where it should always be, where decisions can be properly made. And if it results in congestion of courts, extend the courts."[83] Thus, acting on the premise that judicial review of administrative practices, even when it existed, was a "mere empty shell," the Committee on Administrative Law concluded that "to be effective, review of an administrative decision must not only be by an independent body (i.e., a body having no interest in the outcome, either as legislator, prosecutor or otherwise) but must extend to the determination of issues of both law and fact."[84]

Having established its principled position, the committee's *operational* proposal in 1934 was to support the Logan bill, which was by then pending in Congress. The Logan bill substituted a United States Court of Administrative Justice for the then-existing United States Court of Claims, for the court of Customs and Patent Appeals, for the United States courts that reviewed the decisions of the Board of Tax Appeals, and for some of the functions of the Supreme Court of the District of Columbia.[85] In endorsing the Logan bill, the committee had in mind an administrative court, which in itself would be "subjected to judicial review to the full extent permitted by the Constitution."[86] McGuire, member of the committee and its chairperson in 1936, was the main champion of the idea and spread it in a series of articles in the *American Bar Association Journal.*[87] The decision to endorse the Logan bill, however, reflected an agenda that lagged far behind the heated rhetoric of the committee and its vision of an overall administrative reform. The Logan bill did not impose a mechanism of judicial review on those administrative agencies about which lawyers complained the most, nor did it propose to segregate their judicial from legislative functions. Rather, the bill represented an effort to reform some administrative agencies which were in fact already quite "judicialized." Louis Caldwell acknowledged this fact in 1935. Responding to the argument that the proposed bill would have abolished operating administrative courts that proved their efficiency, he defended the plan by arguing that the bar needed a strategy of gradual judicialization, starting with administrative agencies that were "working well": "They have achieved judicial independence, they do enjoy public confidence. We badly need such a nucleus if we are to have any prospect at all of ultimately persuading Congress gradually to divest other administrative agencies, which are not working well, of their judicial functions and to lodge them in a single court with branches."[88] Further, support for the idea of an administrative court was based on a conscious understanding that no immediate results could be expected. The plan only represented an "ideal," a "start." In the future, it was hoped, such a tribunal would be capable of "receiving added jurisdiction from time to time over new fields of administrative controversy."[89] The reason for this prudent course of action, according to the committee, was the unanimous belief of its members "that it would be impolitic at this time to attempt more than to establish a nucleus of such a court."[90]

But the ABA could not unite its members even around this very limited proposal. Lawyers who developed specialized practice in those administrative settings which the Logan bill sought to reform resisted the idea of a unified administrative court. Albert MacBarnes, the president of the Customs Bar Association, and Addison Pratt, the vice president of the Customs Bar Association of the City of New York, protested "most strongly against the abolition of the United States Customs Court and the United States Court of Customs and Patent Appeals" and argued that it would only result in inefficiency and confusion.[91] William Grogan, from the Washington, D.C., Bar Association, argued that there was neither any need nor any reason for the abolition of the exiting administrative tribunals, and the national Federal Bar Association voiced its opposition through John Dickinson, Justin Miller, and William Roberts. Addressing the ABA's General Assembly, Roberts argued that "the necessity for the establishment of a general administrative court was not present, [and] . . . many administrative courts are now functioning [well]."[92] The opposition was serious enough to prevent the Committee on Administrative Law from submitting any report to the annual meeting of 1935.[93] Louis Caldwell complained that "rumblings began to be heard" not only from the Federal Bar Association and the Customs Bar but also from the ABA's Special Committee on Federal Taxation and its Patent, Trademark and Copyright Law Section. Frustrated with these "obstructions," Caldwell remarked that "if there were an organized bar of lawyers practicing before the Court of Claims I now feel sure we should have heard from it also."[94] Still, the committee kept insisting that the creation of an administrative court was the best solution to the problem of administrative law.[95]

In 1936, alternative proposals of reform began to float around the ABA. These new proposals were based on the premise that the cure for the administrative malaise was a procedural reform that would correct the deficiencies of various administrative tribunals. These proposals were mainly advocated by those who opposed to the creation of an administrative court. Addison Pratt argued that "our efforts should be directed to the regulation of these administrative agencies and not merely to the consolidation of certain specialized courts and their functions," and William Roberts, of the Federal Bar Association, called on the ABA to adopt the following resolution: "The Association deplores the procedural confusion and inadequacy existing in federal and other executive departments and separate administrative agencies. It believes that the improvement of these conditions should be by a gradual process of correction, rather than by a sudden and complete destruction of existing agencies and the creation of a wholly experimental tribunal of general powers and functions."[96]

Accordingly, the proposed resolution focused on "the gradual establishment of uniform administrative procedure for the review of administrative and executive action."[97] The new effort, in other words, resembled the efforts of solo practitioners to reform the administrative space from below, rather than subjecting it to the hierarchy of the judicial system from above. This proposed solution, which was not approved by the ABA's General Assembly in 1936, had in fact been a visionary one. In years to come, it was indeed through procedural reform that lawyers succeeded in taming the administrative machinery of the state.[98]

The administrative process was launched by open-ended legislation, which delegated some authority to more or less autonomous bodies of state-employed officials and experts. These empowered bodies and agencies, in turn, created mechanisms of rulemaking that were not directly checked by the legislature and mechanisms of adjudication that were not directly subjected to the hierarchy of the judicial system. Together with statutory law, the administrative process was an instrument that marked the expansion of governmental powers.[99] The process was also an orientation that carved out a space for competitive ideas and practices about law, professionalism in law, and legal authority. This space was a site where the dichotomy of law and politics dissolved, thereby creating a boundary problem that triggered renewed struggles over the power and influence of lawyers. The purpose of lawyers who tried to bring controversies back into the judicial system was to redraw the boundaries between law and politics, and this effort was one of the major forces that shaped the politics of the bar.

The administrative space, of course, was also a site of competitive ideas about bureaucratic order, democratic theory, and economic control. Looking at the administrative space, therefore, one could identify an affinity between the movement from laissez-faire capitalism to state monopoly capitalism and the movement from the "catch-as-catch-can" adversarial method in law to the planned and socially informed legislative process. In 1934 Supreme Court Justice Harlan Stone publicly described elite lawyers as highly skilled servants of business who tainted the profession "with the morals and manners of the market place in its most anti-social manifestations."[100] Throughout the New Deal, elite lawyers had to defend themselves against accusations of overidentification with clients and overzealous pursuit of commercial interests. "In a climate of hostility toward 'economic royalists,' " wrote Auerbach, "lawyers who had enjoyed immunity from public criticism during a decade of prosperity suddenly found themselves vulnerable. Any reassessment of the American business system was bound to generate a parallel reconsideration of the profession that served it so conspicuously."[101] Yet it is noteworthy that in responding to the criticism of the bar's leaders of the administrative process, New Dealers made no attempt to account for it in terms of the alleged subservience of lawyers to commercial clients. Both advocates and adversaries of the expanding administrative process realized that they were negotiating over an issue which had to do with the distinct professional concerns of players in the legal field. The views of the bar's leaders concerning the power of administrative tribunals may have corresponded to the interests of commercial clients, but they were by no means determined by these interests; this distinction is important if one wishes to trace the dynamic by which truly strong coalitions are formed.

My analysis showed that the organized bar had serious difficulties in articulating a unified response to the emergent administrative space. One source of difficulty had to do with the existence of different interest groups, pursuing their own distinct agendas, within the practicing bar. First, the different market situation of solo practitioners and law-firm corporate lawyers led them to treat the new opening as a field of potential opportunities and as a field of potential threats, respectively. Solo practitioners had a pretty good idea about the course of action that should have been taken: eliminate lay competition and consolidate a lawyers' monopoly over a space that promised to provide new sources of income. Elite lawyers were more ambivalent. Faced with an unwarranted threat to the centrality of courts, they could respond by withdrawing into what Gordon terms "purified zones of practice."[102] This option, however, was unrealistic. Elite lawyers, like solo practitioners, were pulled into the administrative apparatus by clients who needed representation at all stages of the process. The Wall Street lawyer, like the Main Street lawyer, simply could not ignore the vast market opportunities created by the newly opened space. Hence the elite lawyers' drive to mold the administrative process in ways that would subject it to their own already established grammar of law.

A second split within the bar developed along the lines of specialized expertise. The Committee on Administrative Law faced opposition to its plans from lawyers who already established specialized practice before various administrative tribunals. Professions, writes Abbott, cannot just grow as they please; they cannot accommodate expanding areas of professional work and uncritically absorb new methods and forms of knowledge without thereby diluting the "cognitive structure" that binds the profession as a whole. "The more abstract the binding ideas," writes Abbott, "the more vulnerable they are to specialization within and to diffusion into the common culture without."[103] The latter evil—that of diluting the professional aura of expertise—triggered the bar's leaders attempt to rewrite the grammar of the administrative process; the former one, however, obstructed their plans. The diversity of opinion within the bar, rooted in the position of specialists with their own distinct interests, undermined the hierarchy of influence within the bar, prevented the ABA from developing an agreed-upon course of action, and ultimately weakened the political influence of the organized bar as a whole.

Finally, it is perhaps ironic that the grammar upon which elite lawyers so insisted during the first years of the New Deal, to no avail, was ultimately written by the administration itself. Even in the early years of the New Deal, some farsighted jurists predicted the fate of the envisioned autonomous administrative space: "Periods of great scientific and governmental activity," argued Leon Green, "[are] necessarily periods of administration, while periods of stabilization are periods of law."[104] Some observers therefore predicted that with the passing of the transitory period of experimentation in law and government the administrative machinery would be eventually brought under the umbrella of judicial hierarchy. The stabilization of the political and economic order in the early 1940s indeed created new conditions in which the somewhat deliberately chaotic nature of the administrative space gradually gave place to a renewed interest in objectifying the new established order. As the story of the Administrative Procedure Act shows,[105] when the political pendulum swung back in the direction of stabilization, the legal pendulum followed suit. A process of judicialization and a gradual return to formal and "autonomous law" was again set in motion.

Excursus II
Professionalism and Monopoly of Expertise

The General Framework

Insofar as the developent of administrative law during the New Deal posits a strong measure for the expansion of state powers, the response of various segments of the bar to this development clarifies the conditions under which lawyers tend to either resist or support state-building processes. The approach developed here, explains the politics of lawyers in terms of their position within the legal field. In this excursus I will recast the findings of chapter 5 in broader theoretical terms.

Two principal arguments, or foundational prisms, run throughout the chapter. First is the premise that law is largely developed, shaped, interpreted, and manipulated by that specialized group of experts that we know as lawyers. Law may be conceived of not only as the language by which the state communicates its commands but also as a body of knowledge, a resource, by which lawyers construct and reproduce their claims to exclusive expertise (with all the material and nonmaterial rewards that ensue). This knowledge/power dimension of law is an important element in the political economy of lawyers, and consequently, changes in the organization of the legal system are evaluated by lawyers in light of the prospective effects such changes are likely to have on the internal and external conditions of their professional lives. In particular, the response of lawyers to the development of administrative law can be explained independently of their ideological dispositions toward the politics of the New Deal and of their commitment to clients who may have resisted the policies of the New Deal for their own economic reasons. This theoretical approach follows Bourdieu's proposition that the analysis of the legal field should proceed without falling prey, on the one hand, to a formalist conception which asserts absolute autonomy to the force of ideas in shaping the trajectory of law or, on the other, to an instrumentalist conception that conceives of law as "a tool in the service of dominant groups."[1]

The second foundational prism is that the bar is stratified: theoreticians and practitioners, academics and judges, lawyers in the service of the state and lawyers in private practice, solo practitioners and partners in big corporate law firms. The considerable variation in the relative social status, wealth, and political power among American lawyers necessarily leads to variation in the response of different segments of the legal profession to changes in the legal environment. Especially important is the by-now classic observation of Heinz and Laumann that the American bar is comprised of two "hemispheres" of lawyers whose nature of practice, socioeconomic background, education, and clientele differ considerably.[2] The most basic distinction is between lawyers who are partners in law firms that cater to corporate clients and lawyers who work as solo practitioners or in small partnership firms and cater to individual clients. Although a minority in comparison to the vast number of solo practitioners, it is this group of corporate lawyers, predominantly partners in big law firms, that first established and then controlled the major bar associations of America. Traditionally, the voice of this elite was more often than not presented as the voice of the profession as a whole.[3] This is not surprising given that the overwhelming majority of lawyers in private practice are too busy with economic survival to engage in the politics of the bar and to be actively concerned with the long-range interests of the profession. It is mainly lawyers who are economically secure who can dedicate time and energy to public activities and to projects that transcend the immediate demands of clients.[4]

The difference between these two hemispheres of the bar also finds expression in their politics of response to legal change. Solo practitioners are more driven by market considerations than are the bar's elite. The latter, in contrast, are more concerned with the image and status of the profession and with the character and organization of the legal system. In short, solo practitioners are driven by market anxiety, while established corporate lawyers tend to be driven by status anxiety. Let it be immediately said, however, that elite lawyers are not free from market considerations. On the contrary, the organization of the market for legal services is very much on their minds. Nonetheless, the market position of elite lawyers predisposes them to a different social-action orientation than that of solo practitioners. In the New Deal, this meant that solo practitioners were inclined to support measures that would have resulted in the outright exclusion of nonlawyers from practice in administrative arenas, while the upper echelons of the bar were inclined to be more concerned with the form and character of administrative practice and with the overall relationship between the administrative and judicial apparatuses of the state.

How well does the above proposition interact with contemporary theories of the political economy of lawyers? Three theoretical models obtain. The first is that which is commonly referred to as the "market-monopoly" approach. It asserts that the primary aim of occupational groups in a capitalist society, in fact the defining characteristic of professions, is to control the market for their services.[5] The basic questions this model posits thus concern the strategies that professional elites invoke in order to establish exclusivity in given areas of practice and to expand their control over new areas of work. Richard Abel offers the most systematic analysis of the historic trajectory of the American legal profession in terms of the market-monopoly model and is treated here as a prototypical example of the market-monopoly approach.[6] Christine Harrington offers an insightful revision of Abel's original formulations that is especially important here because she invokes the market-monopoly model in order to explain the response of the bar to the development of administrative law during the New Deal.[7]

By focusing on the internal stratification of the legal profession and the unequal distribution of material and nonmaterial benefits among its members, Abel has made his most illuminating contribution by subverting the homogeneous and collegial image that lawyers strive to present to their relevant audiences. Abel's analysis demonstrates the way in which American lawyers developed a set of strategies whose purpose was to control the number of practicing lawyers, to autonomously regulate competition among practicing lawyers, and to exclude "unqualified" competitors from areas of work in which lawyers enjoyed a monopoly of practice. Abel conceptualizes these set of strategies by speaking about the efforts of lawyers to control both the "production *of* producers" (i.e., the number and "quality" of newcomers) and the "production *by* producers" (i.e., regulating competition among lawyers and excluding outside contenders).[8]

Abel's model, however, provides that lawyers do not merely defend and regulate established areas of practice but also seek ways to exploit new opportunities.[9] Lawyers, in other words, are also interested in the creation of demand. In his treatment of the state as a source of new legal technologies, for example, Abel discusses lawyers' efforts to encourage the development of subsidized legal-aid services as means to enhance the demand for legal services. More generally, a key factor that ensures a growing demand for legal services involves the "progressive legalization of social life."[10] The implicit assumption here is that the general expansion of state powers through, for example, increased reliance on statutory intervention and administrative regulation creates precisely such a generalized legalization and a corresponding growth in the demand for legal services. We may therefore conclude that the market-monopoly model employs the assumption that lawyers will embrace, and in turn will try to monopolize, new professional opportunities that result from the state's legalization practices. The market-monopoly model, in short, also subverts the unproblematic conception of legal work as an objective phenomenon of the market's complexity and replaces it with a view of legal work as a social construction of expertise through the manipulation of discrete knowledge.

The second model I consider has been articulated by Terrance Halliday, who in 1987, with the publication of *Beyond Monopoly: Lawyers, State Crises, and Professional Empowerment*, assumed the unpopular task of critiquing the monopoly thesis as a "new orthodoxy."[11] Halliday's work is consciously situated within a tradition that has tended, since Durkheim's *Professional Ethics and Civic Morals*, to address questions of professionalism from a perspective that asks about the contribution of professionals to social integration and to the stabilization of the social, economic, and political order.[12] Halliday's work challenges the market-monopoly model's assumption that in their relations with the state, lawyers are interested only in appropriating privileges through state-granted monopolies. Halliday distinguishes between two phases of professionalization and argues that the attempt to monopolize the market for legal services characterizes the legal profession only in its early, "formative" years. As the legal profession reaches maturity and its control over the market becomes an established fact, it moves "beyond a preoccupation with monopoly, occupational closure, and the defense of work domains."[13] In their "established" stage, lawyers become sensitive to their civic responsibilities and to their capacity to contribute to solutions of human problems that lie within their domain. The civic responsibilities of the legal profession, says Halliday, find expression in the profession's ability and willingness to nurture "contributory relations" with the state; lawyers shape legal development in ways that facilitate an ever-growing legal rationalization by contributing to the upgrading of the state machinery and by modifying "the constitution to facilitate the problem-solving ability of the state."[14]

Halliday, in contrast to earlier models in the theoretical tradition that he continues, does recognize the reality of the stratified bar and incorporates it into his analysis. Not all segments of the bar, he argues, are equally geared toward devouring potential areas of work. There are situations in which one segment of the bar seeks market control, while another is ready to dismantle it (e.g., established lawyers who embraced no-fault laws). In what follows, I show that the major strength of Halliday's approach lies not in the concept of "contributory relations" but in opening the way for a more sensitive discussion of the relationship between the location of lawyers within the legal field and their respective professional dispositions towards various areas of practice.

The third perspective that I examine has been methodically formulated by Andrew Abbott in his *System of Professions*.[15] The fundamental strength of Abbott's model is that it establishes a strong theoretical link between a given profession's "knowledge" and its ability to control the market for its services. Further, the model posits that the study of a profession cannot be undertaken independently of the activities of other professions because all occupational groups are situated within a system in which there is an ongoing interprofessional competition over turf. This competition is largely played out in the domains of competing systems of knowledge that claim to provide better or more effective solutions to various problems. Central to this model is the concept of jurisdiction. A jurisdiction is a kind of an authorized area of market control established when particular social problems are associated with particular forms of solutions and with a more or less exclusive group of experts who are capable, or perceived as capable, of providing them. In order to establish a jurisdiction, professional work has to be perceived as requiring more than a direct connection between tasks to be performed and people capable of performing them. An unambiguous relationship between a problem and its solution diminishes the ability of professionals to prevent the routinization of their work and the dissolution of their distinct identity as a bonded community of experts. Simple problems and obvious solutions are not conducive to the monopolization of expertise and lead to the deprofessionalization of practice.

Central to a profession's ability to sustain a jurisdiction, therefore, is the development of an abstract and theoretical system of knowledge that transcends the particularities of practice and provides scientific legitimacy to actual practice.

This formulation marks the most important difference between Abbott's model and the market-monopoly thesis. In Abel's approach, the theoretical knowledge of lawyers is not much more than an auxiliary ideology whose purpose is to enhance the social status of lawyers.[16] The intricate ways in which the ideology of law as a science may become a strategy of invading new areas of practice, or a condition that affects the way lawyers respond to changes in the legal environment, is not incorporated into Abel's analysis. Abbott, in contrast, argues that the relationship between knowledge and practice complicates the market-monopoly model's expectation that professions tend to engage uncritically in monopolistic practices. Professions, says Abbott, cannot just grow as they please, because unchecked expansion may compromise their distintive identity as communities of experts. Below, I show that Abbott's theoretical model provides useful conceptual tools for interpreting the political economy of at least some segments of the bar. However, the application of the model to the present case requires some modifications, because the model overemphasizes interprofessional competition and downplays the significance of intra-professional competition.

Application to the "Case"

The theoretical expectation of the market-monopoly model is that lawyers will try to monopolize the areas of work in which they practice. Accordingly, the fact that lawyers sponsored legislation that would have guaranteed them exclusive rights to practice before administrative agencies seems to confirm the assumptions of the market-monopoly model. The growing reliance on administrative practices created a perceived enhanced demand for legal services and opened a new space of professional opportunities. But along with the recognition that new professional opportunities had been created came concerns about fierce competition from lay practitioners, who were also allowed to practice in administrative forums. The sponsorship of legislation to eliminate lay competition, therefore, is in accord with the expectations of the market-monopoly model.

However, complaints about the destructive effects of lay competition came almost exclusively from the weaker segments of the bar; the bar's leaders did not support this direct monopolization move. The theoretical question, therefore, concerns the ability of a market-monopoly model to offer a plausible explanation of the fact that the bar's elite resisted the attempts of solo practitioners to monopolize administrative practice. While Abel's general model does not seem to anticipate such a case, Harrington's study of the bar's response to the emergence of administrative law does suggest a promising solution.[16]

Harrington draws a distinction between an attempt to gain monopoly *to* practice before administrative bodies and an attempt to gain monopoly *over* the practice of administrative law. Harrington argues that the bar's strategists faced "ideological barriers" in entering the administrative field and opted for various strategies of judicialization whose purpose was to gain monopoly *over* the practice of administrative law.[17] In speaking about "monopoly over practice" Harrington refers to the efforts of the bar's leaders to judicialize the administrative process—to subject the administrative field to judicial standards of practice and procedure, to "rationalize" and "formalize" administrative decisionmaking, to separate the "fact finding" powers of administrative bodies from their "law finding" and adjudicatory functions, and, in general, to subject administrative decisions and regulations to comprehensive judicial review by federal courts. Harrington thus interprets the bar's emphasis on the need to subject administrative practices to strict judicial review as a practice of "monopolization from above," thereby preserving the basic assumption of the market-monopoly model that the primary concern of lawyers is to take over and control potential markets while offering the corrective whereby the way in which monopolization takes place may vary. In contrast to Abel's model, which assumes that the legal profession first establishes market control and only then moves to justify it by invoking a relevant ideology, Harrington argues that in the case of administrative law, lawyers "needed first to establish ideological justifications for [their] dominance in the field."[18] This strategy was needed, says Harrington, because the profession lacked the special body of knowledge needed in order for it to assert its "intellectual superiority" in the field: "The existence of an administrative practice not yet professionalized posed ideological rather than market barriers for the legal profession."[19]

At first glance, this seems to solve the problem. In fact, by combining Abel's and Harrington's approaches one can develop a pretty elegant market-monopoly model. Different segments of the profession, depending on their differential position within the legal field, develop different monopolizing strategies that ultimately result in a pincer movement: the low end of the bar, less economically secure, operates by way of exclusionary practices from below; the high end, more troubled by long-term considerations, operates by way of exclusionary practices from above.

Yet neither Abel's general model nor Harrington's specific one reveals any tendency to develop such a model. In fact, it is noteworthy that Harrington's analysis was not founded on the observation that elite lawyers not only opted for "monopoly for above" but actually resisted the efforts of others to monopolize the field "from below." Her analysis, therefore, carries the (certainly unintentional) implication that the organized bar was unified behind a single strategy of response. Ironically, Harrington's solution thus succeeds at the expense of the apparent success of Abel's general model in anticipating the actions of those lawyers who did seek direct market control. Both Abel's and Harrington's models confirm Halliday's observation concerning the theoretical shortcomings of the market-monopoly approach. Halliday argues that in analyzing the internal politics of the bar (e.g., standards of entry and ethical codes) the market-monopoly model emphasizes the dynamics and consequences of the bar's politics of stratification. Yet in treating the professional dispositions of lawyers toward the market for legal services in general, the theorists of market monopoly have tended to assume internal cohesion that, "in other sections of their discussions, they have been at pains to deny."[20]

Halliday's theoretical model does seem to provide a new opening. It posits that the legal profession has moved from a formative stage, in which it sought market benefits, to an established one, in which it became free to dispense its civic responsibilities. This progressive model seems to have an interesting vitality when applied "inwardly"; rather than looking at the historical movement of the profession as a whole, it may be used to analyze the differential positions of different segments of the profession at a given point in time. The drive to monopolize the right to practice before administrative forums came from solo practitioners, who, being less economically secure, had a stake in invoking strategies that aimed at direct market control. In contrast, the more influential and economically secure segments of the bar, having reached an established market position, tended to view the attempts of solo practitioners to abruptly and unabashedly monopolize administrative practice as distasteful, crude, and unwarranted. For corporate lawyers, the administrative process did not pose a market-control problem but a problem of *form*, a problem of a field that evaded traditional methods of adjudication and dispute resolution. In Halliday's conceptual vocabulary, we may therefore speak of the upper echelons of the legal profession as consisting of established lawyers who thought in terms of "improvement" and "rationalization" of the administrative process.

It remains to be seen whether Halliday's conceptual framework adequately captures the case under consideration. Still, it must be said that there is nothing in the generic market-monopoly approach that prevents it from considering the connection between a given location within the professional hierarchy and specific market-monopoly strategies. There is some doubt, however, whether the model can explain why one segment of the bar would deliberately undermine the monopolizing efforts of another when both segments ultimately strive to monopolize the same space. The conscious decision of elite lawyers not to join in the effort to prevent nonlawyers from practicing before administrative bodies indicates that market-control considerations were not so decisive in shaping their attitude toward the administrative process. Therefore, we should read the demand for the judicialization of administrative practice in a broader context than that provided for in Harrington's analysis. After all, the operational proposals of the bar's leaders to establish an administrative court were but a small part of a very aggressive campaign against the merits of the administrative process and its effects upon the rule of law. Elite lawyers, in fact, were engaged in efforts to undermine and contain the further expansion of the administrative process as much as they tried to monopolize it. Of course, it is possible to read the hostility of the bar's leaders to the growth of administrative law as part of a strategy whose ultimate purpose was to monopolize the field. Yet such insistence risks ignoring the fact that the response of elite lawyers toward the growth of administrative law was shaped by their interest in preserving the hegemony and centrality of courts in the resolution of disputes. To the extent that the defense of the judiciary, rather than monopolization from above, determined the attitude of elite lawyers, we should strive to go beyond a monopoly model that thinks of the legal profession only in terms of an imperialist organ.

Halliday's expectation that established lawyers would contribute to the rationalization of the legal system and would tend to develop contributory relations with the state should be given further attention. A good example in support of this line of reasoning is provided by the efforts of the bar's leaders to propose various measures that ultimately materialized in the form of the Federal Register Act. Although the actual influence of the American Bar Association in this matter may be contested, it is nonetheless true that the association's Committee on Administrative Law was among the first organs to complain about the lack of rational and orderly publication of administrative regulations. In Halliday's terms, therefore, the efforts to secure publication of administrative regulations may be described as one indication of the contributory relations that the upper echelons of the bar established with the state. Still, a considerable stretch of the imagination is needed in order to argue that the overall response of elite corporate lawyers to the expansion of the administrative process was based on a contributory orientation. Corporate lawyers saw the enhanced strength of administrative bodies and the overall empowerment of the executive branch of government as dangerous trends that had to be tamed. In contrast to Halliday's assumptions, the rationalization of the existing order and the search for methods that would increase the efficiency of the state administrative machinery in providing solutions to social and economic problems were advocated not by corporate lawyers but by law professors and government lawyers, who were by and large identified with the legal-realist movement. As we shall see in more detail in the next chapter, it was this particular segment of the profession that developed contributory relations with the state during the New Deal. Corporate lawyers were determined to discredit these relations and to operate on the premise that the rise of the administration marked the decline of the courts. The actions of the bar's elite in the New Deal do not fit Halliday's theoretical model. Rather than contributing to the administration's efforts to revitalize the legal system, the leaders of the bar consciously sought ways to undermine them and cause them to fail. Curiously, Halliday qualifies his own model in ways that render it more compatible with the actions of the bar's elite during the New Deal yet less conceptually consistent. He asserts that the most important contribution American lawyers render the American legal system concerns their efforts to facilitate the transition to a "more purely autonomous legal system."[21] Borrowing from Nonet and Selznick's conception of autonomous law as a system in which law and politics are formally separated, Halliday argues that the legal profession "has the will and the ability to advocate a general transformation of the legal system toward autonomous law."[22] At the same time, Halliday admits that "the profession has steadfastly resisted any further transformation of law in the direction of responsive law."[23] By "responsive law" Halliday refers, again following Nonet and Selznick, to a legal system that resides on a "higher" plane of evolution than autonomous law. In such a system, law positively responds to pragmatic and functional imperatives and seeks the solution of social problems even at the expense of established patterns of formal legalistic rules and procedures.[24] In fact, Nonet and Selznick's responsive law is consciously based on the legal-realist conception of law. Given that Halliday recognizes the inherent resistance of lawyers to such tendencies, his general model cannot explain the role of the legal profession in one of America's most crucial periods of change.

Lawyers, says Halliday, are inclined to invoke legalistic rhetoric when faced with "law on the offensive." This rhetoric, in the name of the rule of law and an autonomous legal system, is the heart of Halliday's model of a legal profession that performs "civic responsibilities." In other words, the assertion that lawyers contribute to the state through their commitment to the idea of autonomous law a priori limits the generalization ability of the model; lawyers contribute to the state only under particular conditions and not as a result of their evolution toward a more responsible social role. Further, the recognition that lawyers are concerned only with the development of a particular form of law, namely autonomous law, suggests that self-serving interests (e.g., market-monopoly and status considerations), not a general sense of civic responsibility, is behind this commitment. Halliday's model would have been much more convincing had it been able to show that the commitment of lawyers to public service transcends their commitment to a particular legal arrangement. But apparently this is not the case.

Finally, Halliday qualifies his model in another significant way. The legal profession, he says, "will commit its monopoly of competence and its organizational resources to state service, *so long as the substance of its service does not directly erode the general control of the market the profession has attained,* although it may be prepared to roll back monopoly in certain areas" (italics mine).[25] This qualifies Halliday's model in a way that compels us to turn again to a market-monopoly model. In practical terms, Halliday's own qualification suggests that whenever the self-serving interests of lawyers are or are perceived to be in conflict with the demands of the state, the former set of interests will take the upper hand. If this is the case, the model loses much of its vitality; state service then becomes an occasional by-product of the profession's effort to secure its market monopoly under historically contingent legal-political arrangements.

At any rate, Halliday's findings concerning the strong commitment of lawyers to a formal legalistic order underscore the need to turn to a theoretical perspective that pays greater attention to the relationship between the profession's system of knowledge and its response to social change. The further away we get from dealing with direct methods of market control, the more we need to be sensitive to the intricate links between lawyers' knowledge and their professional practices. The market-monopoly model tends to underestimate the significance of these links and, in Harrington's concrete analysis, does not sufficiently situate the reform efforts of lawyers in the larger context of judicial defense. Halliday's model, by contrast, ends up exaggerating the altruistic motivations of lawyers or, alternatively, admitting the limited capability of lawyers to adjust to new social conditions.

The decisive conceptual turn needed here has to do with a reformulation of the problematic under discussion. After all, if all that the bar's leaders wished to achieve was a "juridification" of administrative methods, they would have directed their efforts toward procedural reform (as indeed finally happened) and not toward creating a separate judicial apparatus in the form of an administrative court. The market-control model insists on formulating the question in terms of "opportunities," of asking about the actions of lawyers who tried to monopolize the administrative field. Halliday's model formulates the question in terms of potential contributions. An alternative formulation, however, is and should be in terms of "threats": of asking about the dangers that lawyers identified with the growth of administrative practice. This reformulation involves more than discussing two sides of the same coin because it leads to a consideration of the conditions under which lawyers will be inclined to resist, rather than embrace, expanded professional opportunities—conditions under which lawyers will tend to defend their existing jurisdiction rather than penetrate a new one.[26]

Abbott's "system of professions" model seems to offer such an analytic framework. He articulates a model that is highly sensitive to the relationship between a given profession's core theoretical knowledge and its response to potential changes in its jurisdiction. From this perspective, the prime concern of the more "enlightened" segments of a profession (i.e., its elites) is to defend the integrity of its theoretical knowledge against external invasions. Indeed, it seems this was precisely how the administrative process was perceived by the bar's leading elites. The expansion of the administrative arena during the New Deal marked a shift from a centralist to a pluralist paradigm of law and signaled the clear preference of the administration for the latter. In terms of Abbott's model, we may thus describe the growing reliance on administrative methods as a form of practice and knowledge that escaped the paradigmatic core on which lawyers traditionally based their claims of exclusive expertise.

The development of a new source of law, at the direct expense of judicial authority, threatened to undermine both the market and the status privileges that the professional elite enjoyed. More concretely, it threatened to compromise the asserted distinct professional identity of lawyers and to subvert the hierarchical organization of the field around the centrality of courts. Practicing in a field that purposefully escaped legalistic methods threatened lawyers because, as Abbott puts it, "expert action without any formalization is perceived by clients as craft knowledge, lacking the special legitimacy that is supplied by the connection of abstractions with general values."[27] Larson, discussing the representation functions of lawyers, also provides a key to understanding the threat posed by unregulated administrative practices. Informal administrative methods undermined the "asymmetry" between lawyers and clients that had been based on lawyers' "differential knowledge of normative codes, conventional procedures, and interpretive techniques."[28]

Yet whereas the market-monopoly model tends to assume that a profession's ability to sustain the asymmetry fuels a project of expanding market control and consolidating status conquests, Abbott's model is also sensitive to conditions under which the effort to sustain such asymmetry will deter professions from embracing new areas of practice. If professions were simply "carnivorous competitors" that grew in strength as they engulfed new jurisdictions, he argues, the professional universe would have evolved into two or three dominant groups. But since professions function within a bounded interdependent system that contains competing and often conflicting systems of knowledge, professions cannot just grow as they please. One obvious constraint has to do with the limits of abstraction: "No profession can stretch its jurisdiction infinitely. For [the] more diverse set of jurisdictions, the more abstract must be the cognitive structure binding them together. But the more abstract the binding ideas, the more vulnerable they are to specialization within and to diffusion into the common culture without."[29] These two predictions—of "diffusion without" and "specialization within"—were fully realized with the proliferation of administrative methods in the New Deal. The development of the administrative arena threatened the distinct boundaries that separated law work from other forms of commercial counseling, and this threat was in turn one of the most significant incentives elite lawyers had to judicialize administrative forums. Ironically, the failure of the American Bar Association to mobilize its members to support the creation of an administrative court was at least partially a result of the fact that lawyers who specialized in practice before some of the more established administrative forums were reluctant to lose their competitive advantages.[30] The specialization from within that administrative practices brought about, in other words, circumscribed the ability of the organized bar to fight the threat of diffusion into the common culture without.

Abbott's model, however, assigns prime importance to the academic elites of any given profession. The model assumes, quite rightly in the general case, that a profession's theoretical and abstract knowledge is produced and generated by academics whose detachment from practice allows them to develop systematic and abstract propositions. Academic producers of professional knowledge are assigned two primary tasks. First, they are responsible for the selection and training of new professionals and hence for the creation of a symbolic bond between practical work and scientific abstraction. Second, and probably more important, academic work provides professions with the compelling legitimacy of science: "Academic knowledge legitimizes professional work by clarifying its foundations and tracing them to major cultural values. In most modern professions, these have been the values of rationality, logic, and science. Academic professionals demonstrate the rigor, the clarity, and the scientifically logical character of professional work, thereby legitimating that work in the context of larger values."[31]

Abbott's model, in other words, assumes an internal cohesion between theoreticians and practitioners. This assumption does not hold in the present case. On the contrary, the response of elite lawyers to the development of administrative law was particularly hostile precisely because it reflected the internal split, suspicion, and competition between legal academics and legal practitioners. In the particular configuration of the American legal field, legal academics were not those who provided scientific legitimacy to the profession as a whole. That task had been assumed by a federal judiciary that developed legal knowledge through the incremental process of deciding concrete cases and abstracting legal doctrines and principles from established precedents.[32] Insofar as the legal field was a "site of competition for monopoly of the right to determine the law," the hostility of lawyers toward the growth in administrative methods reflected their interest in shielding their particular "judicial-scientific" site of legal production from the dangerous theories of aspiring academics.[33]

This observation leads to another important difference between Abbott's general model and the case of the legal profession in the New Deal. Abbott's model emphasizes inter*professional* competition, the classic case being that of a contending profession that invades the jurisdiction of an incumbent one. Yet the case of administrative law involved an *intraprofessional* competition, between low-end and high-end members of the bar on the one hand and between practitioners and academics on the other. In particular, the threat to the profession's theoretical knowledge came from within—from legal academics who challenged the hegemony of courts in the legal system and granted intellectual legitimacy to the administration's experiments in administrative law. These academics challenged the very idea of a self-referential scientific law and exposed the uncertainty of the judicial process, and with it the fragile cognitive foundation of the profession of law. When the boundaries of the traditional legal field threatened to disintegrate, the leaders of the bar invoked strategies whose purpose was to reassert judicial supremacy.

Viewed from this perspective, it is also understandable why the efforts of elite practitioners were not initially aimed at imposing judicial procedures on administrative agencies but focused instead on subjecting them to judicial review. Simply, this strategy aimed at the preservation of judicial authority as much as it was oriented toward the monopolization of a new professional market. Further, it may be clearer now why elite lawyers not only insisted on judicializing the administrative field but also actively resisted the attempts to exclude lay practitioners from the field. What at first looks like contradictory practices becomes understandable: the exclusion of lay practitioners would have implied that the bar unconditionally accepted the validity and prominence of new methods and techniques for making law and surrendered some of its prerogatives to autonomously define the boundaries of legal practice. At least relatively undisturbed by direct market competition, the calls of the bar's leaders for judicial review and judicial methods in administrative rulemaking and adjudication should be comprehended as practices whose purpose was to restrict the ability of administrators and academic legal experts to enforce a new paradigm on the legal field.

An intraprofessional perspective, rather than an interprofessional one, best captures the strains and struggles around the development of administrative law practice. This is not to say that interprofessional competition was not on the agenda. The lower segments of the bar did suffer from lay competition and responded by trying to secure a statutory monopoly to practice. Their failure, however, owed much to their structural position within the profession's hierarchy. Inter- and intraprofessional competition, therefore, are two distinct conditions that do not necessary lead to corresponding strategies that can be determined a priori. In the most general and tentative terms, and on the basis of the limited case that I considered here, it is possible only to outline some relationships between different types of competition and corresponding types of response.

There are two typical forms of interprofessional competition. One is that in which a contending profession invades established areas of work that are controlled by an incumbent profession. The second type occurs when there is a new area of practice that is not yet fully controlled by either party. Such interprofessional competition may be thought of in terms of a race between parties over who will be the first to control this new space for professional activities. It was this second type of competition that lawyers faced in the administrative arena. As is reflected by the hemispheric split within the bar, those lawyers who suffered most from the economic effects of the depression had a stake in defining administrative practice as a natural legal domain and in eliminating the competition with nonlawyers in this still loosely structured field.

Intraprofessional competition involves a different type of threat. At stake here is the dominance, or at least the secured position, of particular professional segments within the professional hierarchy. Again, this type of competition may be thought of in two analytically distinct ways. Direct intraprofessional competition is the typical condition that each lawyer experiences as a result of an ongoing competition for clients. A second type involves an open struggle for influence and prestige within the professional hierarchy. This type of competition, while rare, is nevertheless extremely destructive to a profession's sense of unity. It was this type of intraprofessional competition that the leaders of the bar experienced during the New Deal. A group of academic jurists, with the blessing of the administration, advanced a new thesis, a new juristic paradigm, that shook the traditional theoretical foundations of the professional jurisdiction. Consequently, the bar's leaders sponsored defensive strategies that were intended to contain the new paradigm as much as possible.

The terminology invoked here may be easily incorporated into both the market-monopoly model and Abbott's system-of-professions model. Despite their different orientations, both establish a link between the practices of lawyers and their distinct interests as an occupational group. But can we accommodate this perspective with Halliday's model? Halliday consciously refused to describe the relations of established lawyers with the state in terms of their self-serving interests. Yet he recognized that elite lawyers were prone to defend and improve the "rule of law." Taking this latter formulation as a point of departure, to the extent that we may legitimately deconstruct the idea of the rule of law, the implications of Halliday's formulations are not that far removed from the other perspectives discussed here. To make this point, let us look at the argument of Robert Gordon, who, not unlike Halliday, distinguishes the "ideal interests" of lawyers from their material ones. These ideals, in general, concern the interest of lawyers in promoting the image of lawyering as a public calling that contributes to the improvement of the legal order for the general benefit of society. The essence of the ideal, Gordon tells us, consists in the wish to develop legal "science." The purpose, he goes on to say, is to create a bridge between professional practices that grow ever more distant from "pure" law and lawyers' belief in their obligations to a universal legal order. While Halliday speaks of an altruistic impulse to contribute, Gordon speaks of a psychological need of elite lawyers to "live in comfort" with themselves.[34]

The overlooked element in this perspective is that the improvement of legal science is itself a result of a particular conception of law. Law as a science, like the rule of law, is not an objective term that exists as an essential entity but rather a social construct whose content and form are historically contingent and discursively negotiable. Those lawyers who wanted to improve law as a science were at the same time defining what law as a science meant, in contrast to the emergent conception of a new legal science put forward by the advocates of administrative law. In their efforts to distinguish politics from professional expertise, the leaders of the bar justified their calls for the judicialization of administrative practice by invoking the general value of the rule of law. As Brint observes, "[P]rofessional influence can be extensive when professionals are able to assert a central cultural value in the absence of a strong counterideology."[35] Yet in the New Deal there was a strong counter-ideology at work; the new emphasis on pragmatic needs and the advocacy of bold legal experiments offered an antidote to the values associated with the rule of law. Consequently, the ability of the bar's leaders to shape the administrative process in the first years of the New Deal was very limited. The desire of lawyers to protect law as a science and their bold defense of the rule of law, in short, reflected their own versions of these notions, and these in turn reflected their own structural positions in the legal field. Lawyers may be well intentioned, and some of them are surely committed to an ideal vision of law as the guardian of social harmony. Still, we have yet to come up with a case in which lawyers put their ideal interests before their own material and status considerations.

6 The Revolt of Academics: Legal Realism and the New Deal

Introduction

I have already argued that the distinction between politics and law was under-girded by a corresponding split between will and reason.[1] The legislative and administrative agenda of the New Deal threatened to expose the vulnerability of this socially constructed distinction and seemed like a nightmare to the bar's leaders: Law, not only as an idea but also in the way it was exercised in the early years of the New Deal, emerged as an authoritative machinery that had no cognitive foundation independent of social, political, and economic context.[2] Force had been infused into the realm of privileged reason, and where will was to govern and guide, the moral foundations of law were also put into question. From the standpoint of the bar's leaders, the legal field became a site for a contest of wills, drifting by the sheer force of interests that in themselves had no anchor in fundamental principles. Legal texts in general, and the Constitution in particular, could not serve any longer as sources for truth that had to be rediscovered and uncovered. The hidden moral meaning of the Constitution that legal reasoning claimed to uncover, and the technique of reason that served the dual function of reiterating the professional identity and finalizing the legal text, gave place to discursive practices that treated legal texts as no more than reference points for the further elaboration of fresh principles and for truth that could be articulated only on the basis of needs.

The Constitution was treated by a new breed of legal thinkers as nothing more than an "experimental text,"[3] and established constitutional doctrines that stood in the way of change had to be reinterpreted or sometimes even avoided. This was the case when the Guffey-Snider bituminous coal conservation bill was pending in Congress in 1935.[4] Doubts as to whether this legislation could survive constitutional scrutiny by the Court had been raised before a subcommittee of the Senate Committee on Interstate Commerce even prior to *Schechter.* These doubts intensified after *Schechter,* and the subcommittee asked the attorney general, Homer Cummings, to offer his views on the matter.

Cummings refused and advised the subcommittee "to push [the bill] through and leave the question to the courts."[5] President Roosevelt sent the committee a letter in which he advised it to prefer considerations of expediency over considerations of constitutionality: "No one is in a position to give assurance that the proposed act will withstand constitutional tests, for the simple fact that you can get not ten but a thousand differing opinions on the subject. But the situation is so urgent and the benefits of the legislation so evident that all doubts should be resolved in favor of the bill, leaving to the courts, in an orderly fashion, the ultimate question of constitutionality. . . . I hope your committee will not permit doubts as to constitutionality, however reasonable, to block the suggested legislation."[6] To lawyers who saw it as their professional and moral duty to subject human affairs to the purifying light of legal reason—as if its hidden yet discoverable rules and maxims could and should objectively determine the course of social change—the idea that expediency came first was simply shocking. Roosevelt's statement, which could have been interpreted as a perfectly reasonable distinction between legislative and judicial functions, deferring to the Court questions of constitutional validity, created a storm among lawyers. They saw it as an open invitation to litigate, as proof that the administration consciously adopted "unlawful practices," and as a sign that there were many among the administration's advisers who lent prestige to the viewpoint "that small constitutional scruples ought not to stand in the way of a great legislative benefit."[7] Underlying all these accusations, however, was outrage at an attitude that exposed legal certainty as a myth and undermined the idea that legal reason was beyond instrumental manipulation. A horrific picture of a world governed by will, in which professional identities, taken-for-granted truths, and established roles were constantly reshuffled and, worse still, doubted, determined the response of many lawyers to the new developments. "With an almost fanatical worship of efficiency," warned one, "some would erect a state, a great machine of government, which with terrifying precision would articulate and control our entire social and economic life."[8] "The men of our time," declared another, were pragmatists who judged "everything from its practical results," while "the founders of the Republic were moralists."[9]

The men who were to blame for the new developments were often the reform-minded law teachers. Earlier I referred to the administration's legal advisers, to academics who lent their support to the administration's plans, to government lawyers who advocated a new approach to law and the constitution, and occasionally to the legal-realist spirit that permeated and guided the New Deal's legal agenda. Out of these referrals emerges an image of a legal field in which corporate lawyers and legal academics were pitted against each other. It is important to stress, however, that this rough dichotomy necessarily ignores some of the complexities of the legal struggles of the times. I am talking here about large groups of professionals who had their own internal divisions of opinions and attitudes. There were corporate lawyers who sided with Roosevelt's plans and identified with the legal-realist mood, as well as those who joined the administration and had a significant voice in shaping legislative policies.[10] Similarly, there were more than a few legal academics who did not share the new vision of law and watched with alarm what they regarded as the destruction of law schools and legal education.[11] Nonetheless, it may still be argued that, by and large, a core of elite corporate lawyers in private practice and a significant core of law teachers from elite law schools were engaged in a struggle over the "right to determine the law," or in the more mundane appearance of this struggle, over professional status and influence both internal and external to the legal field. Consider a telling anecdote. The American Liberty League tried to mobilize support for its opposition to the New Deal by enlisting academics. In 1936, the league published a report whose purpose was to demonstrate that "despite the connection of certain [academics] with the administration 'brain trust,' many scores of them have voiced criticism." Yet none of the nearly two hundred professors from various disciplines whose names appeared in the report was a professor of law—a glaring absence for an organization that enjoyed the support of the bar's elite.[12]

For elite corporate lawyers who saw the events of the times as a nightmare come true, law professors and teachers were the enemy, harshly judged and suspected precisely because of their location within the legal field. Law teachers, as Charles E. Clark flatly admitted, were "suspected in this country" by a group of lawyers who distanced themselves from academic jurists and contributed their share to an ever-widening gulf between the two groups.[13] Law teachers were portrayed by some of the bar's leaders as "dangerous academic theorists" who "refused allegiance" to the American Constitution and form of government and who threatened "the safety and security of constitutional government."[14] Indeed, one could not but pause and either applaud or shudder at the boldness of Yale's Walter Nelles, who opened an article about the nature of law with a quotation from Marx's *The Eighteenth Brumaire of Louis Bonaparte*.[15] Corporate lawyers shuddered; elite law teachers were conceived of as subversive "liberals" who harbored ideas resembling those of Karl Marx and as "dangerous academic theorists" who pretended "to sit in judgment not only upon decisions of the Supreme Court but upon the relative merits of the judges." The real objective of the "academicians" who spoke from the academic halls to other "ever present demagogues," argued one lawyer, "has been and still is the overthrow of our free institutions and the establishment of a new social order."[16]

So far I have concentrated on identifying the network of elite lawyers in private practice who constituted the core of the opposition to the New Deal's legal agenda. In this chapter I take a closer look at those "dangerous academicians" who drew their fire. A description of the animosity between the bar's leaders and this emergent group of academic thinkers that reduces it to a struggle between liberals and conservatives—that is, to idea-shaping forces external to the legal field—would miss the degree to which reform-oriented attitudes on the one hand and attachment to the status quo on the other had their own internal dynamic and sources within the legal field. It is this "threat from within," so alarming precisely because of the professors' standing, that I address here. I discuss the relationship between the New Deal's emergent vision of law and the position of its advocates in the legal field and consider a body of thought as it was embedded, determined, and expressed in concrete practices. In so doing, I hope to provide a conceptual link that has been somewhat understated by those who looked at the new generation of jurists either as lawyers-turned-political-activists (New Dealers) or as lawyer-thinkers (mainly the so-called legal realists). My intention, however, is not to offer new insights concerning the ideas associated with legal realism. The abundant literature about the realists provides a quite comprehensive account of the realists' major heroes, of the relationship of some of the realists with the New Deal's administration, and, in general, of the realists' seemingly incompatible tastes for informed legislative and administrative planning, profound skepticism, social reform, obsessive "behaviorist" focus on judicial decisionmaking, ethical relativism, and cultural hermeneutics.[17]

Although I rely on some sources in this literature, I focus instead not only on the widely recognized *instrumental* connection between the legal realists and the New Deal's administration but also on the *conceptual* links that linked the two. I thus develop Glennon's observation that "while there was no necessary correlation between legal realism and New Deal liberalism," the realists' legal philosophy "fitted well with the experimental and flexible nature of the New Deal."[18] In particular, I would like to stress, on the one hand, that the "experimental" orientation of the New Deal derived legitimacy and was in effect partly shaped by the legal realists' approach to law, and on the other that the "flexibility" of the New Deal played a part in the ability of the legal realists to gain professional prominence. I share Horwitz's insight that the realists' reformist zeal and their critique of legal reason were two interrelated elements of a single trajectory. His innovative assertion that "administrative law is in many ways the culmination of the crisis of legitimacy that Realist criticism produced" is particularly important.[19] Yet the relationship between the legal realists and the political reformers of the New Deal was two-sided. To radicalize an argument:

were it not for the New Deal, legal realism might have remained a relatively obscure body of thought, familiar to academics and theoreticians, perhaps to students under the guidance of such teachers, but essentially foreign to policy makers and state experts. For the bar's leaders, at any rate, the problem was neither that of legal realism per se nor of lawyering at the service of the state as such. Rather, it was the combination of legal thinkers from elite law schools who had a concrete voice in shaping the legal agenda of the state that posed a threat to their self-identity and to their privileged hierarchical position within the legal field. It was this forceful combination of their academic standing and their political influence during the New Deal that enabled the realists to reframe the spatial boundaries of law, to question the internal hierarchy of the legal field, and to assert a new role for academic law teachers within it. Accordingly, I wish to treat legal realism not only as a body of thought, incoherent as it was, but also as the professional praxis of specific carriers. In other words, while the relationship to the New Deal created opportunities, it was the internal organization of the legal field at a particular historical juncture that bred the impulse to exploit them.

Some students of legal realism situate its development in the context of a rather straightforward progression of jurisprudential ideas in "revolt against formalism," or, in what is only another version of this tradition, as part of a series of continuities and breaks with past "classical" legal thought.[20] Certainly, seeds had been planted by some notable forerunners: Holmes, Gray, and Green, three jurist-members of Harvard's Metaphysical Club, had already cast doubt on the determining role of legal logic forty years earlier in the name of pragmatist thought.[21] The German Free Law movement, with which at least some of the realists were familiar, provided intellectual inspiration, with its emphasis on judicial creativity and its insistence on "gaps" in even the most rigidly codified law.[22] And Cardozo's *The Nature of the Judicial Process*, and particularly Pound's sociological jurisprudence, which harnessed social science to the aid of legal science, worked against "mechanical jurisprudence."[23] All, coupled with a subtle yet consistent antiformalist trend in American legal thought since the turn of the century, provided the realists with the conceptual ropes with which to climb out of what they considered to be the choking pit of formal legal thought. Yet intellectual history alone cannot "explain" the realists' trajectory. It cannot account for the conditions of possibilities in which some groups, or individuals, become more open to certain styles of thought; it can only clarify the available repertoire to which disenchanted thinkers can turn for intellectual inspiration. In what follows, therefore, I do not look backward, that is, to sources of inspiration, but forward, to the field of possibilities opened up for the realists through their declared agenda of distrust. The subversion of law's certainty, from this perspective, was a reaction against academic legal thought's powerless isolation and ultimately a crucial step in overturning the established hierarchy of the legal field.

By looking at the relation between the new ideas and the legal field's internal hierarchy, I reconstruct legal realism without privileging any particular set of ideas; rather, partly as a tribute to the realists' own tendencies, I focus not on doctrinal writings but on what they actually did (or at least said should be done). In general, we may think of the realists as an imagined bounded community of acclaimed and self-acclaimed members who, while not formally representing a school, did share a "mood."[24] Yet the diversity of practices and ideas among the realists, the distortions that result from focusing only on some notable individuals, the ambiguity that surrounds the question of who was and was not a "realist," and the seemingly incompatible tastes they displayed for the study and implementation of law limits the analytic value of ideational descriptions.

These ambiguities may be at least partially accommodated by treating the realists as a group of players who occupied the same space within the legal field, namely, by focusing on their institutional roles as law-teachers-turned-experts in the direct and indirect service of the state. From this standpoint, as we shall see, Felix Frankfurter was no less a realist than was Thurman Arnold or Charles Clark. Distinctions among the realists that are important for various scholarly reasons, like the distinction between those who were rule skeptics and those who were fact skeptics, those who were inclined toward behavioral studies and those who were more oriented to critical theoretical thought, or those who were ethical relativists and those who were not, are important in the present context only insofar as they show the different faces and phases of a single project whose consequences, if not orchestrated purpose, had been to temporarily diffuse the centralized power of courts and to crown academics-turned-experts as the bar's new mandarins.

Legal realism will be treated here as an internal "collective mobility project" that enhanced the status and influence of a particular segment of the legal profession, namely legal academics. This project took place *within* the legal field through an intraprofessional struggle over the symbolic and material resources that constituted the field's hierarchy. "The structure of professions," writes Larson, "results from two processes: the process of organization for a market of services, and the process of collective mobility by which the early modern professions attached status and social standing to their transformed occupational roles."[25] Indeed, the collective mobility project of law teachers depended for its success on their ability to benefit from and contribute to the expansion of the market for legal services. Whereas the supply of legal services was traditionally oriented to the market, legal academics allied themselves with the public arena of the state, offering a variety of contributory capabilities that allowed them to assert a leading role within the legal profession.[26] As such, the collective mobility project was an unstable process in the course of which the practices and ideology of law professors led to a partial breakdown of the established order in the field. Therefore, the ascent of academics was perceived with alarm from the perspective of the bar's leaders, as a mark of their own decline as an influential segment of the profession. Legal realism, in short, is treated here as a revolt of academics and as a path of internal professionalization intimately linked with the ascent of the interventionist state.

An Isolated Profession

Legal realism was of course first and foremost an academic affair and a creature of academic culture.[27] It was within the particular location of universities between the market for private legal services and state demand for public law that the professionalization of law teachers took place, and it was in these institutions of higher learning—particularly the elite law schools of Yale, Columbia, and Harvard—that new and provocative ideas about the function and nature of the legal system eventually crystallized into a body of thought transmitted by a group of influential carriers.

"The very idea of a professional teacher of law," writes Purcell, "suggested the role of a specialized expert capable of objectively evaluating the social consequences of legal institutions."[28] He asserts that "the general problem of professional identity, acute for lawyers newly separated from practice, made self definition in terms of the scientific method an obvious recourse."[29] An "obvious recourse" it may have been, yet more than one road led from this principled commitment to science. From its inception in the second half of the nineteenth century, the newly established profession rested its epistemological foundations on deductive rationalism. A systematic study of the "social consequences of legal institutions," on the other hand, remained a road not taken until the 1920s and 1930s. Cognitive identification with the natural sciences notwithstanding, the road that led legal educators to adopt the "case method" of legal education and study—an embodiment of deductive rationalism—reflected academic acceptance of the given order and structure of the American legal field.

Coming of age in a field dominated by the centrality of a common law–based judicial system, full-time law teachers uncritically accepted the basic tenets of the system. Law was portrayed as a gapless system of rules that determined legal results independently of substantive political and economic considerations. Judicial decisions, in the story often told by Judge Joseph Story, were portrayed as merely "evidence of the universal common-law" and as the result of principles inherent in law.[30] Law teachers fed on these particular assertions of scientism. The systematic teaching and learning of legal decisions—comparing the law library to the laboratories of university chemists and physicists—contributing to the practicing bar's aura of scientific expertise, legitimized the judicial system's assertions of coherence and logic, and at the same time advanced the institutionalization of full-time law teachers as a "profession within a profession."[31] The consolidation of a court-centered legal science in the second half of the nineteenth century had been accompanied by a concurrent institutionalization of university-affiliated law schools and autonomous bar associations. The case method of legal education was developed and perfected in Harvard under the deanship of Langdell and Ames between 1870 and 1910, and it was also this period that saw a rapid proliferation of law schools and the establishment of bar associations in New York (1870), Cleveland (1873), Chicago and St. Louis (1874), and Boston (1877), leading finally to the American Bar Association in 1878. The project of the elite lawyers responsible for the creation of these associations corresponded to that of elite law teachers who strengthened their hold on legal education.[32] Although the relationship between the American Bar Association and the Association of American Law Schools was marred by ongoing conflicts and mutual suspicions, the project, at least until the 1920s, was mutual: an intensive process of professionalization based on higher standards of formal legal education, elimination of part-time schools, and standardization of rules for admission to the bar.[33] On the one hand, law teachers suffered from the dominance of elite practitioners in the American Bar Association, and the bar's leaders, for their part, were always on guard against attempts of law teachers to take the lead in shaping and defining the "needs" of law. On the other hand, as Stevens notes, a common culture of professionalism united academics and practitioners in jealously protecting their domains from potential interlopers. " '[S]cience' and the orthodoxy of the case method had given them a solid base for their pride."[34]

Yet there was a marked difference between law and other scientific disciplines. Law may have been a science, but it was one that had not been exclusively produced in institutions of higher learning. Legal science was also the art of judicial decisionmaking at the appellate level. Law was what appellate judges declared it to be: whatever had been created, accumulated, and processed in the course of the exchange between practitioners and judges and presented as an objective inquiry into the realm of reason. The role of law teachers, apart from preparing future practitioners, was to contribute their talents and intellectual faculties to the further perfection of law: to organize and categorize knowledge that had been produced in courts, to rehearse it in treatises, and to identify and clarify the rules upon which it was founded. The role of legal academics, in other words, was to render judicial utterances ever more certain and consistent:

> The best service a professor of law can render the profession, aside from his work of teaching, is to state in treatises, or essays, the rules or principles that after collating legal decisions and using such general knowledge as he may possess he conceives to be sound. This he will do with full recognition that he is not thereby giving to the counselor or to the court all that is necessary for the performance of their respective tasks. He is only giving them aid of the kind that his own work best fits him to give, in a matter that is vital for the successful prosecution of their functions, whatever else may also be needed.[35]

Academics, in this professional configuration, were the librarians, judges the authors. The scientism of law teachers founds its most glaring example not in their abstract contribution to legal theory but in their ability to "save the system and the profession" from the chaos of a legal order that had been based on the flow of endless singular and atomistic cases. Later in the twentieth century the classificatory talents of law professors would be exploited in the restatement projects. Yet even before that, the practical identity between the law and judicial precedent in America turned law teachers, in the service of practitioners and judges on the lookout for the "right" case and the "correct" result, respectively, into valuable information sources and experts at finding and classifying the opinions of appellate-level judges.

Perhaps inevitably, the road taken by the young profession thus had its costs. The study of law from within—consciously reproducing judicial rulings as a clearly demarcated universe of discourse—dictated a kind of intellectual isolation, the unintended consequence of which was the structural positioning of legal academics in a relatively marginal, or at least adjunct, position vis-à-vis the judiciary and the bar's elite. Law teachers, in fact, suffered from a "dual marginality."[36] Within the legal field, it was appellate courts, and not academic scholars, who were the primary source of authority and influence. In fact, the paradox of the new professionalism was that the obsessive focus on appellate cases as the high road of legal learning and "discovery" also served to reinforce, with each case that was dissected, analyzed, and observed, the prominence and centrality of courts in the legal system. Within the academic world, on the other hand, law teachers were often just that: teachers in a professional school whose role was to train future corporate lawyers. In stark contrast to the vivid intellectual activity in the emerging social sciences, the almost exclusive focus of legal education on appellate cases left little room for sustained reflexivity on the project of law as a whole. This could hardly be attained by scholars who were indulging in the opposite project, that is, construing law as a "natural artifice" whose validity as a given order of things had to be assumed and constantly asserted.[37] Law teachers, in short, were not fully integrated—either institutionally or intellectually—into the rest of the academic world. Purcell offers a highly important insight, therefore, in suggesting that the new generation of realists in the 1920s and 1930s "represented both a development of and a reaction against the new professionalism."[38] Just as the response of the bar's leaders to the new vision of law has to be read in light of their distinct professional considerations, so also must the ideas embodied in the disjointed body of thought that we refer to as legal realism be read as an expression of the professional aspirations of legal academics to escape their marginality within the legal field.

A sense of relative isolation and undue marginalization had been building up among law teachers since the Progressive Era, precisely because of the growing discrepancy felt between the professors' "elitist claim of expertise" and their primary role as trainers of corporate lawyers who soon detached themselves from legal theory only to engage in the manipulation of judicial precedents. Consequently, writes Auerbach, "in the two decades preceding World War I a sense of public responsibility and an identification with political reform provided law teachers with their special identity."[39] The development of a shared distinct identity, grounded in the unique strategic position of teachers between the state and the market, reached a climax in the 1930s. Of course, not all law teachers shared these sentiments, and relatively few were actively trying to redefine their position. Ester Brown, for example, reporting on the state of legal education in the 1930s, cited a law school bulletin that confessed that "the faculty has in mind no radical experiments in legal education. . . . We stick to fundamentals. No member is inclined to convert his classroom into an expensive laboratory in which to experiment with novel, radical, or untried theories."[40] Yet the 1930s did see an accumulated mass of law teachers in elite law schools who knowingly or unknowingly contributed to the crystallization of a new collective mobility project; and in the last instance, it is always an elite that speaks for the group as a whole.

The dependence of the interventionist state on science, both as a legitimating vehicle and as an instrument of management, created favorable conditions for this collective mobility project. This project, fragmented and inconsistent as it was, may be considered analytically as a two-tiered assault on the established legal order: first, doubt and discreditation, second, enlargement of the professional space to accommodate new forms of legal production; first, destructive skepticism (also as a form of identity construction), second, constructive positivism (also as a form of destroying the "old" expertise).

Realism as a Collective Mobility Project I: Casting Doubt

The unifying energy that fueled the different programs of the loosely coordinated projects of the realists had been their agenda of doubt, an attitude that Cowan poignantly described as saying that "there is no certainty except this: there is no certainty."[41] Although there seems to have been wide agreement that the realists "differed from as much as they resembled each other," there also seems to be wide agreement that they all shared the attempt to "dissipate the myths of conventional thought."[42] Karl Llewellyn, who insisted that "there is no group" with an official "creed," was nonetheless ready to adopt Jerome Frank's opinion that the realists were related to each other "only in their negations, and in their skepticisms, and in their curiosity."[43] The realists scandalized the all-too-often respectable appearance of law by bringing into broad daylight what had previously been only whispered behind closed doors: law was as chaotic, indeterminate, and inconsistent as the world around it. The idea of law as a certain and consistent body of thought—the ability of both judge and lawyer to know the law, to uncover its hidden truth, to discover and apply the law's rules and logic, and to activate a technology of prediction—constituted the legal profession's paradigmatic core. The certainty of law and the promises of stability and calculability that came with it reinforced the social value of the autonomous legal space and augmented the scientific image of its learned participants. Certainty served as an insurance policy, providing a cover against the risk of instability and the demonic possibility of an unsettled order of things. Certainty, to put it differently, was the objectifying meeting point of the "is" and the "ought," and it was precisely at this paradigmatic core that a new breed of law teachers aimed their most biting critique.

To be sure, a sense that the certainty of law was marred by inconsistencies and confusion had been pervasive in legal circles for quite some time.[44] Various plans to create a juristic center that would unite academics and practitioners in some kind of legal reform had been floating around the American Bar Association and the Association of American Law Schools since the second decade of the twentieth century. For a while, competition between practitioners and law teachers over who was best suited to lead and to conduct a project of legal reform blocked and delayed an early start. Law professors, as Hull reports, were "well aware that their practitioner brethren gave them short shrift in practical law reform." In the 1922 meeting of the American Bar Association, for example, a proposal to create a commission for the reform of federal civil procedure specified that it would be composed of "two Supreme Court justices, two circuit judges, two district judges, and three lawyers of prominence."[45] Law professors had no place in this perceived cherished bond between the bar and the judiciary.

Ultimately, an initiative of the Association of American Law Schools to create an American Law Institute was realized after Elihu Root endorsed it. Root, the "acknowledged leader" of the bar, had been concerned about the chaotic nature of the common law and supported earlier abortive attempts to launch an orderly classification and restatement of the law.[46] In 1923, he recruited some of New York's elite corporate lawyers, arranged for a constitutive meeting in the headquarters of the Association of the Bar of the City of New York, and provided for an initial grant of one million dollars from the Carnegie Foundation, of which he had been a trustee. In the envisioned project of the restatement of the law, in short, elite corporate lawyers played a pivotal role. Although the actual burden of work was assigned to willing academics, it was the bar's elite that provided the legitimacy, prestige, and material resources needed for the project.[47]

The primary objective of the American Law Institute, then, was to conduct a thorough restatement of the law. The restatement project was premised on the recognition that the accumulated mass of legal decisions had reached a critical point of inconsistency, and that in order to bring order and reduce uncertainty, a systematic reorganization of the various fields of law had been called for. As Samuel Williston explained, the restatement of the law in an orderly fashion— bringing out both the latest judicial decisions and the legal principles they embodied—would enable the "true lawyer" to apply legal rules "with constant facility and certainty to the ever-tangled skein of human affairs." True, "to the extent that social needs and mores change, legal principles should change," yet legal principles had to be changed slowly: "[s]o only can reasonable certainty and stability be had."[48] The first statement conveys the vision of a master of rules who casts order on a chaotic social universe, the second acknowledges the force of needs and their determining effect on law only to subject them to the composed gait of legal logic. Together they reproduced the opposition between social will and legal reason and subjected the former to the triad of reason, stability, and certainty. Consider this reproduction in light of Thurman Arnold's way of describing the restatement project as a sham: "Out of the whole confused effort comes the belief that a unified body of rational principles must exist, or else learned men would not be hunting for them with such untiring diligence. Present confusion is explained by showing that the law is an uncompleted science. The analogy of evolution, including the outworn scientific notion of the survival of the fittest, is employed."[49] It was in light of such attitudes that the restatement project was nonetheless regarded by some as an adequate response to the emergent legal realists. George Wickersham, a corporate lawyer and the president of the American Law Institute, expressed similar sentiments upon the completion of the Restatement of the Law of Contracts. The realists represented a school of thought, he argued, that considered the

> effort at clarifying and simplifying the law as a pursuit of a vague idea, because it assumes the fallacious concept that there is such a thing as "the law." The school of thought represented by such a critic is absolutely foreign to that by which this Institute was formed. We believe that there is such a thing as "the law of the land," and, despite the scornful denials of the opposite school, that "the now law," as they term it, can usefully be expressed and understood; and that only when it is so expressed, can it intelligently be modified in its application by judicial decision, or changed by legislation.[50]

Thus, the lawyers and legal scholars who worked on the restatement project shared with the realists the same empirical observation that the law was full of uncertainties and contradictions. Yet whereas theirs was an effort to perfect the system, the realists emphasized this point in order to dethrone the king. The realist challenge consisted in denying the traditional legal way of uncertainty reduction. Their untiring agenda of doubt was different from that of former critics and reform-minded lawyers because it violated the cherished distinction between the discipline's "research frontier" and its "scientific core." The research frontier, writes Cole, "consists of all the work currently being done by all active researchers in a given discipline." The core, on the other hand, "consists of a small set of theories and analytic techniques which represent the 'given' at any particular point in time."[51] Traditional jurists could agree that there were inconsistencies and uncertainties as far as their "research frontier" was involved. They believed, however, that these could be settled from within the system, where a scientific core of solid procedures of legal reasoning provided the means to advance legal science. The realists, in contrast, carried the notion of uncertainty right into the heart of the legal system, denying the very validity of a solid scientific core.

Law's certainty was a myth, argued Jerome Frank, perhaps even a sinister project of concealment. In stark contrast to the distinction between social will and legal reason, Frank asserted that "the law as we have it is uncertain, indefinite," "vague and variable," and could not be otherwise as long as it dealt with the "confused, shifting helter skelter of life."[52] "Distrust of traditional legal rules," "distrust of the theory that traditional prescriptive rule-formulations are the heavily operative factor in producing court decisions," "distrust of verbally simple rules," declared Karl Llewellyn.[53] And Thurman Arnold, often on the verge of treating law-as-a-science as not much more than a parody, ridiculed it as a falsely promised "way of finding out the truth," and as "the shining but unfulfilled dream of a world governed by reason."[54]

Much has been written on the realists' agenda of doubt, distrust, and uncertainty and its philosophical implications. It is often argued that the logical conclusions of the realists' attitude led to radical ethical relativism, which, with the rise of nazism and fascism in Europe, contributed to its fall from grace.[55] Horwitz notes, however, that the "value" or "ethical" relativism of the realists has been exaggerated while their "cognitive relativism" has not been sufficiently appreciated.[56] What sometimes remains obscure, because of the overemphasis on the realists' ethical relativism is that this relativism and distrust, as well as the call to separate the "is" and the "ought" in the study of law, was grounded in the concrete reality of judicial supremacy in the American legal field. The realists' agenda of distrust must be closely read bearing in mind Oliver W. Holmes's oft-quoted maxim—which many of the realists fully shared—that "the prophecies of what the courts will do in fact, and nothing more pretentious, are what I mean by the law."[57] The realists' "doubt" assumes different proportions, if not meaning, when the concept of law becomes synonymous with that of the judicial process. When the realists spoke of law they had in mind a judge-made law, and when they spoke of legal rules they typically had in mind those rules which judges claimed to discover by way of justifying and rationalizing their decisions.[58]

Some of the most diehard critics of legal realism, many of them quite close in spirit to the realist project, did not fail to grasp this point. Both Roscoe Pound and Herman Kantorowicz, for example, blamed the realists for their "exaggerated" notion of law as nothing more than what judges did. The trouble with reducing law to the province of judicial decisions, Pound argued, was that it confused the particular American case with a universal legal order. The realists' view, in short, was not adequate for those, like Pound, who tried to develop a "general science of law."[59] Yet it is not at all evident that the realists were trying to develop such a general theory. Theirs was a practical position which sought to undermine, through the combined force of persuasion and action, a particular professional arrangement and a particular court-centered ethos.

The realists' assertion that law had to be studied as an "is" was another way of saying that judges were not discovering law and were not making decisions on the basis of objective, determinate rules.[60] By emphasizing the relativity and uncertainty of law, the realists had in mind a concrete project of relativizing judicial pronouncements, discrediting the objective, reasonlike nature of the judicial process, and shattering the aura of sanctity that surrounded the judicial forum. The distinction between the "is" and the "ought" was thus a necessary condition for equalizing judicial authority with other forms of legal expertise and for legitimating alternative sources of law. The legal "ought," a system of given rules with a strong moral tone attached to them, was treated by the realists as a social construct, which did not express preexisting essences. True, distrust of pure legal logic left the field open to the recognition of the role of force in determining human affairs, as Holmes had realized forty years earlier.[61] Yet the distinction between the "is" and the "ought" could be sustained without having to resort to ethical relativism. The primary implication of this distinction—in the context of the realists' attack on the moral-reason justification of legal rules—was that judge-made law had been founded on will, not on reason. The purpose, as Arnold and Nelles declared, was to abandon the illusory idea of a depersonalized realm of judicial reason.[62] Judging law by its consequences did not *require* ethical relativism; it only called for removing ethical questions from the metaphysical to the social. Morality did not have to lose either its validity or its importance in checking human affairs; rather, it could be grounded in common sense or in a rational and open deliberation of the social "good" without having to resort to the metaphysical force of legal rules.[63] Edward S. Robinson, a psychologist at the Yale Law School, seems to have clarified this position. Roscoe Pound, he said, wrongly assumed that by emphasizing the "is" of law the realists neglected the "ought." Not so, argued Robinson: "There is a failure to see that moral judgments are themselves conclusions regarding the facts and that, wherever there are widely accepted facts, the moral values will be brought into line with them."[64] A beautiful passage by Felix Cohen—often a critic of realism for its neglect to consider the ethical dimensions of law—also captured this point: "The field of ideal law is not a checker-board. It is rather a sea, as vast, as turbulent, as impatient of restraint, as life itself. Rules and decisions and practical standards we set up in our attempt to draw peace and order out of this Heraclitean flux. Actually we can only chart its currents,—to shape them is past human power. By these charts, indeed, we sail, but not by these charts will this sea itself be bound. The success of our sailing will be measured not by conformity to our maps but by conformity to those powers of the deep that govern the realm we have tried to picture."[65]

The concrete consequence of the realists' position, in sum, was that judicial decisions lost their privileged status over other forms of social deliberation. This latter point tends to disappear from accounts that emphasize the realists' court-centered approach. From the perspective offered here, however, the realists' focus on judicial decisions, while stressing the lawmaking powers of judges, at the same time constantly challenged the grounding of this exclusive authority in the realm of reason and science.

This position had some immediate implications. Distrust of legal rules was a necessary condition for a successful attack on the method and content of legal education. The case method, with its adherence to the firm grip of the judicial text, restricted the intellectual horizons of law teachers and prevented them from pondering the larger context within which law was produced and re-produced. The time had come, they argued, for "a smashing of the mirrors" and for a move away from a spirit that had "choked" the learning and teaching of law.[66] Jerome Frank called for the study of law "in context"; Karl Llewellyn searched for "freak persons and freak policies" that would free the law from "outmoded traditions"; and persons like James McLaughlin, James Landis, Arnold Harno, and Edson Sunderland lamented the wastefulness and excesses of a system that overemphasized, if not canonized, appellate-court decisions.[67] Traditional jurisprudence, wrote Arnold, tried to construct a "logical heaven" behind the courts, whereas the faculty of reason should have taken "a less important place in the hierarchy of ideas."[68]

The attempt to escape the choking environment of deductive reasoning also involved the effort to stoke closer relationships with the social sciences and to incorporate new materials into the curriculum of law schools. "In 1932," notes Kalman, "the Columbia Law School faculty included a professor of finance, a professor of legal economics, and a political scientist. Additionally . . . the law school teaching staff expanded to include a professor of insurance, marketing, philosophy, accounting, and two professors of economics."[69] Here again, co-operation with social scientists who ever more boldly rejected deductive ra-tionalism could only be premised on an approach that considered law's cer-tainty as "transcendental nonsense." The realists' attack on the case method of legal education, in short, both presupposed and reinforced the indeterminacy of law and ultimately led to the questioning of the judicial text as an authorita-tive guide.

It is certainly true, however, that in their enthusiasm over "discovering" the possibility of applying the methods of the social sciences to the judicial process, some realists turned to behaviorism and rigid positivism. Focusing on works like Llewellyn and Hoebel's *The Cheyenne Way*, much scholarly attention has been given to the realists' obsession with the judicial process.[70] This in turn leads some to treat the realist method as a court-centered approach that "places the judge at the center of law."[71] Yet when we read legal realism from the standpoint of the professional field, this court-centered approach had been only part of a broader project whose primary result, certainly unintentional for some, was the ability to break free from the court-centered legal field.

"Every established order," writes Bourdieu, "tends to produce the naturalization of its own arbitrariness."[72] In the field of law, this typically meant the absence of the judge from the judicial text and the objectification of law in such a way that questions of judicial will became irrelevant for the scientific study of law. Both the focus on the judicial process with a social-scientific lens and the departure from the case-method, infused doubt and introduced noise into this presumptive order. Or, to put it in a more precise manner, casting doubt was a necessary condition for shifting one's gaze from the seemingly objective product (i.e., law) to its producers (i.e., judges); this shift, in turn, allowed for further questioning of the field's established hierarchies. The realists' agenda of distrust and its offshoots in legal education and social-scientific studies of judicial performance thus prepared the cognitive foundation for a comprehensive challenge of judicial supremacy on the one hand and the privileged position of the bar's elite on the other.

Courts were portrayed by some of the realists as slow, inefficient, and archaic institutions that could not provide the satisfactory solutions to modern society's problems. "The judicial process," argued Milton Handler, "cannot keep pace with the far-reaching and rapid changes occurring in the world today."[73] Judges, unlike the "competent legislature," argued Cohen, were caught in a discourse that prevented them from appreciating the social, economic, and ethical implications of the subjects upon which they passed judgment.[74] The idea of a "trial by combat," argued Arnold, was fragmentary, inconsistent, and socially irresponsible.[75] Changes were possible, he argued, only on the condition that courts, like the church in the past, lose their unfounded prestige.[76] Others were seeking ways to shift classes of controversy from courts to administrative tribunals and to emphasize the importance of statutory legislation at the expense of judge-made law; and people like Felix Frankfurter, Charles E. Clark, Lloyd Garrison, Thomas R. Powell, and Morris Cohen did not shudder at the thought that Congress would restrict or abolish the judicial review powers of the Supreme Court.[77]

As part of the general agenda of doubt and distrust, the leaders of the practicing bar were also exposed to biting criticism. Supreme Court Justice Harlan Stone, formerly the dean of Columbia Law School, set the tone:

The successful lawyer of our day more often than not is the proprietor or general manager of a new type of factory, whose legal product is increasingly the result of mass production methods. More and more the amount of his income is the measure of professional success. More and more he must look for his rewards to the material satisfactions derived from profits as from a successfully conducted business, rather than to the intangible and indubitably more durable satisfactions which are to be found in a professional service more consciously directed toward the advancement of the public interest. Steadily the best skill and capacity of the profession has been drawn into the exacting and highly specialized service of business and finance. At its best the changed system has brought to the command of the business world loyalty and a superb proficiency and technical skill. At its worst it has made the learned profession of an earlier day the obsequious servant of business, and tainted it with the morals and manners of the market place in its most anti-social manifestations.[78]

Karl Llewellyn, Fred Rodell, Calvert Magruder, Charles E. Clark, Thomas R. Powell, James Landis, Lloyd Garrison, and Abe Fortas, among others, joined in the attack.[79] Consequently, lawyers listened when Harold Laski of the London School of Economics announced the decline of Wall Street lawyers and when Edward S. Robinson predicted the "decay" of the legal profession.[80] The ABA's president, William Ransom, warned his listeners that "if the lawyers of the United States do not want government to organize and control the legal profession, the lawyers better organize, govern and discipline it themselves, in the public interest."[81] The project of the realists was, as far as the bar's leaders were concerned, a subversive one: it cast a shadow of uncertainty over the law in order to justify whole new practices, thus providing law teachers with the symbolic means of rejecting the definition of law and legal authority that had been imposed on them by past generations of legal thinkers, judges, and practitioners. It allowed them, to invoke Bourdieu's terms, to shake the "doxa" of legal discourse and to generate an openly formulated struggle between "orthodoxy" and "heresy."[82] The newly articulated terms of legal discourse that the realists invoked in turn equipped them with the means necessary for challenging the privileged bond between appellate courts and the bar's elite.

A Collective Mobility Project II: A New Legal Science

Casting doubt, however necessary, was insufficient for overturning established hierarchies in the legal field. Doubt without action could well have ended up marginalizing teachers-turned-critics as producers of irrelevant noise, pushing them outside the legitimate discourse in the field. It was only because the casting of doubt was coupled with a constructive agenda of action (at a time when the necessary political conditions for such a move were propitious) that the collective mobility project of academics could be realized. The realists not only discredited the old ideas about the nature of law but also outlined their own alternative vision. At least for some of the realists, theirs was a true science, whereas traditional conceptions of law were false. The old science promised to reduce social and economic uncertainty through the construction of a self-contained and universally applicable system of formal rules. Legal realists envisioned different strategies of uncertainty reduction.

Legal realism, writes Horwitz, assumed two faces, "one critical, another reformist and constructive"[83]—one that showed some realists as iconoclasts and heretics, another that portrayed them as composed experts.[84] In fact, the constructive face of realism was itself oriented in two not necessarily compatible directions. One leaned toward behaviorist and positivist studies of law that substituted scientific inquiries into the way judges made decisions for a focus on judicial opinions.[85] In contrast to Pound's "social engineering" theory, which sought only to bring the social sciences to the aid of law, some legal scholars now affirmed that law itself was part of the social sciences and had to be studied and applied according to their methods. Law professors like Herman Oliphant, Hessel Yntema, William O. Douglas, and Underhill Moore were involved with the Johns Hopkins Institute for the Study of Law, where scientific, "nonprofessional" (i.e., unrelated to the immediate needs of practice) studies of law along functional and behaviorist lines could be assumed in a purely academic environment. Others, however, stressed the importance of "lawyer schools" and legal clinics as a method of treating law from below—looking at the nuts and bolts of the legal process as a way of preparing students for the real necessities of practice. In both cases, the effort and emphasis turned inward, attempting a new way of explaining how law worked and establishing a social-scientific foundation for the study of judicial decisions.

Yet there was a second direction and phase in the constructive agenda of the realists, an outward-looking approach that aligned itself with progressive political forces. Not entirely unrelated to the efforts of the inward-looking strand, this approach treated law as "a science of the compelling power of government to intervene in the relations of human beings."[86] The link between the former and the latter directions of inquiry was articulated by Hessel Yntema. "The simplification of the legal system," he wrote, "requires more than the formal revision or restatement of rules derived from statutes and precedents. It is necessary to know within what limits legislation is practicable and by what means it is effectively administered. This is essentially a scientific problem, upon the solution of which depends not merely the proper restatement of the law but even a reasonable economy in both legislation and the administration of justice."[87] This strand of realism, in other words, focused on the importance of statutory legislation and administrative methods and emphasized the scientific skills needed in order to shape it in light of social ends. A new generation of law teachers thus countered the legal profession's project of reducing social uncertainty through "reasoned" law with a project of uncertainty reduction through "socially informed" law. In both cases, instrumental rationality was the means of asserting intellectual superiority in the field. Yet it was through the constructed relation of socially informed law to the interventionist functions of the state that law professors could spread havoc within the legal field. Moving from negation to action, the shift from judicial cases to a focus on social causes as the engine of legal change was a major, perhaps *the* major, message of the realists. It culminated in the inclusion of the administrative field within the space of law and triggered a vigorous counterattack by lawyers who tried to bring controversies back into the judicial system. Here, suffice it to say that the realists' combined agenda of doubt and action provided the theoretical foundation for these developments.

James Landis argued that "the legislative process, quite distinct from the judicial process, tries to reach a solution on the basis of political or social expediency. It reaches certain balances which the judicial process can't reach because of the limitations that are inherent in that process."[88] As early as 1930 Landis had suggested replacing the "desiderata" of the judge with a "science of statutory interpretation" that made use of "extrinsic aids" such as history and expediency.[89] Milton Handler provided a complementary rationale for the shift to administrative methods: "Obviously, the demand for administrative tribunals arises because of the breakdown of the legal system in particular fields. The demand for those administrative tribunals arises because the problems are too complex, too difficult to be handled by the average judge."[90] This "certitude in administrative efficacy" and a growing confidence in the merits of enlightened legislation was shared by a host of other law professors, from Felix Frankfurter at Harvard to Max Radin at Berkeley and Thurman Arnold at Yale.[91] In its most extreme form—and from today's perspective the most naively positivistic one—the emphasis on statutory legislation culminated in an effort to develop a "legislative science." "To overcome the defects in the form of our existing law and to make possible an enlightened legislative method for the future," wrote Albert Kocourek, a Northwestern University law professor, "there is need of an American Institute of Legislative Science"; a scientific approach to legislation, he assumed, could reduce ambiguity in the law "to an extent that will make litigation unnecessary in the great bulk of cases."[92]

It was here that the fundamental difference between legal realism and Pound's sociological jurisprudence collided. There is certainly more than a grain of truth in Hunt's sociological insight that "the realist movement only took form and character in the process of sharply distinguishing itself from sociological jurisprudence. It is a common feature of intellectual movements that they develop in conflict with those that retrospectively they may be seen to have most in common with."[93] Yet Pound never intended to challenge judicial supremacy. His vision was closer to what Hart called "the noble dream": a holistic system from which a socially sensitive judge would creatively extract law. Pound moved from formal rules to principles, values, ideals and interests without ever departing from the field's established hierarchy. Pound's vision, in short, was that of the judge as a master of balance, a fountain of social wisdom, aided by social scientists but never threatened by them. The professorial-realist "revolution," in contrast, moved toward a socially informed law that was to be produced by Congress and the government's administrative machinery under the guidance of trained experts in the art of statutory legislation and administrative methods. Further, Pound never regarded his own social engineering program as a route for political change. He conceived jurisprudence as an "intellectual matter" unrelated to political struggles, whereas the realists' project had challenged this alleged autonomy of law's universe. What is sometimes presented as the difference between the moralist (i.e., Pound) and the behaviorist and instrumentalist (e.g., Llewellyn) may be thus reformulated as a difference between two different spatial organizations of the legal field: social planning through judicial expertise versus social planning through academic expertise.

The relationship between law professors and the New Deal administration was thus premised on a particular notion of law as a form of socially informed expertise. The concept of experiment, a key political slogan of New Dealers and a "scientific principle" of academics, served aspiring law professors as a bridge between doubt and action and coupled the assertions of law's indeterminacy and uncertainty with a promise of order. Experiments, in short, created a link between skepticism and scientific social planning. Jerome Frank, for example, suggested that "realistic jurisprudence be re-named 'experimental jurisprudence' and that those who lean in that direction be called experimentalists." While he described the experimentalists as those whose ideas were based on constant skepticism and partial ignorance, he also argued that they were "devoted to action." There was little ground to cover from this position to the ideas that the New Deal had to be treated as "an elaborate series of experiments" and that the experimentalists would "help to contrive new governmental agencies to be used experimentally as means for achieving better results in agriculture, industry, labor conditions, taxation, corporate reorganization, municipal finance, unemployment relief, and a multitude of other subjects."[94] Indeed, as Glennon notes, Frank considered writing a new preface to *Law and the Modern Mind* showing the relationship of his ideas to the New Deal.[95]

Legal academics offered a scientific rationale for the administration's policies, countered the bar's and the judiciary's resistance, and contributed their concrete services to the governmental state apparatus. In return, law professors reached positions of influence and prestige they had never enjoyed before.[96] The realist-professorial project benefited from the crisis of 1929 not only because this crisis "unsettled the certainties of their allied enemies" but also because the New Deal "opened an entirely new market of legal services, that of the legal expert in the new governmental agencies, and, in the same act, opened the door of the law school to the social sciences."[97] In other words, conditions external to the legal field facilitated the ability of law teachers to escape their dual marginality in the legal field and in the institutions of higher learning. Yet theoretical caution is called for. I do not mean to suggest that the negotiated meaning of law and authority within the legal field may thus be reduced to events external to it. Rather, the external crisis allowed a ferment that had grown within the legal field since the turn of the century to materialize in the form of concrete practices.

Legal academics provided public defense and justification for many of the administration's key laws, helped in drafting laws and suggesting new forms and types of legislation, wrote briefs, and helped to defend the administration in court. In all this, law professors and many of their fresh graduates acted as policy makers who articulated the general blueprint for the New Deal's experiments.[98] Others took leave of their academic posts and assumed key governmental positions.[99] And Harvard's Felix Frankfurter, who was described at the time as "the most influential single individual in the United States," orchestrated an avalanche of young graduates, specialists in drafting legislation and trained in both commercial and administrative law, who entered government service.[100]

These newly formed "contributory relations" with the state were accompanied by bold assertions of academic leadership and the new role of professors as the "final arbiters of 'the law.' "[101] Lawyers had to become "architects of social institutions" and masters of an "applied science" that determined "whether and how social ideals may be attained by official action, [and] what measures will cost least waste effort and sacrifice of human integrity."[102] Law professors, in turn, considered themselves as best fit for the task. John Dickinson, for example, spoke of the guiding authority of professors of law in constitutional matters: "The constitutional law of many practitioners today, and especially of those who are most vocal, is not the constitutional law of the law professors and not the constitutional law of the law schools . . . I suggest that the practitioner has in comparison decidedly less to contribute, and that the importance of the professor's contribution is relatively far greater, than in almost any other field of law or economics. The professor has, or should have, the better of it in constitutional law."[103] Professors of law, said Charles Clark, were situated in a strategic position that required them to fill a leading role in legal reform. He proudly reviewed the "crowning achievements" of law professors and placed special emphasis on their "spectacular activities" at the service of the New Deal administration. The "activities of our colleagues in the far-flung experiments in governmental control," he declared, were "becoming history at Washington, both in the original conception and organization of the plans and later in the slower moving but possibly more important activities of bringing order out of the chaos of their own or their colleagues earlier efforts."[104] And Leon Green, of Northwestern University, described the professors who worked for the New Deal administration as the legal profession's "Brain-Trust."[105] Legal realists, in short, assertively argued that they were the ones best equipped to coordinate the multiple sources of law and to scientifically "manage" the legal system. The image of the professors as an intellectual vanguard and the assignment of lawyers who were molded in their image as the architects of a new social order thus put a heavy premium on lawyering at the service of the state. Felix Frankfurter, who harbored the idea of law as a public calling, outlined a vision of a new breed of lawyers who could "compare favorably with the representatives of finance and industry" and vigorously acted accordingly.[106] The open invitation to take part in the New Deal, in sum, allowed law teachers to truly become a generation in a sociological sense: a group that was able to generate its own distinct identity through negation, novelty, a sense of exclusivity, and ultimately, a joint agenda of action. Far from being a "jurisprudence of despair," the realist project involved bold affirmative assertions of intellectual leadership largely based on their alliance with the governmental apparatuses of the state.

The professorial-realist revolution was the sum total and accumulation of various loosely coordinated programs: criticizing the bar for lacking in social responsibility, challenging courts for lacking in efficiency and expertise, treating traditional legal education as an intellectual straitjacket, cultivating statutory

legislation and administrative practices as alternative sources of law, and asserting the professors' own constructive role as scientific social-legal planners and
managers. It may be immediately seen that this project, judged from the inclu-
sive perspective of the legal field, was a blend of symmetrical propositions
(diagrammed in the table).

NEGATION	AFFIRMATION
Legal education—case method (law in book)	Legal education—context (law in action)
The bar's corporate elite (private interest)	Lawyers as social planners (public interest)
Judicial process (case)	Legislative & administrative process (cause)

These symmetrical practices amounted to a collective mobility project because,
taken as a whole, they represented the negation of one given hierarchical order
and the affirmation of an alternative one. I do not mean to suggest, of course,
that each of the participants shared in the project as a whole. On the contrary,
while some were dedicating efforts to, say, a critique of legal education, others
promoted statutory legislation. Those who joined forces in criticizing, say,
judicial methods and rulings did not necessarily share a similar vision of an
alternative scientific inquiry of law. Further, those who in retrospect are seen as
separately promoting single aspects of a quite comprehensive whole were pas-
sionately criticizing and distancing themselves from each other. In short, only
by looking at various practices and not falling prey to the participants' own
internal ideational distinctions, may one hope to make sense of the case under
discussion in terms of a collective mobility project that advanced at the expense
of the profession's traditional elites.

The advantage in treating realism from the perspective of the legal field is that
it sets us free from forms of analysis that treat legal theory as if it originated and
developed in separation from concrete practices. Legal actors are not equipped
with a theory of law that they cast over the legal field; rather, they articulate
theories and attempt to define the nature and meaning of law in the course of
their professional lives within the field and in response to various structural and
institutional pressures both internal and external to it. From a doctrinal point of
view, legal realism expressed an instrumental approach to law and a challenge to
legal formalism; from a practical point of view, the principles this challenge
embodied should be analyzed as verbal artillery specifically designed to gore
particular groups within the legal field.

In fact, as Dworkin observes, serious doubts exist as to whether there ever were legal formalists of the sort portrayed by the realists. The realists, no doubt, made every effort to portray a Bealist monster: a formalist legal thinker blind to the social consequences of his logic, a naive believer in the force of objective reason, and a relentless advocate of legal absolutism.[107] Perhaps Dworkin exaggerates when he argues that the battle against formalism was "a famous victory over straw persons."[108] Yet as far as the bar's leaders were concerned, we have every reason to believe that even before the realists formally announced the death of pure reason, their daily professional practices had been based on down-to-earth assessments of the judicial process as a contingent, arbitrary, and haphazard game in which the key to success often resided in the ability to please or impress the right judge at the right place and time. How could they think otherwise after going through a legal training that taught them that the law provided reasonable means to defend and condemn every conceivable dispute with equal force and vigor? The bar did not need the realists in order to understand the nature of the judicial process. Realism, as Grey aptly puts it, is the "implicit working theory of most good lawyers."[109] The announcements of the realists, therefore, scandalized the legal field not because they discovered the indeterminacy of law but because they discussed the profession's inner secrets in public and, worst still, did so in order to advance an unabashed agenda of change. The realists spoiled the show by refusing to stay behind the scenes. Negation was their way of scandalizing the calm waters of the legal field, affirmation their way of asserting their leading position within it.

Yet while in negation lay the realists' strength, affirmation had been their weakness. Stanley Fish has captured this point from a theoretical point of view: "The basic realist gesture is a double, perhaps contradictory one: first dismiss the myth of objectivity as it is embodied in high sounding but empty legal concepts . . . and then replace it with the myth of the 'actual facts' or 'exact discourse' or 'actual experience' or 'rational scientific account,' that is, go from one essentialism, identified with natural law or conceptual logic, to another, identified with the strong empiricism of the social sciences."[110] Thus, from a sociological point of view,[111] the ability to develop a critical discourse is the privilege (some would say the irresponsibility) of those who are not bound to serve and represent interests external to the field. The realists emerged as a loosely coordinated group of academic scholars whose detachment from practice allowed them to assume the posture of the disinterested critic and to develop precisely such a critical discourse. Yet as we have seen, while legal realism had been an affair whose direction and various tones were largely determined by the internal structure and dynamic of the legal field, it truly materialized into concrete forms of praxis owing to external political conditions. The realist program was strongly tied to the agenda of the interventionist state and to the legislative plans of a reform-oriented administration; it legitimated the administration's experiments and in the process allowed the realists to assume positions of power and influence.

Yet the conditions of representation that allowed the realists to transform themselves into a professional vanguard also led them to gradually cast aside the critical posture and to assume the role of the responsible social-legal planner. The realists, in other words, created their own dialectic of representation. The alliance with Roosevelt's administration led the realists away from a critical discourse toward an operational one, from a discourse whose effects undermined the authority of courts to one premised on the realists' own alternative legal-scientific expertise. The movement away from the position of the disinterested critic toward the position of the responsible social-legal planner, in other words, created a gravitational pull leading to the typical subservient politics of the professional in the service of a client, be it a corporation or a governmental agency.[112] The theoretical double gesture of dismissing the myth of objectivity and simultaneously asserting the merits of positive legislation thus reflected the tension between the position of the disinterested critic and the position of the jurist in the service of the state. Having the state as their sponsor, the realists gained entry to the halls of power and influence but may also have planted the seeds of the deradicalization of their program.

Although realism had an irreversible impact on jurisprudential and practical legal thought in America (Hunt writes, "We are all realists now"), it all but vanished as a policy-oriented agenda of action.[113] The realist retreat from the halls of political power, the "reemergence of proceduralism" in law, the surfacing of a "process-oriented" method in constitutional law, the "deradicalization" of New Deal laws, and the intellectual decline of "pragmatic instrumentalism" are often attributed to the realists' own inability to develop a comprehensive legal-scientific agenda for the interventionist state and to their naive belief in government and legislation.[114] It is interesting to note that the failures of realism are thus attributed precisely to that part of their program which concerned their constructive-scientific posture. This point is important if we are to grasp the trajectory of legal realism and, in particular, what had come to be seen as its "failure." As much as the realist ability to produce a crisis within the legal field had to do with the general conditions of crisis in the economic and political spheres at large, so did the realists' failure have to do with changing political conditions on the one hand and their new position of power within the legal field on the other hand. The realists' version of law best served the interests and needs of New Deal politics during the transitional period in which new methods of administration and new forms of legitimation for these new methods were called for. Toward the end of the 1930s the New Deal began to lose its rather aggressive reformist zeal, and the drive for change was gradually replaced with a desire to stabilize (i.e., formalize) its achievements. The political interest in using law as an open-ended experimental instrument, in other words, was gradually replaced with a renewed interest in law's objectifying force. It was the coupling of these changing political conditions with the representation functions many of the realists assumed that ultimately dulled their critical edge.

If we accept this basic proposition, then the "failure" of realism cannot be attributed simply to a successful counterattack by legal formalists and to realism's ideational weakness. This proposition opens up questions concerning the relationship between the internal dynamic of the legal field and the political conditions external to it and concerning the force of realism as a critical posture and its weakness as a professional assertion of expertise. In the final chapter of this book I provide some conceptual keys to answering these questions.

7 Lawyers as Servants of Power

It is quite appealing to cast the role of lawyers in the New Deal in terms of what is generically known as a class-centered approach. This approach may be invoked from the perspective of both the sociological literature on professionalism and political sociology. In the professionalism literature, a class-centered approach has played an important role in refuting the optimism of earlier generations of scholars who hoped that the professions would serve as a mediating haven between the state and the individual in an anonymous and anomic mass society and as social clusters that could "salve the wounds of the modern capitalist order."[1] Beginning with the work of Johnson and reaching a certain climax in the work of Larson, the literature on professionalism in America partially joined forces with the general neo-Marxist position that refused to treat professionals as if they stood outside the class structure of society, as if they were neutral in class conflicts, and as if they somehow transcended the conflicts and self-serving interests that accompanied the social-action orientation of other social groupings.[2]

Larson, who provides one of the most sophisticated and penetrating accounts of the rise of professionalism in America, essentially treats experts and professionals as a service class that lacks a unifying class consciousness. One of her principal arguments is that the professions infuse the logic of science into the logic of capitalism and in the process accomplish a collective conquest of social status and market control. Yet, Larson argues, professionals as a whole function by and large as mere agents of power: they accept a subdominant role under the aegis of corporate capitalism because it is consistent with their ideal and material interests and because it allows them to enjoy a privileged lifestyle as merit and certified knowledge become legitimating and rationalizing principles in the ideology of late capitalism. Professions are thus driven by an expectation for a career, and this in turn is a "powerful factor of conformity with the existing social order and a source of basic conservatism."[3]

The legal profession, in particular, receives unambiguous treatment at Larson's hands. Elite lawyers reach positions of influence along with the growing political and economic power of their corporate clients, and it is "the organic connection of the legal profession with the propertied class" that has to be taken into account in analyzing the profession's historical development in the American scene.[4] It is interesting to note, however, that Larson does attribute somewhat different characteristics to academic lawyers and lawyers in the service of the state. Largely relying on Auerbach's thesis that the marginality of academics within the legal field drove them to embrace the political ideals of the Progressive Era, Larson mentions in passing that in their public duties these lawyers were not exposed to "the compromising connections of the legal marketplace."[5] Nonetheless, the general conceptual scheme leads to the conclusion that lawyers in general, even those in the service of the state, are no more than servants of power. Given that the state itself is considered essentially capitalist, the general treatment of professionals as a service class of the bourgeoisie remains intact throughout Larson's analysis.

To treat lawyers as servants of power implies that power does lie somewhere, in the hands of a class or social stratum of one kind or another. Yet can we really reduce the force and logic of capitalism to any given site or to any identifiable, coherent class that sustains and promotes it in an organized and collective manner? Can we really speak of capitalist power as if it is concentrated somewhere, at the level of the state or at the hands of corporate executive boards? Larson's answer seems to be that lawyers, like members of other professions, constitute a "heterogeneous category of the occupational structure"; they lack the capacity to transcend their service functions and serve powerful clients whose own class power may indeed be disorganized and fragmented. Yet if we submit to the view that the force of capitalism lies precisely in the facts that it cannot be captured in a unified discourse, that it operates simultaneously on various levels and in various settings, and that it is sustained through its irreducibility, it remains to be seen whether the treatment of lawyers as servants of power (i.e., the propertied class) fully captures the role of the legal profession in the New Deal.

As mentioned above, a class-centered approach is also a high road of inquiry in political sociology. Of particular interest are the attempts of the neo-Marxist class-centered approach to "explain" the New Deal. In its most straightforward version, this approach posits that the New Deal was a capitalist plan that had been carved out by farsighted business leaders who had direct access to the state machinery and cleverly used it to shape state policies to their own advantage—to rationalize capitalism, dismantle working class discontent, and defend the privileges of the propertied classes.[6] This approach, generally referred to as a "corporate liberal" approach, was effectively criticized in Skocpol's seminal 1980 essay about the politics of the New Deal.[7] In contrast to the class-centered argument that the more enlightened and more powerful segments of the capitalist class had a considerable impact on the federal administration's policies, Skocpol argued that "[m]ajor New Deal measures were passed and implemented over the opposition of capitalists. Not only did capitalists fail to control the political process during the mid-1930s, they even lost their ability to veto major legislative enactments that touched directly upon their accustomed prerogatives. Corporate-liberal theory cannot explain why or how this could happen."[8]

This conclusion is affirmed in the present study as well. In fact, in contrast to the often vague discussion about a capitalist class "out there," the focus on corporate lawyers allows us to speak—from a corporate-liberal point of view—about a relatively coherent group of professionals whose activities, at least to the degree that they were coordinated, reflected the interests of their capitalist clients. Indeed, the New Deal highlighted the "organic connection" between corporate lawyers and their clients. In opposing laws such as the National Labor Relations Act, the Public Utility Holding Company Act, and the securities laws, corporate lawyers clearly acted as a capitalist vanguard: they displayed a remarkable degree of cooperation, effectively mobilized bar committees to provide professional support for their actions, participated in the activities of the American Liberty League, and invoked a combination of professional rhetoric, populist zeal, and utilitarian arguments in trying to represent the interests of their corporate clients. Treating corporate lawyers and their activities as a barometer of capitalist cooperation with or resistance to various New Deal measures, however, also exposes the shortcomings of the corporate-liberal approach. First, we have seen that influential segments of the business community benefited from the National Industrial Recovery Act, and that, accordingly, corporate lawyers tended to suppress their own misgivings about the law. Ironically, it was precisely this law, which fits the general theoretical assumptions of the corporate-liberal approach about the ability of capitalists to shape public policy, that failed to pass the constitutional test of the Supreme Court, an institution that at the time symbolized the alliance between conservative forces and the legal system. Second, in their opposition to numerous other New Deal laws in the failure of which the propertied class had a stake, the opposition of lawyers was largely ineffective. The failed attempts of corporate lawyers to block, subvert, or dismantle the New Deal's legislative agenda serves as testimony to the inability of capitalist interests to directly shape the course and content of New Deal politics.

A possible way out of this theoretical impasse is to argue that New Deal reformers and their own army of professional experts were also operating in the service of capitalism—that one should not look at the direct actions of the capitalist class but indirectly, at the actions of supposedly neutral and class-free agents. Applied to the case of legal realists, one may well argue that they never intended a departure from the basic principles of free-market competitiveness and private property sacredness, and that their reform agenda represented a conscious attept to rationalize capitalism rather than subvert it—that legal realists, in other words, were the truly enlightened representatives of capitalists. This is not a far-fetched argument. The realists were far from being the wild-eyed radicals that their adversaries depicted. To the contrary, in their research activities, their teaching agendas, and their role as administrators, many realists displayed the opposite tendencies. Jerome Frank, the uncompromising skeptic, was also "a confirmed capitalist of the liberal persuasion"; Thurman Arnold, the relentless critic, was an ardent supporter of a truly free market economy; and Felix Frankfurter reminded critics that even in the heyday of the New Deal he still placed more of his students in Wall Street than in government.[9] The "organic" connection of the legal realists with the propertied class had been nowhere more evident than in their teaching functions. Judging by their actions as educators, the legal realists were not only ideologues of a new legal order but also active reproducers of corporate lawyers and "capitalist" law. Laura Kalman argues that "regardless of what he said, the overriding concern of the average realist was to make the study of law more 'realistic' by making it more closely approximate practice." This meant that the realist teacher tried to portray a "more accurate picture of the business world" rather than shift attention away from it. Any radical departure from established methods of teaching law and established fields of study threatened to undermine their promise to produce a "better training of attorneys in the fields of business and property."[10] The realists, in other words, were captives of their own legal training and their own institutional position and ended up reproducing future generations of corporate lawyers and a highly developed system of business-oriented law.

In sum, the underlying assumptions in this particular version of political sociology are similar to those of the concurrent variant in the sociology of professions. Lawyers, like other experts and professionals, are treated as no more than agents of power. The roles of lawyers may vary, yet this variation simply reflects the interests of those whom they happen to represent: the propertied class or, alternatively, state managers who are themselves not much more than capitalists in disguise.[11] This approach, as Manza recently observed, "leads to the rather strange result" that state managers and politicians who promoted legislation against the perceived interests of the capitalist class "are somehow still representing a fraction of that class."[12]

Curiously enough, the implicit treatment of professionals as mere servants is also retained in class-centered analyses that move away from assuming the presence of an organized capitalist class (or fractions thereof) that is able to shape state policies, as well as in the analytic perspective commonly referred to as a state-centered approach. The first to develop an approach of the former type was Nicos Poulantzas, and it was Fred Block who applied it, with some notable modifications, to the New Deal.[13] The central figure responsible for the advance of the latter approach is Theda Skocpol, who developed her state-centered analysis in direct reference to Block's way of explaining the New Deal.[14] Block's basic thesis is that the two forces that lead reformers to initiate policies that run contrary to the immediate concerns of capitalists are working-class pressure from below and the "will to power" of state managers from above. The model posits that extensions of the state's role in the economy take place at times of crisis when "state managers can pay less attention to business opinion and can concentrate on responding to popular pressure, while acting to expand their own power."[15] The Poulantzian idea of objective and functional capitalist reproduction by relatively autonomous state managers is concretized by Block: politicians in liberal democracies seek reelection, and their ability to retain their positions of power depends "on the maintenance of some reasonable level of economic activity."[16] To the extent that the level of economic activity is determined by private investment decisions, state managers are routinely discouraged from taking actions that might seriously deter investors. State managers, in short, operate under a systemic pressure to "aid the investment accumulation process." While this systemic pressure loses some of its vitality during times of crisis, it reappears with the restabilization of a given social and economic order. The popular reforms of state managers thus gravitate toward protecting capitalism's vested interests and pacifying and neutralizing working-class pressure.

The important point here is that in referring to state managers Block seems to be talking about *politicians*, not about the scientific experts that state managers typically recruit to carry out and legitimize their preferred policies. It is the interest of politicians in reelection, according to Block, that creates the structural constraints that work to "increase the likelihood" that effective measures will be taken by politicians to facilitate investment and business confidence.[17] Yet what about state experts who do not share the politicians' reelection anxieties? How can we account for their role in reestablishing an order that "increases the likelihood" that effective measures will be taken to facilitate business confidence? To what types of systemic pressures, if any, do scientists, policy experts, intellectuals, and technocrats have to respond? What were the external pressures, to put it more concretely, that led the legal realists away from a more radical agenda, and the external forces, if any, that ultimately brought about the gradual decline of legal realism? Block's model does not provide answers to these questions but rather employs the silent assumption that state experts are servants of state managers in the same way that the corporate-liberal approach treats them as servants of the propertied classes.

Block's approach, at any rate, has been both criticized and perfected by Skocpol, who, unsurprisingly given her theoretical focus, tried to refute the class-centered element in Block's model.[18] Skocpol agrees with Block that state managers develop their own distinct agendas and interests, but she insists that "independent initiatives by liberal politicians" and a particular set of political conditions account for the passage of Wagner's act as much as working-class pressure from below. Skocpol's essential argument with Block, in other words, is that class-centered theories do not go far enough in analyzing the state as an independent constellation of forces with its own history and institutional structures.

But Skocpol's approach fares no better when it comes to the role of experts in the service of the state. In fact, Skocpol explicitly denies the relevance of the Poulantzian assumption—that the ability of the state to contribute to the repro- duction of capitalism derives precisely from the real separation between capi- talists on the one hand and a host of experts and civil servants who have their own working procedures on the other—to the analysis of the New Deal. The U.S. federal government in the early 1930s, writes Skocpol, lacked the admin- istrative capacity that Poulantzas outlined as a necessary condition for the realization of an autonomous state.[19] Autonomy in Skocpol's theory as well refers mainly to the independent capacities of politicians and to the indepen- dence of the political apparatuses of the state. Skocpol's arguments concerning the lack of administrative autonomy in the New Deal, however, may be ques- tioned. Skocpol is right that the administrative capacity of the American federal government in the New Deal was still very far from that of European nations. Yet she understates the degree to which the New Deal was a concentrated effort to create a federal administrative apparatus in which experts could make and implement policy on the basis of their scientific expertise. At least as far as legal expertise was concerned, we have seen that the New Deal did create favorable conditions for the emergence of a group of legal experts who assumed key roles within the administration, had their own professional stake in the expansion of state power, and were dedicated to the idea of civil service. Throughout this study we saw how the academics both provided the legitimacy for the expansion of the administrative process and actively assumed operational roles in managing the new administrative agencies. The legal realists, in short, fit well into the Poulantzian model of a "relatively autonomous" administrative apparatus.

Concretely, the question of law's autonomy and the role of its carriers thereof has been conceptualized away in Skocpol's analysis. Law is considered the language of the state and a mediating embodiment of either class interests or presumably autonomous political interests (e.g., reflecting popular demands or management tactics of the state's experts and technocrats). In this analysis, the law is simply a medium for transforming objectives and intents into a set of operational rules. Thus, in asserting the autonomy of the state, in both the class- and state-centered approaches, law and its carriers had been reduced to a mere instrumentality. In fact, curious isomorphic tendenices have occurred over the last several years. The corporate-liberal approach, recovering from a long period of neglect, comes to acknowledge some of Block's formulations, while Skocpol's own model is now treated as pratically the same as that of Block.[20] To put it somewhat simply, where Block sees opportunistic political elites who seek to expand their power when they can and respond to systemic pressures when they must, Skocpol sees political elites who go through a rational process of political learning, in the course of which they come to recognize their institutional responsibilities and capacities.

Yet to talk about political learning only begs the question. How do politicians learn? Who are their educators? Where do new ideas originate, and how do they come to shape the consciousness of politicians? What is important here is that the relative autonomy of ideas is not related in any coherent way to the role and position of their carriers. The statist approach, like the class-centered approach, treats the knowledge and expertise on which policy decisions are based as mere tools. If corporate lawyers may thus be seen as the hired guns of the bourgeoisie, legal realists may similarly be seen as the hired guns of state managers. Both have no will of their own and no interests to protect or advance, only masters to serve. In contrast, I submit that once the autonomy of the state and its "managers" is acknowledged, as seems to be the case in both contemporary class-centered and state-centered approaches, the asserted autonomy of law's carriers should also be analyzed as having a history of its own.

The concept of autonomy refers to an area of social practice that is immune to external intervention. The definition of external intervention is less clear and often obscures the analytic value of the concept. While a state-centered approach emphasizes law's autonomy or lack thereof vis-à-vis the state, a class-centered approach insists on talking of it vis-à-vis capitalist interests. Yet to think of autonomy in such terms misses the point, because neither approach fully captures the notion of law's autonomy as an *idea* and as a *claim* rather than as an empirical reality.[21] Thus, the Supreme Court's defiant decisions early in the New Deal did not prove law's autonomy from the state any more than its later affirmation of New Deal legislation testified to its autonomy from capitalist control. To some extent, law's autonomy is always imagined. Even its most diehard defender would concede that law is sensitive to society, at least to the degree that law affirms and reflects foundational social norms and values. Insisting on law's autonomy, therefore, is typically tied to assertions of independence once such values and norms have been infused into the system. More precisely, assertions of autonomy have to do with the claim that it is not total immunity to a surrounding environment that constitutes autonomy but rather a specific type of closure. Luhmann's distinction between normative closure and cognitive openness is useful here.[22] It is not that law denies the relevance of external pressures, interests, and expectations; this would render the law entirely redundant for deciding disputes and shaping public policy issues. It is the way the law absorbs, dissects, and responds to such externalities that makes it an autonomous system; it is law's distinct ways of producing the output, and not law's input, that determines and guarantees its autonomy. Stanley Fish articulated this point with typical clarity: "Legal autonomy should not be understood as a state of impossibly hermetic self-sufficiency, but as a state continually achieved and re-achieved as the law takes unto itself and makes its own (and in so doing alters the 'own' it is making) the materials that history and chance put in its way. Disciplinary identity is asserted and maintained not in an absolute opposition to difference but in a perpetual recognition and overcoming of it by various acts of assimilation and incorporation."[23]

Law's autonomy, then, is a distinctive social construction of imagined boundaries that separate law from other discursive formations and allow law's carriers to establish a *jurisdiction*. The assertion of law's autonomy provides the ideological energy that fuels the project of law's carriers; it is, to put it more crudely, the marketing and public-relations strategy of law's carriers. Autonomy, conceived as part of a process of distinct boundaries formation, is not simply a matter of control over the *conditions* of legal work but also a way of asserting decisionmaking authority over issues that have far-reaching social, economic, political, and cultural implications.

Crucial observations follow once we begin to think of autonomy in terms of jurisdictions. This means that autonomy is an unstable area of designated competence that is forever open to negotiation and conflict. It follows that autonomy is established in the course of a contest over the formal power to make decisions on the basis of distinct types of knowledge. The constitution of a jurisdiction, writes Stinchcombe, determines where judgments should be located—the creation of boundaries within which the power to determine substance is protected.[24] By talking about law's autonomy, therefore, I do not mean to imply that there is some universal essential arrangement in the absence of which law cannot be autonomous. This, to some extent, is the confusing result of Reuschemeyer's otherwise illuminating analysis of the relationship between states and legal professions.[25]

Invoking a state-centered approach, Reuschemeyer argues that the historic relative "statelessness" of the United States (at the federal level) meant that modernizing transformations came from "capitalist entrepreneurial activities," whereas in France and Prussia-Germany the state played a greater role in the process. Accordingly, the American legal profession matured and developed through alliances with powerful industrial and commercial groups and retained a high degree of institutional autonomy from state apparatuses. On the Continent, by contrast, the development of the legal profession came about through strong alliances with various state apparatuses, to an extent that actually turned lawyering into a "profession of the state." Reuschemeyer therefore concluded that conditions in the United States created "the most favorable conditions in the modern world for the autonomy of law," while in Germany law had little autonomy.[26]

Reuschemeyer's logical leap from discussing the institutional and organizational autonomy of law's carriers to a general discussion of law's autonomy goes too far. After all, it was in highly centralized and bureaucratic Germany that the idea of law as a science made its most ambitious appearance, and it was the organization of the German legal system that inspired Weber to formulate the ideal-typical concept of formally rational law, a gapless system of rules that enjoyed a high degree of institutional and cognitive autonomy due to its distinct working procedures. While in Germany the assertion of law's autonomy was regarded as an established fact precisely because of the role played by legal scientists in the service of the "neutral" state in its formation, it was only through a long process of adaptation to market demands that American jurists were eventually able to assert law's autonomy.[27]

Indeed, the New Deal administration reshuffled established jurisdictions by departing from the historical course that allowed law to develop independently of the legislative and administrative apparatuses of the state. The New Deal, from this particular perspective, was an assertion of the state's autonomy that found its expression not only in the ability to intervene in the market despite the resistance of leading capitalists but also in the readiness to invade law's autonomy despite vocal opposition from the corporate bar and significant parts of the judiciary. Economic regulation through administrative methods, as we have seen, came about through an expansion of the legal field to an extent undesired and uncontrolled by law's guardians. In the New Deal, in short, law's autonomy was progressively invaded by a state that wished to establish its own power to make substantive decisions in social and economic policy issues. The carriers of this process, legal realists and lawyers under their influence, in a sense pushed the American legal system in the direction of the continental model, both in their emphasis on the merits of state legislation and in their advocacy of legal work as a public calling. But this should not lead to the conclusion that the realists wished to give up on the idea of law's autonomy— only that they wished to constitute it on the basis of new discursive principles, thereby opening a struggle over the boundaries and nature of the legal field. In other words, the New Deal administration invaded a *particular* arrangement under which the autonomy of law had been asserted. Law's autonomy, as it had come to be conceived of in America, assigned the practicing bar and the courts primary responsibility for producing and developing law. In its New Deal phase, law's autonomy assigned legislators, legal planners, and administrative commissions growing responsibilities for developing and shaping the law.

It is only by thinking of autonomy as a discursive practice on the one hand and as a professional project on the other that we can make sense of the muddled uses and abuses of the notion of law's autonomy. The symbolic construction of distinct boundaries is particularly necessary for the organization of law because its proximity to "politics" forever threatens to expose its extremely unstable cognitive basis.[28] Thus, what is at stake here is not whether law is autonomous or not but rather under what conditions and by which strata of jurists the general movement toward greater legal rationalization and formalization—under whose banner the autonomy of law is asserted—is carried out. Law's autonomy, in short, may assume different institutional configurations. As an *idea*, however, it typically represents the core of the legal profession's project of the formation of distinct boundaries. The possibly shifting arrangements for the organization of law's autonomy *in themselves* tell us little about the actual substance of the judgments and dispositions of law's carriers. Similarly, the inability of interested parties in the market and the state to directly control the outcome of legal decisions and the direction of legal developments says little about the role of law in the reproduction or protection of a given order. But once we place at the center of attention the stake lawyers have in defending their jurisdiction, the great pressure that perceived threats to a given configuration of law's autonomy may exert have to be taken into account when the role of law's carriers in reproducing, changing, or sustaining a given order is assessed. It is essential, in short, to go beyond approaches that treat lawyers as mere servants of power.

There can be no doubt that the representation functions of corporate lawyers were a decisive element in shaping their response to various New Deal measures. Yet it also seems reasonable to argue that no one would have blamed corporate lawyers for being fundamentally hostile to the New Deal had they restricted themselves to common hired-guns practices: faithfully representing corporate clients in judicial and legislative arenas, guiding them through the legal web, and privately advising them on various legal means of adaptation, avoidance, or resistance to the newly created laws and regulations. The point is, however, that corporate lawyers far transcended these routine functions in their response to the New Deal. Corporate lawyers, as we have seen throughout this work, carried their own crusade against the New Deal. They publicly condemned many measures, actively engaged in the activities of the American Liberty League, and mobilized the formal organs of the bar to resist some major New Deal initiatives.

To interpret these activities as a mere response to the direct demands of powerful clients, or, alternatively, as a manifestation of economic laissez-faire impulses which corporate lawyers indiscriminately internalized, is to simplify a more complex reality. Coming to terms with the readiness of corporate lawyers to publicly situate themselves as an oppositional vanguard requires a more thorough understanding of the historical process in the course of which lawyers organized their body of knowledge as a particular type of a scientific discourse. During the second part of the nineteenth century the instrumental nature of American law had been replaced by a discourse that emphasized the scientific, objective, and autonomous properties of law, and this had happened in tandem with the changing nature of American capitalism. Horwitz writes: "If a flexible, instrumental conception of law was necessary to promote the transformation of the post-revolutionary American legal system, it was no longer needed once the major beneficiaries of that transformation had obtained the bulk of their objectives. Indeed, once successful, those groups could only benefit if both the recent origins and the foundations in policy and group self-interest of all newly established legal doctrines could be disguised."[29]

It was the ability to rationalize the legal system and render it more scientific that allowed lawyers to become a profession capable of demonstrating its cognitive coherence by pointing to a unified paradigm under which legal activities were undertaken. The underlying power of this professional paradigm, as Mensch observes, must not be trivialized, as if it were only a thin disguise for the protection of capitalist interests.[30] As the ability to pursue the collective interests of lawyers became more and more dependent on the ability to persuade various audiences of the strictly scientific-professional nature of law work, the paradigm acquired a life of its own. Professionalization meant that in order to serve clients in the best possible way, lawyers had to create mechanisms designed to symbolically distance them from the very interests they represented. In other words, direct representation functions were both a source of power and a source of liability. The livelihood of lawyers, of course, depended on their ongoing ability to be retained by interested parties in the market. Their ability to extract the material and symbolic benefits that came with professionalization, on the other hand, depended on their ability not to appear as mere hired guns. The institutionalization of particular forms of organization, the exclusive links of lawyers to the apparatuses of justice, and the assertions of law's autonomy on the basis of distinct modes of legal thinking contributed to the ability of lawyers to distance themselves from particular interests while at the same time increasing the efficacy of the services they were able to perform on behalf of clients. It was therefore not coincidental, as Larson observes, that "the American legal profession should have decisively moved toward professionalization in the Progressive Era. The bureaucratization of the state apparatus, the movements for civil service reform, and the articulation of legitimacy principles which emphasized the role of expertise all contributed to establish the state's 'neutrality.' This, in turn, created a favorable ideological climate for the legal profession's assertion of neutrality and independence."[31]

At this particular historical juncture, in other words, the reliance of the state on scientific and legal expertise operated as a distancing mechanism for the legal profession as a whole. Various recipients of legal services benefited from the scientific aura of legal work, a particular type of logic and practice was infused into corporate capitalism and the state, and lawyers, in turn, secured a position of authority based on their ownership of a distinct type of symbolic capital: learned expertise in the domain of the law.

The politics of corporate lawyers in the New Deal should be analyzed not only in terms of servants performing for masters but also in terms of conscious experts in defense of their symbolic capital. The New Deal sharpened the tension between the idea of law as a positive science and the legal elite's representation functions. The vehement defense of the coherent unifying paradigm in law, the insistence that uncertainty could be reduced only through adherence to conventional forms of legal reasoning, and the efforts to preserve the strict separation between law and politics should all be read as the concentrated yet unsuccessful struggle of the bar's leaders to block a movement and a process in the course of which the power of law as objective knowledge and their own power as its sole carriers were systematically undermined. The dejudicialization of the legal system in the New Deal also created the effect of deprofessionalization. In the particular formation of law's autonomy that existed at least until the New Deal, there was a structural homology between laissez-faire capitalism and what we may term juridical laissez-faire. Laissez-faire capitalism amounted to capitalism's having a stake in minimizing state intervention while retaining the freedom to make substantive judgments concerning economic relations, transactions, policies, and methods. Juridical laissez-faire amounted to the legal system's having a stake in minimizing political (e.g., legislative and administrative) intervention in the production of law and in legal decisionmaking routines.[32] The dejudicialization of the legal system brought about through the intensive reliance on administrative measures shook the unifying paradigm, disturbed the fragile lines that separated law and politics, redirected attention to the instrumental nature of law, and consequently undermined the professional claim of objective and neutral expertise. Hence my suggestion—in fact, one of this book's central theses—that the strong incentive corporate lawyers had in resisting New Deal measures was fueled not only by their individual obligations to corporate clients but also by their collective interest in arresting the tendency of the state's legislative and administrative apparatuses to usurp law-producing and law-controlling functions.

To the extent that corporate lawyers acted as a capitalist vanguard, in other words, they did so through their defense of their own perceived autonomous domain and not because they necessarily embraced the particular values of their clients. It was the structural bias of this autonomous system, not substantive ideological inclinations, that created the bond between the court-centered legal system and laissez-faire capitalism. The assertion of law's autonomy—with its ever-present tendency to depoliticize social relations—systematically denied law's sociohistorical roots, the unequal social accessibility to legal remedies, the prominence of corporate and business law in legal education, and the structural advantages of corporate lawyers in developing areas of the law in ways that reflected the demands and interests of their corporate clients. In time, it would be the professional disposition to innovate in ways that protected their market monopoly and ensured the ongoing dependence of clients on their services that allowed lawyers to adjust themselves to the new conditions in the legal field.

This ability to adjust and innovate was well understood by some farsighted jurists. Carl McFarland, for example, argued that "[t]he public as well as the legal profession may profitably remind themselves that the common law . . . in the course of time has taken over whole fields of administrative or executive justice. Administrative justice has been the trying ground . . . whereby the courts have avoided some of the embarrassments of experimentation in new fields of government."[33]

This observation reflects a deep sociological insight concerning the fate of law. It is through formalization that jurisdictions are created and protected. It is through formalization that the consistency needed for the institutionalization and objectification of a given order are established. It is through their efforts to create, defend, and, when necessary, re-create the formal boundaries of law that lawyers constitute themselves as an influential professional group. It is precisely in their efforts to control their own privileged domain—one based on the idea of law's autonomy—that corporate lawyers serve the propertied class.

The discussion so far seems to imply that the principal carriers of the attack on law's autonomy, namely the legal realists, somehow escaped their own profession's unifying paradigm and developed their own concepts of law independently of their position within the legal field. Following Bourdieu, I believe that an analysis of the legal field should free itself from the constraining terms of debate imposed by jurisprudence: those terms that describe a debate between legal formalism and legal instrumentalism and present the former as a position that preserves the idea of law's autonomy and the latter as one that subverts it. I submit that this ideal division fails to appreciate *both* positions as strategic orientations of players within the legal field; that is, as strategic choices of carriers whose agenda is fundamentally tied to particular conditions of representation, institutional roles, blocked or potential possibilities, and so forth. Law as a social instrument, in short, may also be contained in the idea of law's autonomy, although it then articulates a different way of justifying the efficacy of law and its epistemological status as a rational discourse of uncertainty reduction.

Regardless of what they said and did, lawyers in private practice, lawyers in the service of the state, and academic law teachers were first and foremost players in a legal field within which they were disposed to share some core orientations, despite all the evident differences in opinions and practices among them. The destiny of all these separate segments of the profession depended on the preservation of the legal field as an autonomous space and on the protection of legal knowledge as a distinct resource. They were all positioned, in other words, in interlocking networks of mutual recognition and tacit cooperation.

I partially embrace and partially dispute therefore Brigham and Harrington's assertion that the realists challenged the autonomy of law but not the authority and prestige of the legal profession.[34] I embrace it insofar as it suggests that the realists never intended to give up the distinct privileges that came with the position of the expert. I dispute it insofar as it suggests that the realists did not challenge the privileged position of Wall Street lawyers and, moreover, insofar as it suggests that the realists somehow transcended the idea of law's autonomy. Rather, the realists challenged a particular construction of law's autonomy and sought to replace it with their own vision. While representation functions have been decisive in shaping the practicing bar's vision of scientific and autonomous law, the absence of such functions in the case of legal academics enabled them, in fact encouraged them, to develop an alternative vision of law.

The transgression of the practicing bar's unifying paradigm was not necessarily a result of a principled dissatisfaction with the social order in general but was first and foremost an expression of a certain sense of blocked opportunities that legal academics experienced under a legal regime that marginalized the role of the academic expert. True, the realists displayed a quite explicit antagonism toward the values and ideologies that were voiced by their corporate counterparts. Yet the realists were not anti-capitalists who fought for the socialist cause, nor was there any indication that they saw themselves as the intellectual vanguard of the working class. Rather, their orientation expressed their alienation within the legal field. Having no clients to represent in a system that was organized around the centrality of courts in resolving concrete disputes, a broad vision of law as a social vehicle and academics as legal planners offered an escape route from a position that assigned them responsibility for training future corporate practitioners.

Finally, the principle of representation or lack thereof is key to understanding both the emergence of the realists' critical discourse and the reasons that their revolt was only partial. The growing intervention of the state in the market created a new planning apparatus and offered new opportunities for legal academics and for a host of young lawyers who were educated in the realist spirit. It was through the door that the state opened in the New Deal that the realists were able to escape their alienation, to transgress the boundaries of the unifying paradigm in law, and to dictate an alternative agenda. Their critical discourse, as we have seen, served the realists well. It allowed them to offer an alternative that suited the state's interest in moving from cases to causes, to legitimize the new experiments as a kind of reasoned reflexivity, and, most importantly, to reshuffle the legal field's hierarchy in a way that assigned them a greater voice in shaping the direction of legal development.[35]

Yet the alliance with the state also placed the heretofore representation-free realists in a new position. With the growing reliance of the state on their services, and their own growing involvement with the ongoing affairs of the administration, the realists became trapped in a representation position. In this new capacity, the radical elements of their critical discourse were cast aside by a rational discourse that legitimized their new role as state experts. To be sure, their version of law was not the same as the old. The realists' version represented a kind of social positivism, a promise to solve the problems of society through carefully articulated statutes, administrative methods, and socially informed judicial reasoning. Nonetheless, as a problem-solving and planning orientation the realists' discourse began to resemble the dispositions of their corporate counterparts. With the move from the position of the disinterested intellectual to that of the state expert, the realists came to share with practitioners the metalanguage of the new class, which struggled to convey the impression that experts could solve "the fundamental requisites of the universal grammar of social rationality: to reunite both power and goodness."[36]

The realists, like the practicing elite, were indeed owners of a currency, a form of capital. They were owners of symbolic capital and masters of exclusive knowledge that was not available to lay persons. But the representation functions underlying the privileges of this mastery created, in both cases, a gravitational movement toward assertions of exclusive mastery over an autonomous domain. Representation functions, in other words, pull experts—whether intellectuals or technocrats—away from the emancipatory and hermeneutic potential of a critical agenda and push it toward using knowledge as an instrumental currency. In an age of instrumental reason, the constant pressure is to link ideas to concrete programs and to transform observations into realizable solutions. Under such cultural and economic conditions, lawyers of whatever brand have a great stake in asserting the autonomy of their currency of expertise. The owners of knowledge-turned-into-private-property strive to clearly draw the boundaries of their expertise, to distinguish their body of knowledge from other discursive bodies, and in particular to distinguish it from society's open-ended and unprofessional ideological debates. It is in this sense, therefore, that the realists' counterproject did not dissolve law's autonomy but rather sought to constitute it on the basis of new terms and new institutional arrangements. In the final analysis, the realists came to share with their corporate counterparts the disposition to trade the problem-solving capacities of the expert in return for a comfortable position within the existing order.[37]

Notes

1   Introduction

1   Urofsky and Levy 1991, 521.
2   Hawley 1966, viii.
3   Gramsci [1929–1935] 1971, 276.
4   Calabresi 1982, 5.
5   See, in general, Galanter 1974. On the role of lawyers as innovators in corporate lawmaking, see Powell 1993.
6   Weber 1978, 775.
7   For more on this theme, see Shamir 1993. On Weber's sociology of law in general see Rheinstein 1966; Trubek 1972; Hunt 1978; Feldman 1991.
8   Jackson 1941; Schlesinger 1959; Hawley 1966; Auerbach 1976; Irons 1982; Lash 1988.
9   Notable studies on the rise and current role of large law firms are Smigel 1969; Nelson 1988; Galanter 1983.
10 For a critique of Auerbach's work see Halliday 1983.
11 Cain 1979; Heinz 1983; Nelson 1985. On lawyers in politics see Eulau and Sprague 1964; Nelson, Heinz, Laumann, and Salisbury 1988. On various approaches to the question of the policy influence of experts in general see Brint 1990.
12 Parkin 1979, 44.
13 Abel 1981; 1989.
14 Bourdieu 1987.
15 Terdiman 1987, 806.
16 Bourdieu 1987, 817.
17 Terdiman 1987, 808.
18 White 1949; Glennon 1985, 41; Mensch 1990, 21; Horwitz 1992, 188.
19 Breslau 1990, 421.
20 Isaacs 1933, 226.
21 Foucault 1972, 223.
22 Ibid., 221.
23 Carr-Saunders and Wilson 1933; Goode 1957; Barber 1963; Wilensky 1964; Milerson 1964; Parsons 1968 (on lawyers see Parsons 1964).
24 Johnson 1972, 37, 42. Also see Reuschemeyer 1964; Parkin 1979; Freidson 1983; 1986; Friedman 1989.

25   Larson 1977.
26   See, for example, the brilliant study of Heinz and Laumann 1982.
27   Abel 1981; 1989a; 1989b.
28   Abel 1989a.
29   Nelson 1988.
30   Following Weber, Larson argues that the rationalization of law is crucial for the
     ability of lawyers to construct the image of impartial experts. Yet Larson also notes
     that the cognitive foundation of the legal profession "cannot appear to be as
     immune to class interests" as that of other professions (1977, 168–69). See chap. 7 of
     this book. Elsewhere, Larson invokes the Foucauldian notion of "power-as-law" to
     argue for the connection between the training and practices of lawyers and their
     "state constitutive" functions in cloaking the law with an "aura of legal transcen-
     dence" (1989, 444–45).
31   Lewis 1989, 29.

2   *Subservience to $18,000 Functionaries*

 1   Section 7(a) of the NIRA provided that "employees shall have the right to organize
     and bargain collectively through representatives of their own choosing, and shall be
     free from the interference, restraint or coercion of employers of labor, or their
     agents, in the designation of such representatives or in self-organization or in other
     concerted activities for the purpose of collective bargaining or other mutual aid or
     protection." The provision also stipulated that "no employees and no one seeking
     employment shall be required as a condition of employment to join any company
     union or to refrain from joining, organizing, or assisting a labor organization of his
     own choosing." The main problem of Section 7(a) was that it contained extremely
     vague language. Employers insisted that while the act recognized the right of em-
     ployees to bargain collectively, it did not outlaw individual bargaining, could not be
     construed to forbid merit-based hiring practices, and did not require employers to
     bargain collectively. Most of all, employer groups feared that Section 7(a) would be
     construed to require them to negotiate with outside unions and with individuals
     who were not their own employees. As the NIRA required that the major labor provi-
     sions of Section 7(a) would be included in the industrial codes that were then being
     negotiated, many companies rushed to establish their own company-dominated
     unions with which they would bargain. Another problem concerned the choice of
     employee representatives with whom employers were to negotiate. The statute did
     not provide any explicit mechanism for choosing representatives. In labor disputes
     that followed, the National Labor Board (NLB) adopted the secret ballot as an ad-
     ministrative device for the selection of representatives, ruled that employees could
     vote for outside unions, and adopted the majority principle of representation. Em-
     ployers resisted these rulings. Leading the opposition to the board's powers and rul-
     ings were the National Association of Manufacturers and the steel industry. Em-

ployers scored success in lower courts in at least two cases: *United States v. Weirton Steel* and *United States v. Houde Engineering Co.* A further blow to the authority of the NLB came when President Roosevelt abandoned the majority principle and allowed proportional representation in the automobile industry. Thus, by the beginning of 1934 it became clear to labor supporters that Section 7(a) and the NLB could not guarantee the rights of labor. In February 1934, Wagner introduced his labor disputes bill, whose purpose was to correct the deficiencies of Section 7(a) and to put teeth in the National Labor Board. When this bill failed to pass Congress, Wagner introduced a new version in the National Labor Relations Act of 1935 (see chap. 3). For a detailed review of the Wagner Act legislative history, see Irons 1982; Cortner 1964.

2 For an elaborate discussion of the NIRA's corporatist tendencies see Hawley 1966; also see Irons 1982.

3 Vadney 1970. Reviewing the events that lead to the Schechter case, in which the NIRA was invalidated by the Supreme Court, Richberg later wrote: "I had expressed my grave doubts of our success to everyone with whom the case had been privately discussed" (Richberg 1954, 190–91).

4 Lash 1988, 122.

5 Ibid., 123.

6 Ibid., 116. Jerome Frank, a corporate lawyer turned New Dealer and a leading advocate of the legal-realist approach in jurisprudence, later recalled that Felix Frankfurter urged New Deal lawyers to be "slow" in testing the law. When Frank asked him how to handle the daily situations where the act had in fact been challenged, "he was kind of nettled and had no answer" (cited in Lash, 1988, 128; also see Irons 1982, 81).

7 The NIRA raised issues related to the Constitution's commerce clause because it opened up questions regarding the administration's powers to regulate manufacturing conditions under its constitutional powers to regulate interstate commerce. These questions involved a debate concerning the type of businesses that could be regulated under the commerce clause and, moreover, whether businesses whose activities were purely or mostly intrastate could be regulated under the theory that their trade affected interstate commerce. Questions concerning the Constitution's due process clause were relevant in order to determine whether the NIRA provisions amounted to being an "undue deprivation of liberty" because of their interference with the freedom of contract and the sanctity of private property. In this regard, the licensing provisions of the act, under which the president could forbid the operation of businesses that did not obtain a license, created the major problem. The delegation doctrine was relevant for determining whether the act was too vague and general and thereby allowed for an illegitimate delegation of lawmaking powers to private groups or to the executive in breach of the separation of powers principle.

8 Arnold 1933, 989. Thurman Arnold was another law professor turned New Dealer and another leading advocate of the legal-realist cause. For an elaborate discussion on the relationship between legal realism and the New Deal see chap. 6.

9   Handler 1933, 482. Milton Handler taught at Columbia University Law School and
     later became the general counsel of the National Labor Board.
10   Ibid., 444. The *Harvard Law Review* (Nov. 1933) noted the doubtful constitu-
     tionality of the NIRA and also defended it in terms of an emergency doctrine.
     Dealing with the commerce clause, it suggested that "it may cogently be argued that
     while, in normal times, the causal connection between interstate shipment and
     manufacturing conditions is not sufficiently close to permit congressional regula-
     tion, in a depression, industry in one area is far more sensitive to standards else-
     where, so that interstate competition will more directly affect local conditions"
     (85). Similarly, the commentary suggested that "due process is admittedly a crea-
     ture of time and circumstance; interference with private rights in the public interest
     to a degree which would be invalid under normal conditions may be justified dur-
     ing an emergency period" (91). It also noted that the only possible way to uphold
     the sweeping "grant of power with so indefinite a guide given to a congressional
     enforcement agency" would be on emergency grounds. However, particular atten-
     tion was given to the fact that if this delegation "should be held constitutional, the
     Court would, in effect, be nullifying the maxim altogether, since *it is difficult to
     conceive of greater powers being given to an administrative agency* during the active
     operation of a congressional form of government than have been conferred upon
     the President under the Recovery Act" (95; italics mine). It is interesting to compare
     this statement with the view expressed in the Nov. 1934 issue of *Yale Law Journal*.
     That article maintained that the NIRA could be constitutionally sustained "without
     much difficulty" and dismissed the delegation issue altogether. "The problem of
     delegation of legislative powers to the President, though concededly serious, seems
     to be *the least important of the constitutional considerations* . . . the Supreme Court
     has never held an act of Congress unconstitutional on this ground, and the lower
     courts have been reluctant to say that there is an unwarranted delegation of power
     by the Act" (*Yale Law Journal* 1934a, 97; italics mine). Five months later, the Su-
     preme Court unanimously struck down the NIRA, establishing the unconstitu-
     tionality of the delegation of legislative powers under the law.
11   Clark 1934c, 269. Charles Clark, the dean of Yale University School of Law, was
     another legal realist turned New Dealer; see chap. 6.
12   Ibid., 272. Also see Clark 1934a, 1934b. The fact that Clark tried to define the court's
     substantive jurisdiction is highly important for the argument I develop in chap. 6.
     Briefly, while attention has been given to the realists' court-centered approach,
     their efforts to restrain judicial powers have been somewhat overlooked. But see
     discussion in chap. 6 and Urofsky 1991 for a discussion on Frankfurter's advocacy of
     judicial restraint.
13   Podell 1934, 281–82.
14   Richberg 1934, 292.
15   But see, e.g., Dickinson 1933, 1095. Dickinson asserted that "to sustain the constitu-
     tionality of the Recovery Act requires no change in or departure from the principles

of our constitutional law" and dismissed the part the emergency doctrine played in justifying the act.

16   Arnold 1933, 990.

17   The most systematic study of the NRA machinery was conducted by the Brookings Institution (1934). Also see Himmelberg 1976.

18   National Recovery Administration release 1933.

19   Ibid. Not many lawyers stayed "at home." A partial list of lawyers who represented interested parties in their respective codes may give some sense of the range of issues that the codes involved and the degree to which they created professional opportunities for lawyers. The list is compiled from occasional reports in the *New York Times* and mainly refers to code-drafting negotiations in the New York area: A. Kheel, Diamond Setters Association; N. D. Baker, Pennsylvania Grade Crude Oil Association; A. Ballantine, National Association of Wool Manufacturers; M. F. Carlee, Independent Association of Clothing Manufacturers; T. E. Corcoran, counsel for six retail associations; E. H. Davies, National Association of Wholesale Clothing; D. Drechsler, Clothing Manufacturers Association; W. Flugelman, National Restaurant Managers Association; J. Gould, Greater New York Sawdust Dealers Association; E. Hanson, American Newspaper Printers Association; M. Hillquist, International Ladies Garment Workers Union; W. Klein, Cloak, Suit & Skirt Manufacturers (Industrial Council); M. D. Kopple, Kalamein Industry; C. R. Latham, Star Peerless, Century & Continental Wall Paper Mills; E. B. Edward, for 200 jewelry manufacturers; H. R. Lhowe, National Knitted Outerwear Association; A. Lindey, for several newspaper guilds; C. E. Charles, Metropolitan Garage Board of Trade; J. Panken, New York Local 505 Independent Bakers Industry; J. H. Reiman, National Association of Retail Tailors, Cleaners & Dyers; Roseman, Weil, Gotshal & Magnes, for Eastern Millinery Association, Ribbon, Silk & Velvet Association, National Association of Lady Hatters & Women's Group; S. Rosenman, for fourteen department stores and New York City Retail Dry Goods Association; L. Shapiro, Association of Delicatessen Stores; Tachna & Pinkussohn, National Association of Slipper Manufacturers; D. A. Teichman, Association of Dancing Teachers.

20   McCarran 1933, 587; Rowell 1933, 65; Benton 1934, 213.

21   Beck 1933b, 498. For some biographical background on Beck see chap. 4, n. 52.

22   Beck 1933c, 48; 1933b, 496; Also see Beck 1934; Thatcher 1934.

23   The terms of the debate were clearly demarcated in an April 1934 meeting of the ABA's Commerce Committee in New York City. This meeting was dedicated to considering the legal aspects of the NIRA, and various prominent lawyers were invited to voice their opinion. New Dealers like David Podell and Charles Clark defended the NIRA, while prominent corporate lawyers bitterly attacked it as a complete change of constitutional doctrines and an unwarranted expansion of state powers. See Wood 1934; Smith 1934.

24   The most striking example concerned the avoidance of constitutional issues by a

committee that the ABA established with the specific mandate to pass on the constitutionality of various New Deal laws; see chap. 3.

25 Association of the Bar of the City of New York 1934, 231.

26 Miller 1934, 351.

27 Philips 1934, 96. For similar ambivalent comments see Fletcher 1934; Vaught 1935.

28 Benton 1934, 214. Also see Davis 1934, 3; McCarran 1933; Robinson 1935.

29 New York State Bar Association 1935b, 174. The committee was chaired by Gilbert H. Montague, a New York lawyer who was an authority on the Recovery Administration. He advised the Recovery Administration to promulgate the National Recovery Blanket Code and appeared on behalf of many clients before the NRA.

30 Justice Louis Brandeis, for example, "always opposed to bigness, was unrelenting in his criticism of the NIRA" (Urofsky and Levy 1992, 522, n. 9). For an elaborate discussion of the NIRA's corporatist tendencies see Hawley (1966). But see Himmelberg (1976), who disputes the notion that the NIRA favored big over small businesses.

31 Irons 1982, 18–19.

32 *New York Times*, May 4, 1933, 1, 3.

33 *New York Times*, May 23, 1933, 16.

34 *New York Times*, May 19, 1933, 4.

35 *New York Times*, May 16, 1933, 23; and June 23, 1933, 7.

36 *New York Times*, May 14, 1933, 1, 5.

37 U.S. Congress, Senate 1933, 277.

38 It is certainly true that as businesses regained their confidence support for the NIRA diminished. Two major legal battles of the time involved a challenge to Section 7(a) of the NIRA, which concerned the right of employees to organize: *United States v. Weirton Steel Co.*, 7 F. Supp. 255 (D. Del. 1934) and *United States v. Houde Engineering Co.*, 9 F. Supp. 833 (W.D.N.Y. 1935). It is also noteworthy that some big industries secured a favorable interpretation of the NIRA's labor provisions. A particularly telling story was the ability of the auto industry to secure an interpretation that allowed them to retain proportional-representation plans in company-sponsored unions. Moreover, the general talk about diminished support sometimes fails to mention that some of the most disillusioned critiques of the NIRA came from liberals and friends of labor who worried about the ability of business to shape the NIRA in ways that served their own needs at the expense of labor. On this growing sense of resentment, see Urofsky and Levy 1992, 533, 540–44 (in some of the letters of Justice L. Brandeis to F. Frankfurter).

39 *Fortune Magazine*, 1934, 91.

40 Shouse 1934a, 8.

41 For a detailed analysis of NIRA-related litigation, see Excursus I. The underrepresentation of big business and major law firms in NIRA-related litigation also resulted from the fact that the NRA consciously sought to avoid open confrontation with big business. In its enforcement efforts, the NRA mainly targeted small busi-

nesses that declined to comply with the codes' provisions. For a thorough discussion of this issue see Irons 1982.

42 *New York Times*, June 4, 1933, 14 N. The Trade and Commerce Bar Association proposed to substitute the term "unfair competition" with the term "harmful competition," thus expanding the scope of situations under which groups could devise business agreements. The group included Richard E. Dwight, Walker D. Hines, Charles H. Tuttle, William J. Donovan, Kenneth Dayton, William M. Chadbourne, Benjamin Javits, Allen Wardwell, and Rush C. Butler. Dwight was a partner in Hughes, Schurman & Dwight, of New York City. Hines was the vice president of the Association of the Bar of the City of New York (ABCNY), with connections to Roosevelt. Tuttle, an active member of the ABCNY, was a senior partner in Breed, Abbott & Morgan, of New York City. Donovan, a member of the executive committee of the ABCNY, was the senior partner in Donovan, Leisure, Newton & Lumbard, of New York City. Dayton was a member of Cohen, Gutman & Richter of New York City, whose senior partner was Julius H. Cohen. Chadbourne headed Chadbourne, Hunt, Jackel & Brown, of New York City. Wardwell was a partner in Davis, Polk, Wardwell, Gardiner & Reed, of New York City. Butler was the chairman of the ABA's Committee on Commerce and a senior partner in Butler, Pope, & Ballard, of Chicago. Notably, the group also included Milton Handler, an active New Dealer, and David Podell, who coauthored the NIRA.

43 *American Bar Association Journal* 1933a, 314.

44 American Bar Association 1933b, Exhibit F.

45 Report of the Standing Committee on Commerce 1933, 344.

46 Ibid., 339–45. Also see Butler 1933, 128.

47 *New York Times*, May 24, 1933, 1, 13.

48 On the problem of administrative law as a major concern for lawyers in the New Deal, see chap. 5.

49 The American Liberty League was created in 1934 by a group of disenchanted Republicans, Democrats, financiers, industrialists, and lawyers. The league received financial and moral support from the Du Pont Corporation and from John Raskob and Alfred P. Sloan of General Motors. The group included an impressive number of prominent lawyers who established their own National Lawyers Committee within the League (see Excursus I). The activities of these lawyers in the league contributed to the fact that the American legal profession as a whole was labeled not only an enemy of the New Deal, but also one that surrendered its autonomy to powerful financial clients. On the American Liberty League see Wolfskill 1962.

50 Shouse 1934a, 8.

51 Colby 1933, 417.

52 See Roosevelt's inaugural speech, *New York Times*, Mar. 5, 1933, 1.

53 Parker 1933, 570.

54 Mississippi State Bar Association 1933, 77.

55 Cross 1933, 219; *American Bar Association Journal* 1933c, 741; Oklahoma State Bar Association 1933, 1; Nyce 1933, 633.

56 Rush 1933, 312.

57 Q. O'Brien 1933, 69.

58 Martin 1933b, 547.

59 *American Bar Association Journal,* 1933c, 737.

60 Sturges 1933, 51.

61 P. O'Brien 1933, 11. O'Brien made these remarks in an address before the National Conference of Attorneys-General. His remarks drew some bitter criticism; see Diggs 1933, 128.

62 Clark 1934a. Donald Richberg, the general counsel of the NRA, argued that judging by the opinions of many federal judges across the nation, the constitutionality of the NIRA had already been decided in favor of the government. Citing Richberg's arguments, *United States Law Week* responded by saying that this contention "may well be received by many members of the legal profession with some surprise and considerable dissent." The editorial reminded the readers that the Supreme Court had yet to decide upon the issue and that the reason it had not yet spoken was that "the bar generally was not disposed during at least the first 6 months of the NIRA to interfere with or retard in any way the recovery program by the initiation of litigation. During the like period the recovery administration appeared disposed to avoid any challenge of the constitutionality of the statute and any judicial review of its administrative acts" (*United States Law Week,* July 3, 1934, 1). Also see Benton 1934.

63 *Appalachian Coal Inc. v. United States,* 288 U.S. 344 (1933). The Court upheld the right of coal operators to create a collective marketing agency and refused to treat it as a violation of the antitrust laws. To many observers, this decision signaled the readiness of the Court to adapt its doctrines to the necessities of emergency (Ledwith 1934, 76; Jackson 1941, 158). *Nebbia v. New York,* 291 U.S. 502 (134). The Court rejected the due-process challenge of the milk price-fixing law. The decision was interpreted as particularly important in light of the 1932 Oklahoma Ice case (*New York Ice v. Liebman,* 285 U.S. 262 [1932]), in which the Court refused to consider an ice-producing business "affected with public interest" to a degree justifying its subjection to state regulation. The Nebbia case, however, was seen as one that reopened the type of businesses that could be legitimately regulated. In fact, even the Oklahoma Ice case was perceived by some to open the way to the future regulation of businesses in cases of "paramount public importance." Thus, Orville Rush argued that "it appears that the case is the beginning of a series of decisions that will cause serious inroads to be made in our past conceptions of the constitution" (Rush 1933, 292). With the Nebbia case having thus decided, this expectation was further augmented. The *ABA Journal* expressed a widely held view when it commented that "the significance of the decision with respect to various provisions of the National Recovery Program will hardly be overlooked" (*American Bar Asso-*

ciation Journal 1934, 225). The Minnesota Moratorium case (*Home Building and Loan Association v. Blaisdell,* 290 U.S. 398 [1934]) was interpreted as another sign that the court would uphold the NIRA. On the response of NRA lawyers to the *Minnesota* and *Nebbia* decisions see Irons 1982, 38. It is noteworthy that the *United States Law Review* carefully distinguished the facts of the case from those surrounding the NIRA and warned against the tendency to view it as a significant precedent. See *United States Law Review* 1934b, 1–4.

64 Report of the Standing Committee on Noteworthy Changes in Statute Law 1933, 387.
65 Finkelstein 1933, 428.
66 Rush 1933, 292.
67 Rowell 1933, 62. It is interesting to note that the notion that a recalcitrant Court might face the threat of packing was expressed as early as 1933, four years before President Roosevelt actually moved in this direction; see chap. 4.
68 Ibid., 68.
69 Caulfield 1933, 154.
70 Beck 1933c, 48.
71 See Stevens 1935.
72 Richberg 1954, 190–91.
73 Raoul Desvernine was a partner in Hornblower, Miller, Miller & Boston, a New York firm with strong connections to the American Liberty League. Desvernine himself was a leading member of the league's Lawyers Committee (see chap. 5 and Excursus I).
74 The notion that big business turned against the NIRA from mid-1934 on is the principal argument that Skocpol (1980) invokes in refuting the corporate-liberal's way of explaining the New Deal (e.g., Domhoff 1970). The basic terms of the debate center on whether a class-centered approach or a state-centered approach better explains the reforms of the New Deal. Skocpol argues that the fact that major business leaders turned against the NIRA shows the "strong and misdirected political influence of . . . insufficiently class conscious capitalists" (Skocpol 1980, 164) on the New Deal, thus refuting the idea that well-organized, farsighted capitalists were responsible for many of the New Deal's reforms. My purpose here, however, is not to engage in this debate but simply to point out that the particular critique that rests on the presumed capitalist opposition to the NIRA is not well founded.
75 American Bar Association, Report of the Committee on Commerce 1935, 1–4. It is interesting to note that the Executive Committee instructed the Commerce Committee not to appear before committees of Congress with respect to the extension of the NIRA (ibid., 16). This, to my mind, is another indication that the bar's leaders were reluctant to engage themselves on issues that had a political character. A similar report was submitted to the New York County Lawyers Association. This report abstained from elaborating on the legal aspects of the NIRA and strongly implied that it shared the views of the ABA's Commerce Committee (New York County Lawyers Association, Report of the Commerce Committee 1935, 350).

76   American Liberty League 1935g, 4.

77   American Bar Association, Report of the Committee on Commerce 1935, 4.

78   American Liberty League 1935a, 2.

79   The NIRA was struck down in May 1935 in *Schechter Poultry Corp. v. United States*, 89 U.S. 495 (1935). On the response to the decision see chap. 4.

80   Brigham and Harrington 1989.

81   Ibid., 43.

82   Grey 1990, 1590; cited in Rorty 1991, 89.

83   Posner 1991, 41.

84   On this distinction see Bourdieu 1987, 814.

3   The Dilemma of Representation

1   The reaction to the National Labor Relations Act and the Public Utility Holding Company Act is discussed in the next chapter.

2   Larson 1989, 428 (following Pitkin 1967). On the idea of lawyers' citizen-constitutive functions and the political function of representation in general, see ibid., 441–42.

3   For example, I do not distinguish here between an "early" and a "late" New Deal. It is common to distinguish between the first two years of the New Deal—in which the administration sought the active cooperation and consent of business leaders to its agenda—and the period from 1935 onwards, when some measures, most notably Wagner's Labor Act and the Public Utility Holding Companies Act, were passed over the active and vocal resistance of employers. A more detailed discussion on the response of lawyers to these last two measures is offered in the next chapter.

4   I use the term "legal field" to describe a more or less stable set of institutional arrangements, routine procedures, relational hierarchies, and dominant ideas around which the autonomy of law in general and the autonomy of the legal profession in particular are constructed, asserted, and sustained. See chap. 1.

5   See chap. 2, n. 1.

6   See in particular the testimony of Henry Harriman, of the United States Chamber of Commerce, who asked for greater discretion in the administration of the act (U.S. Congress, House 1934, 440).

7   Cited in Lash 1988, 168.

8   Report of the Standing Committee on Commerce 1934, 442.

9   For more details on the litigation campaign that followed the enactment of Wagner's Labor Act and the Public Utility Act see chap. 4. For more details on the litigation campaign that followed the enactment of the securities laws, see Excursus I.

10   Gay 1971, 363. Thomas Gay was a partner in Hunton, Williams, Anderson, Gay & Moore.

11   Ibid., 363.

12   298 U.S. 1 (1936). The Jones case involved the constitutionality of the Securities Act of 1933 and was argued by James Beck and the firm of Saye, Smead & Saye. See Excursus I.

13   But see the minority opinion of Justice Stone, who was joined by Brandeis and Cardozo in condemning this harsh language.

14   Report of the Special Committee on Amendments to the Federal Securities Act 1936, 796.

15   See the complaint of Hal Smith, a partner in Beaumont, Smith & Harris, in U.S. Congress, Senate 1934, 715.

16   Justin Moore also warned that the power industry would carry its struggle against the proposed law to the courts (U.S. Congress, Senate 1935, 402). Moore was a partner in Hunton, Williams, Anderson, Gay & Moore. He was personally committed to the cause, being the vice president and general counsel of the Virginia Electric & Power Company. John MacLane was a partner in Simpson, Thatcher and Bartlett, a firm that served as general counsel for the Electric Bond and Share Company, the company that was to lead the legal challenge to the Public Utility Act.

17   U.S. Congress, Senate 1935, 1100. William White was a senior partner in the Birmingham, Alabama, firm of Bradley, Baldwin, All and White, one of the biggest firms in Alabama and general counsel for the Alabama Electric Company. Charles Rosen was the senior partner in the New Orleans firm of Rosen, Kammer, Wolff and Farrar, who counseled many important industrial and financial institutions in Louisiana. Henry McCune was the senior partner of the Kansas City, Missouri, firm of McCune, Caldwell and Downing, who were legal counsel for the Electric Bond and Share Company, the Kansas Gas and Electric Company, and the American Power and Light Company.

18   U.S. Congress, Senate 1935, 249.

19   U.S. Congress, House 1934, 1–941; U.S. Congress, Senate 1934, 6594. On Gay's later position see n. 9 above.

20   Report of the Special Committee on Amendments to the Federal Securities Act of 1933, 1934; Report of the Standing Committee on Commerce 1934.

21   It is also in light of this reluctance that we should interpret the uproar that followed the public report in which fifty-eight prominent lawyers "ruled" against the constitutionality of the National Labor Relations Act shortly after the Supreme Court invalidated the National Industrial Recovery Act. See chap. 4.

22   U.S. Congress, House 1933, 159.

23   U.S. Congress, House 1934, 1–941; U.S. Congress, Senate 1934, 6421–7758.

24   See the testimony of William Lockwood for New York Curb Exchange, Lothrop Withington for a committee of New England dealers and brokers, and Richard Babbage for the Real Estate Board of New York. Others played an even more indirect role, such as Harry Covington, who submitted a brief for the American Institute of Accountants, and Fred Oliver, for the National Association of Mutual Savings Banks (U.S. Congress, Senate 1934, 6421–7758).

25   See n. 16 above.

26   A number of these lawyers were even willing to *assume*, for the sake of argument, that the bill could survive a direct constitutional attack, but they nonetheless stressed the "unfair" administrative aspects of the bill. Lawyer after lawyer bitterly attacked the arbitrary nature of the board's powers. James Emery, who represented the National Association of Manufacturers, argued that the administrative powers of the Labor Board violated "elementary principles of justice and fair play"; "If that be due process of law, God save us," he said (see n. 18 above). Another prominent lawyer, Nathan Miller, noted that the powers of the board did not "even approximate due process" and that its judicial review procedures were "a farce" (U.S. Congress, Senate 1934, 889). Also see the testimony of Hal Smith, n. 14 above. These arguments were along the lines of those that characterized the general attack that the American Bar Association's committees on commerce and administrative law launched on the expanding field of administrative law; see chap. 6.

27   U.S. Congress, Senate 1934, 404; U.S. Congress, Senate 1934, 562.

28   Walter Carroll for the New Orleans Association of Commerce (U.S. Congress, Senate 1934, 611); Walter G. Merritt, counsel for the League for Industrial Rights (U.S. Congress, Senate 1935, 310); Raoul Desvernine for U.S. Steel (U.S. Congress, Senate 1935, 362). Such opposition to the rights of employees prompted Martha Minow to remark that the charges that rights introduce conflict and adversariness are routinely "levied by people who do not want to change existing patterns of domination" (1987, 1873).

29   U.S. Congress, Senate 1935, 310. The League for Industrial Rights was the successor of the American Anti-Boycott Association. Among its founders was also James Beck, who played a leading role in opposing the New Deal. Daniel Ernst (1988) argues that Merritt held relatively liberal opinions on labor issues. He was certainly at odds with the old arguments against collective bargaining and favored outlawing yellow-dog contracts. Indeed, Merritt adopted somewhat conciliatory rhetoric in his nonetheless explicit opposition to Wagner's bill.

30   U.S. Congress, House 1933, 1–298. William Breed was the senior partner in Breed, Abbott & Morgan. He represented the Investment Bankers Association of New York, New Jersey, and Connecticut, and the Investment Bankers Association of America. Arthur H. Dean was with Sullivan and Cromwell, one of the biggest firms in New York; it represented a large number of financial institutions.

31   U.S. Congress, House 1933, 121; U.S. Congress, House 1933, 137. Notably, the opposition of lawyers rested on the same grounds after Congress unanimously passed the Securities Act in May 1933. Arthur Ballantine discussed the Securities Act in the *American Bar Association Journal* and based his analysis on the premise that the act "in its present form has a tendency to deter adequate functioning of the securities market" (Ballantine 1934, 85). Accordingly, he suggested amendments that were designed to ease the liabilities of directors. Charles T. Donworth reviewed the act for the *Washington Law Review* and also argued that the liability and revocation

sections of the act were "a serious deterrent to raising capital for established business as well as for highly speculative enterprises" (Donworth 1933, 61). Arthur Dean also carried his crusade against the act from Congress to the press; *Fortune Magazine* played host in publishing Dean's critique of the act and Felix Frankfurter's response to it. The debate again boiled down to two basic arguments: Frankfurter justified the act in terms of its contribution to the protection of investors, and Dean responded by pointing out the unreasonable burden the act placed on the financial community and the consequences this would have on the prospects for economic recovery (Dean 1933, 50; Frankfurter 1933, 80). It is also interesting to note that lawyers may have had their own reasons to amend the liability provisions of the act. It provided that purchasers of securities could file suit against every person "whose profession gives authority to a statement made by him, if named with his consent as having prepared any portion of the registration statement." Moreover, directors were responsible for inaccurate or false statements, and many lawyers actively served in the capacity of directors.

32 Donald Richberg was then the general counsel of the National Recovery Administration. For biographical details of Richberg, see Irons 1982, 28–29.

33 McGuire 1935, 239–42.

34 Flexner 1934, 232; Rodell 1933, 272.

35 American Bar Association 1934b, Exhibit N. Silas Strawn, a former president of the U.S. Chamber of Commerce and an influential member of the ABA, was a senior partner in the Chicago firm of Winston, Strawn and Shaw. This firm was deeply involved in the affairs of the ABA and led the opposition to some New Deal measures.

36 Report of the Special Committee on Amendments to the Federal Securities Act 1934, 565–87.

37 Dodd 1935, 199. In another article Dodd was more blunt: "The suggestions for amendment of the act . . . are typical of many recent proposals by conservative lawyers, bankers and accountants in that by introducing a non-conductor between the persons responsible for the original issue and the ultimate investor, they would so weaken the act as to make it largely fail to accomplish its primary object" (Dodd 1934, 248). It would be a mistake, however, to reduce the ABA's opposition to a mere reflection of clients' demands. The Securities Act drew fire from unexpected sources as well. William O. Douglas, for example, a reputed Yale legal realist and a future member of the Securities and Exchange Commission, also criticized the "uncertainties" of the law and its exaggerated *in terrorem* provisions. Nathan Isaacs of Harvard, a moderate antiformalist, also described the law as one that strained both "words" and "principles." See Douglas and Bates 1933, 171; Isaacs 1933, 218.

38 The attempt to limit the jurisdiction of federal courts with regard to utility rate commissions had not been new. Felix Frankfurter had written on the merits of removing this jurisdiction as early as 1928, and a bill to this effect circulated in the 72d Congress. When the Johnson bill became law in May 1934, the *Yale Law Journal*

commented that "a quarter of a century of agitation to eliminate federal court interference with state control of public utilities rates" had finally ended (*Yale Law Journal* 1934b, 119).

39 Report of the Standing Committee on Jurisprudence and Law Reform 1933, 378.

40 U.S. Congress, Senate 1933, 1–33; U.S. Congress, House 1934, 1–319.

41 All three lawyers were prominent members of the bar, and all three were corporate lawyers. Harry Covington was the senior partner in Covington, Burling, Rublee, Acheson & Shorb, one of the biggest law firms in Washington, D.C.; Edward Everett was a senior partner in Winston, Strawn & Shaw, the biggest firm in Chicago. Clarence Martin, who was the president of the ABA, later chaired its committee on the New Deal.

42 Butler was the senior partner of Pope and Ballard, a big Chicago and Washington, D.C., firm. Harry Dunbaugh was a partner in the Chicago firm of Isham, Lincoln and Beale, a leading utility firm. George Lee was a partner in the Nebraska firm of Flansburg, Lee and Sheldahl; he was also a vice president of Northern Natural Gas Company. Robert Coulson was a partner in the prestigious New York firm of Whitman, Ransom, Coulson and Geotz. And George LePine was a partner in the New York firm of Travis, Brownsback and Paxson.

43 U.S. Congress, Senate 1933, 3.

44 U.S. Congress, House 1934, 120.

45 U.S. Congress, House 1934, 175; U.S. Congress, Senate 1933, 25; U.S. Congress, House 1934, 159; U.S. Congress, House 1934, 133.

46 U.S. Congress, House 1934, 123.

47 American Bar Association 1934a, Exhibit B.

48 For a summary of Norris's acrimonious remarks see *American Bar Association Journal* 1933b, 388.

49 William Ransom in American Bar Association 1934e, 310.

50 American Bar Association 1934d, 153.

51 Only a year earlier the Executive Committee of the ABA failed to pass a resolution expanding the objects of the association as defined in Article 1 of its constitution. A proposed amendment to authorize the association "to express and advocate its views on such questions of public interest or pertaining to the general welfare as it shall deem proper" was enthusiastically endorsed by the *ABA Journal*, that described it as being "in line with the admitted duties and responsibilities of the public profession of the law" and expressed its confidence that the amendment would not hurt the traditional "absence of political, sectional and other divisions in its ranks" (*American Bar Association Journal* 1933d, 398). When the proposed amendment was brought before the ABA's General Assembly in August 1933, however, it generated a heated debate and failed to be approved (American Bar Association 1933c, 9–15). The creation of the New Deal Committee, therefore, marked an indirect attempt to expand the ABA's scope of inquiry without a formal authorization to do so.

52   American Bar Association 1933a.

53   American Bar Association 1934a, 300.

54   Ibid., 306.

55   Ibid., 305.

56   Ibid., 300.

57   Frank Hogan reminded the Executive Committee that while the "whittling away of the rights of American citizens" was in process, the association was busy "wringing [its] hands about catching a few gangsters," referring to the intensive focus of the association on crime (American Bar Association 1934a, 302). Frederick O'Connell described the disappointment of many lawyers "in the crowd here" that the ABA had failed to address the fundamental issue of the New Deal's legislative agenda.

58   Martin 1933a; 1933b.

59   See n. 38 above.

60   *United States v. Butler*, 297 U.S. 1 (1936).

61   I could not find any biographical notes on Owen D. Young, a New York lawyer who played a small part in the events that followed, or on Charles Taft, a lawyer from Cincinnati, Ohio.

62   American Bar Association, Interim Report of the Special Committee 1935, Exhibit Z.

63   This reluctance also fits the argument of the previous chapter that lawyers tended to be careful in discussing the Recovery Act because of clients' support, popular backing, and a sharp sense of constitutional uncertainty as to how the Supreme Court would treat the law. Still, there might have been another, more mundane, reason for the reluctance of the committee to discuss the specifics of various New Deal laws. Two other ABA committees established themselves as authoritative speakers on New Deal issues: the Committee on Administrative Law and the Committee on Commerce. It seems that the executive committee found itself in a potential jurisdictional competition with at least one of these two committees. Rush C. Butler, the chairman of the Committee on Commerce, was concerned about a potential conflict of interests and held a joint meeting with Clarence Martin in order to clear up mutual "suspicions." The New Deal Committee reported that these suspicions were "cleared," perhaps at the price of limiting the scope of its work (American Bar Association, Interim Report of the Special Committee 1935, Exhibit Z).

64   American Bar Association, Interim Report of the Special Committee 1935, Exhibit Z.

65   American Bar Association 1935a.

66   On the events that followed the decision and the effect it had on the legal field, see chap. 4.

67   American Bar Association 1936e, 170–80.

68   American Bar Association 1936d.

69   Ibid., 174.

70   Ibid., 21.

71   Ibid., 20–24.

72   Ibid., 21.

73   Ibid., 33.

74   Report of the Sub-Committee to Consider and Report upon the Report of Special Committee 1935.

75   American Bar Association 1936d, 17.

76   Ibid., 14.

77   Ibid., 22–24.

78   Ibid., 47–51.

79   Ibid., 62–65. The General Council voted 26–14 and the Executive Committee 6–4 in their decision to resume the work of the New Deal Committee.

80   Ibid., 66.

81   *American Bar Association Journal* 1936b, 148.

82   American Bar Association, Report of the Special Committee to Study Federal Legislation 1936.

83   American Bar Association 1936e, 83. In a way, the differences of opinion among the members of the committee could be exploited to the association's advantage if it chose to emphasize the plurality of views among its members as proof of its nonpartisanship. The bar's leaders, however, preferred to suppress the whole affair.

84   American Bar Association, Report of the Special Committee to Study Federal Legislation 1936, 385.

85   Ibid., 386.

86   Ibid., 373–79.

87   Ibid., 379–80.

88   American Bar Association 1936e, 342.

89   In order to do so, the Executive Committee had to overcome two procedural problems. First, the 1935 resolution called upon the Executive Committee to consider the reports in a joint meeting with the General Council. Second, both the majority and the minority reports recommended that their respective reports be adopted. Given that the reports contained no substantive recommendations for action, adopting the report would have implied that the governing body of the ABA embraced every idea contained in the majority report. Nobody on the Executive Committee wanted it.

90   American Bar Association 1936e, 160.

91   Gordon 1984, 53.

92   Halliday 1987, 40.

93   Brint 1990, 375.

4   *Lawyers in the Shadow of the Court*

1   295 U.S. 495 (1935). *Schechter* involved the Live Poultry Code, which was promulgated under Section 3 of the NIRA, subsection (a) of which provided that "[u]pon

the application to the President by one or more trade or industrial associations or groups, the President may approve a code or codes of fair competition for the trade or industry or subdivision thereof." The Live Poultry Code was approved by the president on April 13, 1934, as "a code of fair competition for the live poultry industry of the metropolitan area in and about the city of New York." The appellants were operators of slaughterhouse markets in Brooklyn who were convicted on eighteen counts of code violations. On appeal, the Supreme Court overruled the convictions on grounds that the NIRA as a whole was unconstitutional. One of the unexpected elements in the unanimous decision was the killing of the NIRA on the grounds of illegitimate delegation of lawmaking powers to the executive branch of the government (the delegation doctrine, which had been based on the separation of powers principle). Only a few months earlier, in Nov. 1934, an article in the *Yale Law Journal* maintained that the NIRA could be constitutionally sustained "without much difficulty" and dismissed the delegation issue altogether: "The problem of delegation of legislative powers to the President, though concededly serious, seems to be *the least important of the constitutional considerations* . . . the Supreme Court has never held an act of Congress unconstitutional on this ground, and the lower courts have been reluctant to say that there is an unwarranted delegation of power by the Act" (*Yale Law Journal* 1934a, 97; italics mine). A few months later the court also invalidated the Bituminous Coal Act on grounds of delegation, this time attacking the delegation of lawmaking powers to private groups (*Carter v. Carter Coal*, 298 U.S. 238 [1936]). Horwitz notes that *Schechter*, in fact, also involved delegation of lawmaking powers to private groups because of the NIRA's reliance on self-promulgated codes, in which the executive often served as a mere rubber stamp. Horwitz ties the "collapse" of the doctrine after these decisions to the blurring of the private-public distinction in American constitutional law (Horwitz 1992, 208). The role of ideas notwithstanding, it seems that this later "collapse" also was the result of the growing pressure exerted on the court by the administration's vigorous regulatory programs and the heated rhetoric which accompanied them. On *Schechter* as a turning point in the history of the New Deal, see Hawley 1966.

2 For business and big industry, however, the decision had probably been a mixed blessing. Indicative of this fact was the response of the ABA's Committee on Commerce. The committee was quick to propose new legislation whose purpose was to preserve those sections of the NIRA that relaxed the antitrust laws (Report of the Standing Committee on Commerce 1935, 439).

3 Davis 1936, 245; Beck 1935a, 163. The book Beck referred to was Corwin's (1934). John Davis was a senior partner in the New York City firm of Davis, Polk, Wardwell, Gardiner & Reed. Davis was a disenchanted Democrat, a forceful blend of lawyer-politician, a member of the Lawyers Committee of the American Liberty League, and a prominent member of the New York Bar and the American Bar Association. On Davis's role in New Deal-related litigation see below and in Excursus I. On James Beck see chap. 2 and Excursus I.

4   Cortner (1964) described the reaction of President Roosevelt to the decision: "Roosevelt expressed surprise at the Schechter decision and at the fact that the Court liberals had joined in the opinion. When notified of the decision by telephone, he had asked, 'Well where was Ben Cardozo? How did he stand? And what about old Isaiah [Brandeis]?'" (1964, 70). Roosevelt, presumably, should have known better. The NIRA was based on a corporatist philosophy, which was distasteful to Justice Brandeis. For a person who wrote on the "curse of bigness" (Brandeis 1934), the NIRA could not but be regarded as a "kunststucke" (clever trick), one that was not only harmful but also that "restored to the big boys confidence and power, instead of destroying them when they were at his [Roosevelt's] feet" (see a private letter of Brandeis dated Apr. 11, 1934, in Urofsky and Levy, 1992, 544).

5   *United States Law Review* 1935b, 282.

6   *American Bar Association Journal* 1935b, 430.

7   E.g., Blair 1935; Dodd 1936.

8   Farnum 1934, 393; Farnum 1935, 728. George Farnum, a Boston lawyer, specialized in admiralty and maritime law. He was a member of the Standing Committee on Admiralty and Maritime Law of the American Bar Association and lectured on these subjects at Boston University Law School.

9   Blair 1935, 65.

10   See chaps. 2 and 3.

11   Lisagor and Lipsius 1988, 115. A vigorous litigation campaign soon followed. John Davis, already fully committed to attacking the New Deal on every possible ground, was retained by Edison Electrical Institute to plan a constitutional attack on the Holding Company Act. Three other experienced corporate lawyers were also recruited: Forney Johnston, Newton D. Baker, and James Beck. Johnston, a partner in the Birmingham, Alabama, firm of Cabannis & Johnston and at one time a vice president of the American Bar Association, was also an avowed enemy of the New Deal. Like Davis and Beck, he was a member of the American Liberty League. Baker was the senior partner in one of the nation's biggest firms, the Cleveland, Ohio, firm of Baker, Hostetler, Sidlo & Patterson. A distinguished member of the American Bar Association and the Ohio state bar, he addressed the bar on various issues relating to the expansion of the administrative process and its implications for the bar, the judiciary, and democracy in general. A Democrat who contended for the presidential nomination of 1932 and at one time an admirer of Roosevelt, Baker turned increasingly hostile towards the New Deal and considered most of the new measures unconstitutional (see Schlesinger 1959, 483. Baker was also involved in litigation on behalf of private power companies that challenged the constitutionality of using federal money to develop public power companies; see Glennon 1985, 26). The first opportunity to challenge the act came in Sept. 1935, when the American State Public Service Company, represented by the firm of Piper, Carey and Hall, asked a Maryland District Court to determine the act's constitutionality. The American States Public Service Company was a holding company under a

bankruptcy reorganization plan. James Piper, counsel for the company, asked the court to decide whether the company had to register with the Security and Exchange Commission as the law stipulated. Concurrently, he asked Ralph Buell—an attorney who represented Burco Inc., which held bonds of the American States Company—to intervene in the proceedings and to argue that the debtors of American States would benefit most if the company were liquidated in accordance with the provisions of the Holding Company Act. In fact, Ralph Buell's firm was counsel to the International Utilities Corporation, a company that had a stake in striking out the Holding Company Act. Further, James Piper also approached John Davis and asked him to appear in the case on behalf of a straw man who held securities of American States. There was a dual purpose behind these proceedings: first, to compel the court to determine the constitutionality of the Holding Company Act, and second, to obtain a ruling in a case that did not involve the United States as a party. The government's role, therefore, was limited to presenting an *amicus curiae*. The strategy proved successful. The court declared the Holding Company Act unconstitutional in its entirety (Re *American States Public Service Co.*, 12 F. Supp. 667 [D. Md. 1936]; affirmed in *Burco Inc. v. Whitworth et al.*, 81 F. 2nd 721 [4th Cir. 1936]). Other challenges to the act soon followed. In a series of cases various holding companies asked courts to issue injunctions against the enforcement of the act and to declare it unconstitutional. These cases (e.g., *Consolidated Gas v. Hardy* [unreported] no. 81/377 [S.D.N.Y. 1936]; *Cities Services v. Hardy* [unreported] no. 81/384 [S.D.N.Y. 1936]; and *United Corporation v. Hardy* [unreported] no. E81/383 [S.D.N.Y. 1936]) were dominated by two leading Wall Street firms: Davis, Polk, Wardwell, Gardiner & Reed, and Whitman, Ransom, Coulson and Goetz. This latter firm included some of the ABA's most influential members; see n. 61 below. They were aided by two other firms: Freuauff, Robinson & Sloan, and LeBoeuf, Winston, Machold & Lamb, see Excursus I. Another major battle involved the Electric Bond and Share Company, which was represented by the prominent corporate firm of Simpson, Thatcher & Bartlett. (Thomas D. Thatcher was an influential leader of the bar. Apart from activities in the American Bar Association and the New York State Bar Association, he was at one time the president of the Association of the Bar of the City of New York.) The Securities and Exchange Commission took the lead here and filed suit against Electric Bond for failing to register under the provisions of the act. The judicial struggle ended in March 1938, when the Supreme Court upheld the constitutionality of the Public Utility Holding Company Act (*Electric Bond and Share Co. v. Securities and Exchange Commission*, 303 U.S. 419 [1938]).

12 Cortner 1964, 87.

13 Chandler 1936, 248.

14 Cortner 1964, 95–97.

15 In chap. 2 I discussed the ambivalence of the league's lawyers toward the NIRA. On other occasions as well these lawyers used a relatively restrained language. For

example, the public utility holding company bill, the labor relations bill, the Guffey coal bill and the farmers' home bill, all discussed by the league's lawyers prior to *Schechter*, were rather carefully described as constitutionally "doubtful" and "questioned" (American Liberty League 1935e; 1935f; 1935c; 1935d). Following *Schechter*, these terms were replaced by a more aggressive tone: the National Labor Relations Act and the Agriculture Adjustment Act were flatly described as unconstitutional (1935i), and the potato bill was described as "ridiculous" and unconstitutional (1935b).

16   American Liberty League 1935h, 10 (see also National Lawyers Committee of the American Liberty League 1935). The eight drafters of the report were Earl F. Reed (who chaired the project), Harold Beacom, Harold Gallagher, Hal Smith, Randolph Williams, Gurney Newlin, Daniel Kenefick, and Harrison McGraw. Reed was a partner in the Pittsburgh, Pennsylvania, firm of Thorp, Bostwich, Reed & Armstrong, which was involved in a number of highly visible cases (e.g., *Weirton Steel* and *Jones & Laughlin Steel*; see Excursus I). Harold Beacom was a partner in the Chicago firm of Winston, Strawn & Shaw. The firm was affiliated with the American Liberty League through three other partners as well: Silas Strawn, Edward Everett, and Ralph Shaw. Strawn was also an influential member of the American Bar Association (see chap. 3, n. 35). Gallagher was a senior partner in the New York firm of Hornblower, Miller, Miller & Boston, another firm that featured two other partners in the league's National Lawyers Committee: Raoul Desvernine and Nathan Miller. Smith was a partner in the Detroit firm of Beaumont, Smith & Harris. The firm handled the Houde case, which involved the labor provisions of the NIRA, and represented the National Automobile Chamber of Commerce in the Senate hearings on the Labor Act; Williams was a partner in the Virginia firm of Hunton, Williams, Anderson, Gay & Moore, which was deeply involved in efforts to resist the financial legislation of the New Deal.

17   National Labor Relations Board 1936, 47. A number of the bar's biggest firms had been involved in challenging the constitutionality of the act, among them Thorp, Bostwick, Reed & Armstrong; Davis, Polk, Gardiner & Reed; Butler, Pope & Ballard; and Cravath, DeGersdorff, Swaine & Wood. For more details, see Excursus I.

18   Frankfurter 1935; Powell 1935a; Johnson 1936; *United States Law Review* 1935c.

19   George Roberts, for example, a member of the committee and legal counsel for Commonwealth & Southern Corporation, asked John Davis to omit his name from the planned report on the Holding Company Act. Davis eventually withheld publication (see Harbaugh 1973, 351).

20   Frankfurter 1935, 92.

21   The Ethics Committee also issued an opinion in response to a complaint by Carl N. Davie of Atlanta. The complaint concerned the statement of Earl Reed that "when a lawyer tells a client that a law is unconstitutional, it is then a nullity and he need no longer obey the law." The Ethics Committee did not find that the practices of the league were unethical (*American Bar Association Journal* 1935a). It is hard to con-

clude that the opinion of the ethics committee reflected its approval of the National Lawyers Committee. A few months earlier, the Ethics Committee had considered a complaint against Donald Richberg, who reportedly used "derogatory" statements in talking about the legal profession. When the Ethics Committee asked Richberg to respond, he refused in extremely rude language. However, the Ethics Committee, upon the recommendation of the Executive Committee, buried the complaint in an apparent effort to avoid confrontation with a senior lawyer of the administration. It seems to me that in both cases the ABA simply tried to avoid the rough and tumble of politics. For more on the Richberg affair see American Bar Association 1935c. At any rate, some leaders of the bar had been aware of the potentially problematic connection between the association and the Liberty League. When the ABA launched its campaign against Roosevelt's court-packing plan, it was careful to distance itself from lawyers who were affiliated with the league (Auerbach 1976, 196).

22   *National Labor Relations Board v. Jones and Laughlin Steel Corp.*, 301 U.S. 1 (1937). There were other reasons for the silence. Labor law had been extremely marginal to mainstream legal thought and practice, and its low prestige and slow development reflected the concentration of lawyers in business-related fields. Between 1933 and 1936, for example, the *ABA Journal* dedicated one article to labor issues before the National Labor Relations Act became law, and one such article afterwards (see McGuire 1935, Chandler 1936). Other professional forums fared no better. Few lawyers discussed labor-law issues, and those who did were mostly lawyers who supported the rights of employees to organize and to bargain collectively with employers. For example, see Rabinowitz 1933; 1934; Handler 1934a; Thomas 1935a; 1935b; Biddle 1935; Fuchs 1935. Two exceptions were articles by a couple of corporate lawyers: Merritt 1937; C. Wickersham 1935 (also see Landis 1934).

23   Cited in Irons 1982, 106. The 6–3 decision of the court to invalidate the Agricultural Adjustment Act further contributed to the growing spirit of defiance against the powers of the court (*United States v. Butler*, 297 U.S. 1 [1936]).

24   Alsop and Catledge 1938; Leuchtenberg 1963; Leuchtenberg 1969; Irons 1982.

25   Boudin 1935.

26   Association of American Law Schools 1935, 74.

27   Ibid., 64. Garrison offered the following amendment: "Congress shall have power to promote the economic welfare of the United States by such laws as in its judgment are appropriate, and to delegate such power in whole or in part to the states. Existing state powers are not affected by this article, except as Congress may occupy a particular field" (ibid., 69). Another supporter of the idea favored this option over curbing the review powers of the court, because these, he said, were still important for the protection of free speech rights and other civil liberties (Fraenkel 1935a, 2; 1935b, 42).

28   Association of American Law Schools 1935, 65–66.

29   Frankfurter's plan, however, was not favored even by some of his closest allies. Irons writes that many "agreed that the approach that Frankfurter and others favored

raised the frightening prospect of major surgery on the heart of the Constitution and risked upsetting the massive body of precedent behind these central clauses" (Irons 1982, 274). It was ironic that both those who favored amendments and those who opposed them framed their arguments in terms of "legal uncertainty," thus sharing the main concerns of private practitioners who attacked the New Deal for undermining the certainty of law (see chaps. 5 and 6).

30 Association of American Law Schools 1935, 52. In talking about four justices who already thought of the United States as "a nation" Powell referred to Chief Justice Hughes and Justices Brandeis, Stone, and Cardozo. These four justices dissented in a May 1934 decision invalidating the Railroad Retirement Act as an undue federal regulation of intrastate commerce (*Retirement Board v. Alton*, 295 U.S. 330 [1934]). On a different occasion Powell opted for a different strategy. He simply referred to *Schechter* as unimportant: "It may well be that unanimity was possible only because some of the Justices did not regard all of the issues as so far-reaching as many commentators seem to assume. In some respects it is a big case. In other respects it is a less big case" (Powell 1935b, 48).

31 Association of American Law Schools 1935, 52. The "two men" to whom Powell referred were Chief Justice Hughes and Justice Roberts, who were considered to be the Court's swing votes.

32 E.g., Richberg, 1934; Cummings 1933. For the academic legal-realist view see, in particular, Frank 1930. For discussion see chap. 6.

33 See chap. 2.

34 These contradictions had to do with some of the internal inconsistencies of what had come to be known as legal realism (see chap. 6). Horwitz maintains that some realists criticized classical jurisprudence for being too political, others for being insufficiently sensitive to political and social matters, and still others for expressing "bad politics." Some of these contradictions are reflected in the above views on the "problem of the court." For now, suffice it to note that these contradictions point to the problems involved in the attempt to define legal realism on the basis of some common framework of jurisprudential ideas. In chap. 6 I reconstruct the realist project on the basis of the realists' similar structural position within the legal field.

35 New York State Bar Association 1936b, 160, 167. Arnold provided another interesting argument against constitutional amendments. He claimed that all jurists, irrespective of their political convictions, should reject the idea that a constitutional debate, heretofore handled and controlled by the legal profession, would be resolved by an appeal to the political arena. It is precisely this type of reasoning, marginal and seemingly insignificant, through which one may see how the force of the professional field may at times overdetermine the attitude of lawyers to various issues. I will return to this point in the next chapters as well (see n. 29 above and chap. 5, n. 29).

36 Dickinson 1936, 268.

37 Association of American Law Schools 1935, 63.

38   Ibid. Exerting pressure on the court by invoking a subtle threatening rhetoric had been a common practice. See the remarks of Garrison and Powell, above.

39   Boudin 1935, 40.

40   See chap. 3, n. 77.

41   See n. 18 above.

42   The views of Frankfurter on this issue, however, were far from clear. I believe that some of Frankfurter's private and public views reflected, above all, sensitivity to political delicacies and sensitivities. It seems, for example, that Frankfurter did not know how advanced the court-packing plan was until he received a letter from President Roosevelt, shortly before the plan became publicly known, from which he should have guessed what was coming. After the plan became known Frankfurter supported it in private, in spirit if not in all the details, but he did not support it in public. Trying to remain loyal to both Roosevelt and Justice Brandeis, who was personally offended by the plan, Frankfurter "walked a tightrope" throughout the period (see Urofsky and Levy 1992, 592; Urofsky 1991, 40–43).

43   Boudin 1935, 40.

44   Cohen 1935.

45   Cited in Beck 1935b, 162.

46   Clark 1935b, 120. This position was voiced by Clark shortly after *Schechter* in an article written for the *New Republic*. By December 1935, when he chaired a symposium on the subject, he favored constitutional amendments (see n. 26 above).

47   Comprehensive compilations of congressional proposals to curb the powers of the Supreme Court were prepared by various sources. See New York State Bar Association, Report of the Committee on Proposed Amendments to the Federal Constitution 1937; American Bar Association, Report of the Standing Committee on Jurisprudence and Law Reform 1936; *United States Law Week*, Jan. 21, 1936, 2.

48   Reed 1936, 601; Cummings 1936; New York State Bar Association 1936a.

49   The plan, as is well known, was a colossal political failure. Within days, writes Irons, "support from all but the most die-hard New Dealers evaporated" (1982, 276). The plan was too abrupt, shook the public's basic notions of "fair play," and "attacked one of the symbols which many believed the nation needed for its sense of unity as a body politic" (Leuchtenberg 1963, 235). Although the court-packing plan was eventually killed, it nonetheless exerted enormous pressure on the Court. At least indirectly, therefore, the threat of packing the Court contributed to the "switch in time that saved nine": In 1937, while the plan was pending in Congress, the Court upheld the National Labor Relations Act and began the process of aligning itself with the dominant political forces of the day.

50   On the opposition of the American Bar Association to the elimination of federal jurisdiction in public utility rates see chap. 3. For Brandeis's letter see Urofsky and Levy 1992, 576. Brandeis's position, of course, was based on a radically different philosophy from that which guided the critics of the Supreme Court. For Brandeis,

the abolition of the diversity principle was important in the struggle against the power of big corporations.

51   Ransom 1936d, 23.

52   Richberg 1934, 287; Cummings 1933, 577.

53   Beck wrote a number of books about constitutional matters. In 1932 he published *Our Wonderland of Bureaucracy: A Study of the Growth of Bureaucracy in the Federal Government and Its Destructive Effect upon the Constitution.* Beck had a brilliant legal career, moving from private practice to the attorney general's office, only to return to private practice as a partner in the prestigious Wall Street firm of Sherman and Sterling. A few years later, President Harding nominated him solicitor general, a position he held until 1925 when he turned to a political career as a Pennsylvania representative in Congress. By the time the New Deal was initiated he had aleady served three terms as a congressman. Political opposition was also not new to Beck. He was one of the most ardent adversaries of the Eighteenth Amendment (Prohibition) and a supporter of the Association against the Prohibition Amendment (AAPA), the spiritual if not the institutional predecessor of the American Liberty League. Beck was also a member of the American Liberty League's National Lawyers' Committee (Wolfskill 1962, 43–45). As far as opposition to the New Deal was concerned, James Beck was everywhere: speaking against New Deal legislation in Congress, arguing before the Supreme Court, writing numerous articles in scholarly and popular publications, and addressing bar associations, professionals, politicians and the general public. For a sample of Beck's speeches see Beck 1933b (reprint of an address delivered by Beck at a meeting of the Bar Association of Tennessee), June 9, 1933; Beck 1933c and 1933a, addresses to the American Bar Association; Beck 1934, address to the New York State Bar Association; Beck 1935b. Beck was an active member of the American Bar Association and chaired its Committee on Citizenship. In this capacity, he routinely spoke about the connection between "respecting the past, understanding the Constitution, and becoming a good citizen."

54   Beck 1933b, 493; 1935c, 8.

55   Shouse 1934b, 3; Desvernine 1935, 4; Miller 1934, 353. For the firm affiliation and the role of Desvernine in the American Bar Association see chap. 2, n. 73. On his role on behalf of U.S. Steel see chap. 3, n. 28. On Miller see chap. 2, nn. 25, 73, and chap. 3, n. 26 for his role on behalf of utilities.

56   Beck 1935c, 3; 1934, 624.

57   See, e.g., Epstein 1936; Riley 1935; Black 1936; Bouve 1936; Dodd 1936; Gilmore 1936; Ritchie 1935; Sutherland 1936; Vold 1936.

58   Notably, this happened prior to the formal announcement of the court-packing plan in 1937. The plan, however, did enhance the ability of the organized bar to "identify with the popular side of a national issue" (Auerbach 1976, 197).

59   Loftin 1935; Faville 1935, 92.

60   Day 1935.

61 William Ransom became the president of the American Bar Association after a close race with James Beck. Ransom had been elected a judge at the age of thirty; he held this position for three years. He resigned to become chief counsel for the Public Service Commission of the State of New York. In 1919, he joined the Wall Street firm of Whitman, Ransom, Coulson and Goetz and specialized in corporate practice. Apart from his activities in the ABA, he was a member of the three major New York bar associations, the Judicature Society, and the American Law Institute.

62 Ransom 1936c, 519.

63 Ransom 1936a, 297.

64 Ibid.

65 Association of the Bar of the City of New Yor 1936, 204.

66 Chicago Bar Association 1936a, 137; 1936b; The referendum was ordered by the association's board of managers. A postcard was mailed to 4,000 members of the association; 1,770 were returned. Of those, 1,521 members were against legislation limiting the Supreme Court's judicial review powers, 151 were in favor. In addition, 1,490 were against the proposal to allow judicial review when two-thirds of the court's members concurred, 239 were in favor. Also, 1,587 were against the proposal to prevent the Supreme Court from invalidating a law unless the proceeding commenced within six months after the enactment of the law, 86 were in favor. The American Bar Association later adopted the Chicago Bar's referendum initiative as part of its campaign against the 1937 court-packing plan.

67 *American Bar Association Journal* 1936a, 741.

68 Report of the Committee on Jurisprudence and Law Reform 1936, 193.

Excursus I

1 On the troubled career of the National Lawyers Guild see Auerbach 1976, chap. 7; Glennon 1985, 26–27.

2 I offer a partial "correction" to these omissions by treating lawyers and firms who were involved with cases concerning some of these laws at the level of the Supreme Court.

3 U.S. Congress, House 1933, 1–321; U.S. Congress, Senate 1933, 1–439. These lawyers were Fayette B. Dow for the American Petroleum Institute, the National Petroleum Association, and various regional petroleum associations; and Russel B. Brown, Jack Blalock, and Luis Titus for the Independent Petroleum Association of America. Another lawyer, Charles C. Collins, represented the American Automobile Association.

4 See chap. 2.

5 For the reaction to *Schechter* see chap. 4. A total of 593 cases were instituted (including some involving the Agricultural Adjustment Act), but the overwhelming majority of cases were still pending by the time *Schechter* was decided. Out of 91

decided cases, 60 were decided in favor of the government (65.9 percent). Source: *United States Law Week*, March 5, 1935, 48.

6 Appealed cases were considered a single case for the purposes of this analysis. The data is based on published decisions that were periodically reported by the *United States Law Week*. The legal counsel in each case was identified by locating the relevant case in the *Federal Supplement*. It should be noted that the number of cases to which I refer is greater than the number of cases compiled by Irons (1982). Irons found only 19 cases in which the decision rested exclusively or largely on constitutional grounds. The total of 38 cases, in contrast, was reached by looking at cases in which constitutional questions were raised by the parties.

7 Marked exceptions were cases that challenged the labor provisions of the NIRA (e.g., *Weirton Steel*) and its oil-related provisions (e.g., *Panama Refining Co.*). For a discussion on the reasons for this lack of enthusiasm to challenge the NIRA see chap. 2.

8 The number of "members" refers, unless otherwise stated, to both partners and associates in the firms. Source: *Martindale-Hubbell Law Directory* 1933; 1934; 1935; 1936; 1937.

9 Even the *Schechter* case, in which the Supreme Court ultimately invalidated the NIRA, involved a small business, which was represented by the Heller brothers, two solo practitioners from New York. It was only when the case reached the Supreme Court that the Hellers approached Frederick Wood, of the Cravath firm, for legal assistance.

10 In this table and others that follow, the number of members includes, whenever possible, a separate count of partners and associates. It was sometimes impossible to make this distinction, in which case the number reflects the total number of lawyers in the firm. Source: *Martindale-Hubbell Law Directory* 1933; 1934; 1935; 1936; 1937.

11 U.S. Congress, House 1933, 1–298; U.S. Congress, Senate 1933, 1–349. These lawyers were William C. Breed, of Breed, Abbott & Morgan, for the Investment Bankers Association of New York, New Jersey & Connecticut, and for the Investment Bankers Association of America; R. V. Fletcher, general counsel of the Association of Railway Executives; C. Clinton James, a New York attorney and chairperson of the Federal Legislative Committee of the United States Building & Loan League; Huston Thompson, an attorney-at-law from Washington, D.C.; Arthur H. Dean, of Sullivan & Cromwell, who said that he was not appearing on behalf of any particular client but acknowledged that his firm represented "a large number of industrial and public utility clients and investment bankers"; William S. Bennett, a New York attorney who represented the Continental Coal Company of Fairmont, West Virginia; Herbert S. Friedman, a Chicago attorney, for Senator Bulkley; Thomas Creigh, general counsel for the Cudahy Packing Company of Chicago.

12 Source: Securities and Exchange Commission, 1941. The commission compiled all Court decisions on the Securities Act, the Securities Exchange Act, and the Public Utility Holding Company Act. The compilation included both published and un-

published decisions. Appealed cases are counted as a single case for the purposes of this analysis.

13   Sources: Securities and Exchange Commission 1941; *Martindale-Hubbell Law Directory* 1933; 1934; 1935; 1936; 1937.

14   U.S. Congress, House 1934, 1–941; U.S. Congress, Senate 1934, 6421–7758. These lawyers were Roland L. Redmond, for the New York Securities Exchange; J. G. Mitchell, an attorney for the Wetsel Advisory Service, Incorporated; Franklin Leonard, of Leonard, Cushman & Sydam, with interests in the mining industry, the New Jersey Exchange, and the New York Curb Exchange; Richard G. Babbage, a New York attorney, for the Real Estate Board of New York; R. V. Fletcher, for the Association of Railway Executives, of Washington, D.C.; William Lockwood, counsel for the New York Curb Exchange; Thomas B. Gay, of Hunton, Williams, Anderson, Gay & Moore, for the New York Stock Exchange; and Lothrop Withington, for New England Securities Dealers & Brokers. Briefs were presented by Fred Oliver for the National Association of Mutual Saving Banks, Noel T. Dowling for the National Automobile Chamber of Commerce, and Harry Covington of Covington, Burling, Rublee, Acheson & Shark for the American Institute of Accountants.

15   *Securities and Exchange Commission v. Torr*, 15 F. Supp. 144 (S.D.N.Y. 1936).

16   U.S. Congress, Senate 1934, 337–1028; U.S. Congress, Senate 1935, 238–890. Opposition to the bill was voiced by Robert T. Caldwell, attorney for American Rolling Mill Company of Kentucky; Raoul Desvernine and Nathan L. Miller, of Hornblower, Miller, Miller & Boston, for U.S. Steel and the Iron and Steel Institute; Walter G. Merritt, for the League of Industrial Rights; Arno Mowitz, an attorney for the Philadelphia Full Fashioned Hosiery Association; James Emery, for the National Association of Manufacturers; James Deffenbaugh, an attorney for the Hocking Glass Company of Ohio; Elisha Henson, an attorney for the American Newspaper Publishers Association; Franklin S. Edmonds for the Philadelphia Chamber of Commerce; Philip R. Van Duyne, an attorney for seven chambers of commerce of New Jersey; Roy F. Hall, an attorney for the National Lock Company of Rockford, Illinois; Walter Carroll, for the New Orleans Association of Commerce; Ivan Bowen, of Boutelle, Bowen & Flanagan, for the Pacific Greyhound Lines of San Francisco, and the Greyhound management of Chicago; Hal Smith, of Beaumont, Smith & Harris, for the National Automobile Chamber of Commerce; and William S. Elliott, an attorney for the International Harvester Company of Chicago. Briefs were presented by Wager Fisher and Joseph A. Kean; William J. Matthews for the Linoleum and Felt-base Manufacturing Industry; L. H. Sessions for Muskogen Employers Association; and Walter Drew for the National Erectors Association. Opposition to the bill from the Left was voiced by Isador Polier, who presented himself as the executive director of the International Juridical Association, a group of five hundred lawyers who supported the rights of labor.

17   Sources: National Labor Relations Board 1936; *Martindale-Hubbell Law Directory* 1933; 1934; 1935; 1936; 1937.

18   For example, the Houston, Texas, firm of Baker, Botts, Andrews & Wharton, with thirty-three lawyers, the Chicago firm of Cassels, Potter & Bentley, and the Syracuse, New York, firm of Hiscock, Cowie, Bruce & Lee. Also absent from the table is the Detroit firm of Stevenson, Butzel, Eaman & Long (22 lawyers), which at a certain point handled the case of *Freuhauf Trailer Company v. National Labor Relations Board*, 85 F. 2d 391 (6th Cir. 1936).

19   U.S. Congress, Senate 1935, 1–1132. These lawyers were Ralph B. Feagin, a Houston, Texas, attorney for a committee representing the natural gas industry; Justin T. Moore, of Hunton, Williams, Anderson, Gay & Moore, and John MacLane of Simpson, Thatcher & Bartlett, for the Committee of Public Utility Executives; J. J. Hedrick, for the Natural Gas Pipeline Company of Chicago; Fred N. Oliver for the National Association of Mutual Savings Banks of New York; R. V. Fletcher for the Association of Railway Executives; George A. Lee for the Northern Gas Company of Nebraska; and John Benton for the National Association of Railroad & Utilities Commissioners. The Electric Bond & Share Company presented a brief written by William White (a senior partner in the Birmingham, Alabana, firm of Bradley, Baldwin, All and White, one of the biggest firms in Alabama and general counsel for the Alabama Electric Company), Charles Rosen (the senior partner in the New Orleans firm of Rosen, Kammer, Wolff and Farrar, who counseled many important industrial and financial institutions in Louisiana), and Henry McCune (the senior partner in the Kansas City, Missouri, firm of McCune, Caldwell and Downing, which also represented the Kansas Gas and Electric Company and the American Power and Light Company).

20   Examples, some of which will be considered in the next part of the book, concern the prominent Wall Street firms of Cadwalader, Wickersham & Taft; Milbank, Tweed; Shearman & Sterling; and Root, Clark, Buckner & Ballantine.

21   *Carter v. Carter Coal Co.*, 298 U.S. 238 (1936).

22   Morris Ernst to President Roosevelt, cited in Auerbach 1976, 199.

23   Larson 1977, 227.

5   Administrative Law

1   Auerbach 1976, 159.

2   Miller 1936, 330. On the effect of the depression on lawyers, see Gifford 1933, 236–37. In contrast, see Auerbach's comments on the relatively limited effect the depression had on the bar's elite (Auerbach 1976, 160). It is also important to distinguish between the general belief that the profession was overcrowded and the actual conditions. A survey by Lloyd Garrison, for example, demonstrated that lawyers had yet to realize whole new areas of unfulfilled demand for legal services (Garrison 1934).

3   *United States Law Week*, August 13, 1935, 1; Montague 1933, 23; Jackson 1934, 119. On the New Deal as an era of professional opportunities, see also Chamberlain 1933; Handler 1934a; Llewellyn 1933; Manton 1933; Moris 1935; Rogers 1934.

4   Miller 1936, 330.

5   See chap. 2, n. 17.

6   A letter from Evan H. Hammett to William Ransom, American Bar Association, *Proceedings of the Executive Committee* (Jan.): 1–2, typescript. This is only an example. The American Bar Association's Committee on Jurisprudence and Law Reform compiled various legislative attempts to restrict legal representation before governmental agencies.

7   Chenoweth and Whitehead 1934. Of the fifty-eight lawyers who signed the brief, six practiced law in firms with four members or more, twenty-four practiced law with one partner or two (often family members), and twenty-four were solo practitioners.

8   The Chenoweth brief triggered the following resolution from the ABA's Committee on Jurisprudence and Law Reform: "Be it resolved that the ABA, at its annual meeting held at Milwaukee in 1934, urges the repeal of all portions of the National Economy Act of March 20, 1933, which limits the jurisdiction of the United States District Courts over contracts of government insurance and also urges that all laws be repealed which restrict the right of an insured to employ counsel in all stages of the proceedings where the claim or suit is brought on a government insurance contract" (Report of the Committee on Jurisprudence and Law Reform 1934, 74).

9   Robinson 1935, 277–80; American Bar Association, Report of the Committee on Unauthorized Practice of Law 1936, 74.

10 An early bird in this direction was a petition the Ohio State Bar Association submitted to the Ohio Supreme Court. It asked the court to prohibit a local administrative body from permitting persons to practice before it unless they were "properly and duly admitted to practice law" (*United States Law Week*, July 24, 1934, 8).

11 Ransom made this remark as part of a general effort to dissuade ABA members from assisting the FBA in its effort to exclude lay practitioners from the administrative arena. Ransom warned his listeners not to confuse the FBA with another lawyers' organization that carried the same name, "that of D.C., which is a national organization," and one that presumably had more power and influence (American Bar Association 1936c, 84–92). On the isolation of the FBA and its inability to influence ABA's policies see below.

12 U.S. Congress, Senate 1935, S2944.

13 Ransom 1936b, 1.

14 American Bar Association Resolutions Committee 1936, 134.

15 The bill was adversely reported on July 30, 1935; ibid.

16 American Bar Association 1936c, 84–92. For biographical details on Davis see chap. 4, n. 3.

17 American Bar Association 1936c, 87. The two lawyers were Sidney Teiser, who headed the Portland, Oregon, firm of Teiser, Keller & Teiser, and Armwell W. Cooper, a state senator who headed the Kansas City, Missouri, firm of Cooper, Neel, Kemp & Sutherland. Teiser argued that the bill was too sweeping and might

lead to the exclusion of accountants appearing before the relatively highly professionalized Board of Tax Appeals, which had a relatively high level of professionalization.

18   American Bar Association 1936c, 88.

19   American Bar Association 1936c, 209.

20   Ransom interpreted the referral of the Resolution to the Committee on Unauthorized Practice as a form of "modification" of the original resolution and
cleared the way for a vote on a referendum.

21   American Bar Association 1936c, 211–12.

22   Miller 1936, 331; New York State Bar Association 1936c, 331.

23   New York State Bar Association 1936c, 331.

24   New York State Bar Association 1937, 213–14.

25   This was not very surprising given that some influential corporate lawyers were
active in both associations: John Jackson, Julius Henry Cohen, Thomas Beardsley,
and Frederick Coudert, to mention a few who were directly involved with the issue
of administrative law and practice.

26   Heinz and Laumann 1982, 384. Heinz and Laumann studied Chicago lawyers in the
early 1980s. Nonetheless, it seems that this hemispheric division was already well
established in the 1930s, although the size and business volume of law firms in the
1930s was considerably smaller; see Auerbach 1976. In the 1930s, corporate lawyers,
predominantly partners in big law firms, already enjoyed a position of leadership
within the bar and were able to mold the bar's policies according to their own
particular interests.

27   The findings were reported in the American Bar Association Journal, see Jackson
1934, 407–9. The survey was meant to be, and had been presented as, a national
one. Clearly, few lawyers bothered to answer, and the results, accordingly, have to
be viewed with extreme caution. Thus, for example, one open-ended question
was, "What other types of unauthorized practice are also prevalent?" Not one of
the thirty-three lawyers who responded to this question mentioned administrative
practice by laymen as a problem. The results of this very limited survey may have
helped the Committee on Unlawful Practice to conclude that competition from
lay practitioners was not such a grave problem. John Jackson, who conducted the
survey for the American Bar Association, was also the chairperson of the New York
State Bar Association Committee on Unlawful Practice.

28   Miller 1936, 333–34.

29   New York State Bar Association 1936c, 326. In a previous chapter I discussed
Thurman Arnold's argument that to amend the Constitution in order to force the
Court to develop new constitutional doctrines amounted to a transfer of powers
from the legal to the political arena. The logic of Arnold and Cohen, otherwise far
apart in their views on law, was similar. It illustrates the degree to which the force
of the professional field may at times overdetermine the attitude of lawyers to
various issues (see chap. 4, n. 35).

30   The committee also included Pierce Butler Jr., Walter F. Dodd, O. R. McGuire, and Melvin G. Sperry.

31   Jackson 1934 (also Franklin 1934; Fox 1935). Robert Jackson was the solicitor general and later became a Supreme Court justice. His views on constitutional and administrative law were most advanced. Also see his *The Struggle for Judicial Supremacy* (Jackson 1941).

32   Handler 1934b, 138. Milton Handler was a Columbia law professor who became the general counsel of the National Labor Board; see chap. 6.

33   Arnold 1934, 913–47. Thurman Arnold was a Yale law professor who joined the New Deal administration; see chap. 6. Note the similarity of these arguments to the ideas expressed four years later by James Landis, the dean of Harvard Law School and formerly another law professor at the service of the New Deal's administration (see Horwitz 1992, 213).

34   Arnold 1934, 935. On the full development of such ideas see Landis 1938.

35   See the discussion in chap. 4 on the defense of the judiciary by corporate lawyers and on their perception that the New Deal administration launched a frontal attack on judicial authority.

36   See chap. 3 on congressional hearings on the Johnson bill and the National Labor Relations Act.

37   U.S. Congress, Senate 1934, 889.

38   American Bar Association, Report of the Standing Committee on Commerce 1934, 442; *Jones v. Securities and Exchange Commission*, 298 U.S. 1 (1936). But see the minority opinion of Stone, Brandeis and Cardozo. For some bitter critiques of administrative agencies see also: American Bar Association, Report of the Special Committee on Amendments to the Federal Securities Act 1936, 796; Vanderbilt 1937; Rogers 1935.

39   American Bar Association, Report of the Special Committee on Administrative Law 1934, 539–49.

40   Ibid., 547.

41   McFarland 1934, 612.

42   Arthurs 1985, 1, 3. Contemporary sociolegal scholarship devotes considerable attention to the issue of "legal pluralism" (see, for example, a special issue on the subject in *Social and Legal Studies* 1, no. 2 [June 1992]). Yet the main focus of contemporary studies in legal pluralism is the divorce of law from the state, the nature of community justice, and the emergence of informal law in various social settings. Here, in contrast, the paradigm of legal pluralism is invoked to analyze a competing system of law within the state.

43   Ibid., 6.

44   Of course, administrative agencies were by no means an invention of the New Deal (see n. 63 below). A growing interest in the administrative method as a mode of government intervention stretched back to the Progressive Era. Nonetheless, it seems that the creative flood of numerous administrative agencies in the New Deal

justifies the view that this period represented a kind of quantum leap in state regulatory intervention through the administrative method. It is in this respect that I speak about the creation of an "administrative space." Felix Frankfurter became a leading advocate of the administrative state in the second half of the 1920s and enlisted both Louis Jaffe and James Landis in the cause (for a brief account see Horwitz 1992, 236–37). In 1932, shortly before Roosevelt assumed office, James Beck's work on "the wonderland of bureaucracy" and the hostility it displayed toward the development of administrative practices foreshadowed the upcoming crisis.

45   Skowronek 1982, 27. On the contribution of the judicial system to the consolidation of capitalism in America see Horwitz 1977.

46   For a critique of this distinction see Arnold 1936b, 46–52.

47   On the fierce opposition of the legal profession to the codification movement see Horwitz 1977, 257.

48   Botein 1984, 49; Arthurs 1985, 4.

49   Horwitz 1977, 256.

50   Radin 1935; Horwitz 1977, 256.

51   On the legal profession's unstable cognitive basis and its search for "transcendent values" that will legitimize the profession's prerogatives, see Larson 1977.

52   Calabresi 1982, 5.

53   Jackson 1934, 119.

54   Wickersham 1934, 634. George Wickersham was a partner in Cadwalader, Wickersham & Taft. He was at one time the president of the American Law Institute (see chap. 6).

55   Wickersham 1935, 344.

56   Radin 1935. Jacob Lashly described the nature of negotiations between industry and the administration in the NRA code-drafting phase: "Businessmen were said to be about to meet around the conference table with each other and arrange the complex and vital affairs pertaining to their business interests . . . without the intrusion of the legal profession. There can be little doubt that the slogans on each of the occasions introduced the legal profession to the public in the light of unwanted parasites" (Lashly 1939, 657).

57   Larson 1989, 434.

58   Robinson 1935, 278; McNutt 1934, 231.

59   Whitman 1934, 104. Charles Whitman was a former governor of New York and a former president of the ABA. He was the leading partner of Whitman, Ransom, Coulson, & Geotz, a New York firm that also featured the ABA's president, William Ransom. For details, see Excursus I.

60   Ibid. Of course, lawyers' business was to keep clients *out* of court, not to represent them *at* court. Nevertheless, my point is that the talents of the lawyer—as a negotiator and an advisor—were molded and expressed in the shadow of the court. The aura of the judicial process, in other words, was the prime distancing

mechanism of lawyers in private practice. In previous chapters we have seen the efforts of lawyers to retain the aura of exclusive expertise. The administrative process threatened these efforts as long as it was not "normalized" (i.e., regulated and shaped according to the needs and demands of lawyers).

61   See Verkuil 1978, 265; he mainly frames the antipathy of lawyers to the administrative process in terms of their lesser ability to win cases for their clients.

62   See Jackson 1934, 119.

63   Root 1916, 736. Many lawyers could agree that the problem was how to tame the administrative process, not how to reverse it. O. R. McGuire, a member of the ABA's Committee on Administrative Law and its future chairman, quoted Henry M. Bates, dean of the University of Michigan School of Law, before the California Bar Association: "There can be no reversal of the present trends as long as the conditions of life remain substantially as they are today" (McGuire 1933, 471). Thomas D. Thatcher, the president of the Association of the Bar of the City of New York, quoted Elihu Root's old and often-cited ABA presidential address in 1916, in which he analyzed the rise of administrative law and predicted that "there will be no withdrawal from these experiments." Thatcher acknowledged that the expansion of governmental powers "has been going on for more than fifty years" and was the inevitable result of the growth of the country's needs (Thatcher 1935, 94–104). Thatcher's address was delivered before members of the New York bar and was followed by an elaborate discussion. All participants agreed that the necessity to develop expert bodies reflected the growth and complexity of national problems and yet searched for ways to regulate the regulators (New York State Bar Association 1935a, 104–21).

64   American Bar Association, Report of the Special Committee on Administrative Law 1933, 409.

65   The creation of the committee began on a happy note. The president of the ABA wrote President Roosevelt that the committee was about to study federal administrative law, and the president's secretary was reported to have extended the president's blessings. Louis Caldwell also announced that the attorney general had assigned one of his officers to work in cooperation with the committee (Martin 1934, 1–4).

66   Caldwell 1933, 199.

67   American Bar Association, Report of the Special Committee on Administrative Law 1934, 549.

68   Ibid., 544.

69   The composition of the committee changed in 1934. It was joined by Felix Frankfurter, who never actively participated, and Thomas B. Gay, a senior partner in the Richmond, Virginia, firm of Hunton, Williams, Anderson, Gay & Moore (see Excursus I). On Felix Frankfurter's prominence in issues concerning the administrative process see chap. 6 and Horwitz 1992, 236–37.

70   American Bar Association, Report of the Special Committee on Administrative Law 1934, 564.

71   American Bar Association, Interim Report of the Committee on Administrative Law 1935. Frankfurter, as far as I have been able to discover, neither disputed nor affirmed this statement.

72   American Bar Association 1934e, 121.

73   These lawyers were Joseph David and Clarence Goodwin; see American Bar Association 1934c, 178–92.

74   American Bar Association 1934c, 178.

75   American Bar Association, Report of the Special Committee on Administrative Law 1933, 421.

76   Butler 1934, 99. The Committee on Commerce was chaired by Rush C. Butler, a senior partner in Pope & Ballard, the biggest law firm in Chicago. He was a declared critic of the New Deal and, like Caldwell, a member of the American Liberty League's National Lawyers Committee (see Excursus I).

77   American Bar Association, Report of the Standing Committee on Commerce 1934, 439; Report of the Special Committee on Administrative Law 1934, 539–64. The Committee on Administrative Law first suggested that the ABA publish its own "administrative handbook," which would be available to members at no cost. The ABA's Executive Committee, which met to discuss the report, devoted its whole meeting to this proposal. The proposal was eventually dropped because of the projected costs (American Bar Association 1934c, 115–21). Also see a similar proposal in the New York State Bar Association's Report of the Committee on the National Industrial Recovery Act 1935, 174.

78   The AALS recommended that "the federal government should provide for the compilation, publication, and indexing of existing federal executive orders and regulations"; see Association of American Law Schools 1934, 154. Also see Griswold 1934, 198–215. Griswold, a future dean of Harvard Law School and a future member of the U.S. Civil Rights Commission, was then a special assistant to the U.S. attorney general.

79   U.S. Congress, House 1936, 1–38. This does not mean, of course, that the Committee on Administrative Law was the principal advocate of the act. R. J. Glennon writes that Jerome Frank and Erwin Griswold discussed the problem several times and that they approached Roosevelt with a solution. Roosevelt eventually asked Jerome Frank to assemble a committee to produce the draft statute of the federal register (Glennon 1985, 92–93).

80   *United States Law Review* 1934a, 338.

81   Ibid., 337.

82   Baker 1935, 5; McGuire 1933, 471–74. Newton D. Baker was the senior partner in the Cleveland, Ohio, firm of Baker, Hostetler, Sidlo & Patterson, one of the biggest firms in this state. He was an active and influential member of the ABA and a member of its Special Committee on the Coordination of the Bar (see Excursus I).

83 Thatcher 1935, 94.

84 American Bar Association, Report of the Special Committee on Administrative Law 1934, 546. This proposal, in fact, went beyond the established doctrines of the Supreme Court. In *Federal Trade Commission v. Algoma Lumber* (291 U.S. 502 [1934]), the court distinguished between questions of fact and questions of law and ruled that the former involved the choosing "among uncertain and conflicting inferences," an administrative, rather than a judicial task. The distinction between law and fact was often invoked in order to distinguish administrative from judicial functions. Newton D. Baker, lecturing the Ohio Bar Association on the nature of the administrative process, explained that "as society grows more and more complex, the exercise of the legislative function in detail becomes more difficult, if not impossible . . . so because of the inability of the legislature to deal in detail with rapidly changing situations of *fact*, there has grown up the practice of having the legislature announce the principle and permit *fact-finding* bodies to make the determination of the *fact* upon which the application of the principle is to depend" (Baker 1935, 5; italics mine). New Dealers, however, argued that the distinction was highly problematic and mainly served the interests of lawyers. John Dickinson, the assistant secretary of commerce and the chairman of the Committee on Administrative Law of the Federal Bar Association of the District of Columbia, suggested that the judicial and legislative functions of an administrative body could not be segregated without "amputating from the administrative agency many, if not most, of its central functions" (Dickinson 1935a, 78). The report of the Committee on Administrative Law acknowledged that "there may be occasional difficulty in classifying a particular function" but maintained that such difficulties could be overcome (Report of the Special Committee on Administrative Law 1934, 545).

85 U.S. Congress, Senate 1933, S1835.

86 American Bar Association, Report of the Special Committee on Administrative Law 1934, 540.

87 McGuire 1935; 1936a; 1936b; 1936c.

88 Caldwell 1935, 139.

89 American Bar Association, Report of the Special Committee on Administrative Law 1934, 550.

90 Ibid., 209.

91 American Bar Association 1935b, 103, 119; Also see Goodwin 1936, 224.

92 Grogan 1937; American Bar Association 1936b, 221.

93 Frankfurter resigned from the committee in January 1935. In 1935, the committee's members were Caldwell, Gay, McGuire, and the newly appointed Milton Handler, a New Dealer who acted as general counsel of the National Labor Board. The 1935 report singled out Handler as being in disagreement with the majority of the committee over some of its conclusions in 1934. It specifically stated, however, that Handler was in agreement with the committee over the Administrative Court issue; see Caldwell 1935, 137.

94 Caldwell 1935, 138.

95 The position of the committee was particularly striking in light of the fact that the Logan bill itself had never been seriously considered in Congress. The bill was first introduced in the 73d Congress and was referred to the Senate Committee on Judiciary. It resurfaced in the 74th Congress and was again referred to a committee. The Committee on Administrative Law finally drafted its own version of a bill to establish an administrative court (American Bar Association, Report of the Special Committee on Administrative Law 1936, 209).

96 American Bar Association 1936b, 222.

97 Ibid.

98 See Verkuil (1978) on the career of the Administrative Procedure Act of 1946. This act, in a nutshell, passed "in a period of reconciliation and relative agreement" (1978, 277) between the practicing bar and the administration and was, to a considerable extent, a victory for those who sought the judicialization of the administration space. See also Department of Justice 1941.

99 Jaffe 1954.

100 Stone 1934, 7. Such observations were followed by some quite radical proposals. Harold Laski, for example, suggested that the legal profession would be nationalized (1935). The ABA's president, William Ransom thus warned listeners that "if the lawyers of the United States do not want government to organize and control the legal profession, the lawyers better organize, govern and discipline themselves, in the public interest" (1936c; see also chap. 4).

101 Auerbach 1976, 160.

102 Gordon 1984.

103 Abbott 1988, 85.

104 Green 1935, 708. Also see McFarland 1934, 620. Leon Green was the dean of Northwestern School of Law and a strong sympathizer of the administration (see chap. 6).

105 See n. 98 above.

Excursus II

1 Bourdieu 1987, 814.

2 Heinz and Laumann 1982. Also see Carlin 1962.

3 Auerbach 1976.

4 Gordon 1984.

5 Larson 1977.

6 Abel 1981; 1989a; 1989b.

7 Harrington 1983.

8 Abel 1989b.

9 The need to enhance the demand for legal services is particularly important when the control of the profession over the production of producers loses its effective-

ness. One example concerns the shift to formal legal education as the primary vehicle of entry to the bar. This shift dramatically increases the number of practicing lawyers and weakens the ability of lawyers to regulate the number of newcomers; see Abel 1989a. Abel thus talks about "demand creation" in the 1970s, when the profession witnessed an expansion in university education, masssive entry of women, and further growth of the state bureaucratic apparatuses (for a critique see Kritzer 1991). In some respects, the proliferation of law schools, the entry of immigrants, and the growth of the state in the 1930s also led to a weakened control over the production of producers.

10   Abel 1981, 1134.
11   Halliday 1987, 349.
12   Durkheim [1893] 1957.
13   Halliday 1987, 347–51.
14   Ibid., 353, 361. For a further development of this theme see Halliday 1989.
15   Abbott 1988.
16   Abel 1981, 1164. As we shall see, Harrington (1983) does outline a market monopoly model that comes closer to recognizing the importance of knowledge as a resource that affects lawyers' response to change. Nevertheless, Harrington retains the vocabulary of ideology.
17   Harrington 1983.
18   Ibid., 14.
19   Ibid., 15.
20   Halliday 1987, 350.
21   Ibid., 358.
22   Nonet and Selznick 1978; Halliday 1989, 359.
23   Halliday 1987, 358.
24   Nonet and Selznick 1978, 116.
25   Halliday 1987, 370.
26   Osiel (1990) makes a similar observation yet pushes the argument much further. He argues that the monopolistic impulse does not play a decisive role in determining the actions (and subsequent power, wealth, and status) of lawyers. In general, the legal profession's strong aristocratic residues often override market considerations and hence empirically refute the professional project perspective. See a convincing response to this sweeping argument in Abel (1994).
27   Abbott 1988, 103.
28   Larson 1989, 434.
29   Abbott 1988, 88.
30   American Bar Association 1936b, 200–225; For details see chap. 5.
31   Abbott 1988, 54.
32   Bourdieu, who writes on the tension between theoreticians and practitioners, compares the German and French tradition, in which the law is a "law of the professors," to the Anglo-American tradition, which is based "almost exclusively on

the decisions of courts and the rule of precedent" (1987, 822). Also see Reuschemeyer 1973.

33   Bourdieu 1987, 817.

34   Gordon 1984, 53.

35   Brint 1990, 375.

6   The Revolt of Academics

1   On this distinction see Horwitz 1977, 256–57.

2   On American jurisprudence as oscillating between a "nightmare" and a "noble
dream" see Hart 1983, 125.

3   Llewellyn 1934, 1.

4   The bill was one of a series of attempts to stabilize the problematic bituminous
coal industry by means of extensive regulation; Baker 1941.

5   New York Times, July 6, 1935, 2.

6   United States Law Week, July 9, 1935, 1.

7   Black 1936, 286; Sutherland 1936, 146. Also see United States Law Week, July 9, 1935.

8   Gilmore 1933, 103.

9   Beck 1933a, 689.

10   The case of Jerome Frank is probably the best example. Frank became one of the
central figures of legal realism upon the publication of his Law and the Modern
Mind in 1930. Frank was a distinguished graduate of Chicago Law School. He
specialized in corporate reorganization and practiced law in Chicago and then a
Wall Street law firm. He was an ardent supporter of reform and left corporate
practice in 1933 to join Roosevelt's administration, where he first became the
general counsel for the Agricultural Adjustment Administration and later a com-
missioner and eventually chairman of the Securities and Exchange Commission.
Frank, however, was in many respects sui generis. He was also a lecturer in the New
School for Social Research in New York and a visiting research associate at Yale
Law School. He had close ties with some of the most notable academics of his time
(e.g., Morris Cohen, Felix Frankfurter, and Thomas R. Powell) and often expressed disillusionment with corporate practice. Robert J. Glennon, who devoted
a book to Frank's impact on American law, cites a colleague who said that Frank
"was born to be either a professor or a judge, and not to be a practicing lawyer"
(1985, 20). In this respect, Frank was the exception that proved the rule as far as the
administration's inner circle of legal advisers was concerned. Also see Duxbury
1991.

11   This holds true for many nonelite law schools who focused on practical training for
the bar examinations, for some of the old guard at Harvard (e.g., Samuel Williston
and Joseph Beale), and for other concerned law professors like Walter Kennedy of
Fordham Law School ("perhaps the most widely respected Catholic legal scholar in
the country" [Purcell 1973, 165]), who warned that if the "rule of men" sponsored

by the realists were allowed to prevail "there would be no law to teach" (address to the Association of the Bar of the City of New York [Kennedy 1934, 538]), or James G. Rogers, the dean of Colorado Law School and the chairman of the American Bar Association Committee on Legal Education, who warned that legal realism would profoundly alter the profession and the law schools (Rogers 1934, 107). In general see Brown 1938; Kalman 1986.

12   American Liberty League 1936, 2–23.

13   Clark 1935a, 74–75. Charles E. Clark was the dean of Yale Law School, a reputed legal realist, and an enthusiastic supporter of New Deal reforms.

14   Ransom 1936d, 23; Beck 1933c, 49.

15   Nelles 1934, 1041.

16   Miller 1934, 350; Diggs 1933, 130; Beck 1933c, 49.

17   See White 1972; Twining 1973; Purcell 1973; Benditt 1978; Schlegel 1980; Summers 1982; Ackerman 1983; Hart 1983; Glennon 1985; Kalman 1986; Herget and Wallace 1987; Duxbury 1990, 1991; Urofsky 1991; Horwitz 1992; Nelson, Trubek, and Solomon 1992; Fisher, Horwitz, and Reed 1993.

18   Glennon 1985, 84. A number of observers made similar statements; see Auerbach 1976; Hunt 1978; Irons 1982; Lash 1988. Nonetheless, it seems to me that the relationship between legal realism and the New Deal has been too often described as a mere coincidence of *ideas* (e.g., White 1972) rather than as two interrelated forms of *practice* (but see Purcell 1973; Dezalay, Sarat and Silbey 1989; Duxbury 1991; Horwitz 1992).

19   Horwitz 1992, 185.

20   White (1949).

21   Pondering the nature and sources of law in 1909, John Chipman Gray wrote that legal rules "do not preexist the judicial decision: they do not exist eternally in heaven for all time, to be discovered by the judge in an act of *a priori* thinking . . . rather, they are made by judges" (cited in Benditt 1978, 6). On the pragmatism of Charles Pierce, William James, and John Dewey, see Mills 1966. For contemporary debates on pragmatism and law see Brint and Weaver 1991.

22   For a thorough analysis of the impact of the Free Law movement on legal realism and of the relations of Karl Llewellyn with German academic culture see Herget and Wallace 1987.

23   On the complex relations of Roscoe Pound with the realists see Hull 1987; Horwitz 1992.

24   Karl Llewellyn, who engaged Roscoe Pound in a public and much-celebrated debate about legal realism, denied that the realists shared more than a "method" (see Llewellyn 1930; 1931; Pound, 1931). While Llewellyn insisted that legal realism had neither masters "nor even over-mastering ideas," his official and whispered lists of members and recruits created a sense that a secret society of fellows did exist. Llewellyn produced a list of twenty legal scholars whom he considered legal realists: Joseph Bingham, Charles Clark, Walter Cook, Arthur Corbin, William

Douglas, Joseph Francis, Jerome Frank, Leon Green, Joseph Hutcheson, Samuel Klaus, Karl Llewellyn, Ernest Lorenzen, Underhill Moore, Herman Oliphant, Edwin Patterson, Thomas Powell, Max Radin, Wesley Sturges, Leon Tulin, Hessel Yntema. This list served a generation of scholars who studied legal realism and, as Horwitz observes, contributed to a misguided, if not distorted, picture of the realists. The legal historian N. E. H. Hull (1987) exposed additional lists that Llewellyn produced over the years. Thus, for example, persons like Felix Frankfurter, Milton Handler, Thurman Arnold, John Hanna, James Landis, and Robert Hale were mentioned on other, unpublished, lists.

25 Larson 1977, 66.
26 For a similar approach see Dezalay, Sarat, and Silbey 1989.
27 Brigham and Harrington 1989, 44. For a thorough inquiry of the intellectual roots of realism in the academic culture of the times see Purcell 1973.
28 Purcell 1973, 78.
29 Ibid.
30 Glennon 1985, 39. See also Kennedy 1980; Mensch 1990; Horwitz 1992.
31 Sutherland 1967, 175.
32 On the decline of apprenticeship in general and its impact on the American legal profession and legal education see Abel 1989a.
33 Abel 1981; Stevens 1983.
34 Stevens 1983, 101. On rising standards as a form of exclusion, mainly directed against immigrants, see Auerbach 1976.
35 Williston 1933, 609.
36 Auerbach writes, "Law teachers inhabited two worlds but were marginal to both" (1976, 79). Larson also draws on this observation (1977, 172).
37 On the concept of "natural artifice" and the presence of the "stranger" as a condition for its dissolution, see Tester (1992, 32–43), who integrates the ideas of Agnes Heller and Georg Simmel.
38 Purcell 1973, 78.
39 Auerbach 1976, 81.
40 Cited in Brown 1938, 86, and in Stevens 1983, 163.
41 Cowan 1956, 92.
42 Hart 1983, 131. The skepticism of the realists is often the sole criterion used to describe them. Cortner, for example, writes, "I use the term generally to include those who agreed that there was no immutable, transcendental body of law which the judge 'discovered' in rendering a decision and that judges made law by choosing between policy alternatives in deciding cases. Thus, I use the term in its most general sense and do not attempt what the 'realists' themselves cannot do, that is, to determine who is and who is not really a realist" (1964, 34).
43 Cited in Cowan 1956, 159. However, Llewellyn himself produced various lists of "members"; see n. 23 above.
44 Hull (1990) considers Roscoe Pound's 1906 address to the American Bar Associa-

tion to be a historic turning point. In his address as the dean of Nebraska Law School, Pound expressed the sentiment that the declaratory theory of law had lost its vigor under the accumulation of contradictory data. There is little doubt, however, that what Pound revealed in public had already been experienced by practitioners for quite some time.

45 Hull 1990, 68.

46 Ibid., 74. On Elihu Root see Excursus I and n. 47 below.

47 Hull 1990, 74–77. Hull mentions some "notable practitioners" who were involved: George Wickersham, Henry Taft, Charles Burlingham, and Joseph Chamberlain. Michael Belknap, reporting on the history of the conservative American Judicature Society, adds further information. He describes Elihu Root as one who "had been able to get the [Carnegie] corporation to fund virtually any project he favored" (1992, 90). Carnegie added another one million dollars to the American Law Institute in 1933 on top of the one million that it had contributed in 1923. Newton D. Baker (see excursus I) had also been a trustee of the corporation. On the institutional and personal links between the American Judicature Society and the American Law Institute see Belknap 1992.

48 Williston 1933, 599, 606.

49 Arnold 1935a, 731. Also see Yntema 1934, 207.

50 Wickersham 1933, 328.

51 Cole 1983, 114–15.

52 Frank 1930, 4–11. Frank, in particular, was a leading skeptic, moving from "mere" rule skepticism to fact skepticism; see Duxbury 1991.

53 Llewellyn 1931, 1233–1238. On Karl Llewellyn, the "official" leader of legal realism, see Twining 1973.

54 Arnold 1935, 730. Thurman Wesley Arnold was one of the more extraordinary persons in this group of realist scholars who joined the administration. Arnold had been a law professor at Yale Law School and was first recruited to the administration by Jerome Frank, who brought him to the Agricultural Adjustment Administration. Arnold later headed the Anti-trust Division of the Justice Department, was appointed to the U.S. Circuit Court of Appeals for the District of Columbia, and left the administration to found the law firm of Arnold, Fortas & Porter. Arnold had strong ties to other realist lawyers in the service of the New Deal: Fred Rodell, Wesley Sturges (future dean at Yale), William O. Douglas, Abe Fortas (a future law partner), and Walton Hamilton. He was also close to Jerome Frank and corresponded with Felix Frankfurter. Arnold apparently impressed Justice Louis Brandeis, who wrote Frankfurter that "Arnold did pretty well in his first case. Tell me about him" (Urofsky and Levy 1992, 590). Hawley (1966) provides an interesting account of Arnold as one who underwent an "apparent metamorphosis from cynical critic to militant trustbuster" (as he joined the Anti-trust Division): "In an age of colorful personalities he took a back seat to no one. A large man, somewhat paunchy, generally attired in a disheveled costume, and given to

incessant talking in a loud voice, the new antitrust chief was at first regarded as something of a joke, another Marx brother who had strayed into the government by mistake" (1966, 423). Arnold wrote numerous articles in defense of New Deal policies (see previous chapters) and two important books: *Symbols of Government* (1935) and *The Folklore of Capitalism* (1937). Like Frank, his writing provides a thorough critique of the distinction between will and reason in jurisprudential thought.

55   See Herget and Wallace, who argue that the realist "nihilistic attitude" had been finally "exhausted" (1987, 435), and White, who maintains that "as the Axis powers came to pose a threat to America that had distinct moral overtones, the position of the Realists became a source of acute embarrassment" (1972, 1026). Also see Glennon (1985, 58), who describes the critiques of realism on these grounds by Lon Fuller and Jerome Hall. In general, see Purcell (1973), who describes the implications of the realists' relativism for the moral crisis of democratic theory.

56   Horwitz 1992; chap. 7.

57   Holmes 1897, 457; 461.

58   Jerome Frank, for example, characterized lawyers and judges as a "profession of rationalizers" (cited in Glennon 1985, 44).

59   Pound 1934, 525.

60   This was a point that Herman Kantorowicz, a sympathizer and often a harsh critic of the amoral tendencies of legal realism, refused to accept. He could agree with the realists that judicial discretion was an important source of legal production, but refused to consider it proof of a lack of given rules. Judicial discretion, he said, was not opposed to rules but rather to "an intuitive way of finding rules" (1934, 1240, 1244).

61   See Mills 1966, 110.

62   Arnold 1935; Nelles 1935.

63   For the roots of this position in pragmatist thought, see John Fiske in Mills 1966, 96.

64   Robinson 1934, 235, 263.

65   Cohen 1933, 158 (reprint from Cohen's 1933 *Ethical Systems and Legal Ideas*). In another article Cohen described the distinction between the "Is" and the "Ought" as a healthy reaction to the confusing Blackstonian conception of law. Blackstone, he argued, tried to blend Hobbes's definition of law as a body of commands with Coke's definition of law as the perfection of reason; these, he said, were two inconsistent ideas (1935, 809, 835–36).

66   Frank 1933b, 725.

67   Ibid., 726; 1933c; Llewellyn 1935, 641; McLaughlin 1934, 144; Sunderland 1931, 97. In general see Sutherland 1967, 284; Stevens 1983; Schlegel 1985; Kalman 1986, 67. Brown cites Albert Harno, the dean of the University of Illinois Law School: "The case method tends to train artisans of the law, but not architects of our institutions" (1938, 73).

68   Arnold 1935a, 729; 752.
69   Kalman 1986, 75. Also see Handler 1934a, 133; Hanna 1931, 151. In general see Benditt
     1978; Brown 1938. It also became fashionable to cooperate with scholars from other
     disciplines (e.g., economists, psychologists, political scientists, and business ad-
     ministration and management experts) in writing on various legal issues.
70   Twining 1973; Hunt 1978; Hart 1983.
71   Brigham and Harrington 1989, 46.
72   Bourdieu 1977, 164.
73   Handler 1934b, 138.
74   Cohen 1935, 812.
75   Arnold 1934, 913–47.
76   Arnold 1935a.
77   See chap. 4.
78   Stone 1934, 7.
79   See Auerbach (1976, 162) on the general sentiment among legal realists that the
     bar's elite betrayed their public responsibilities.
80   Laski 1935, 676; Robinson 1934, 235.
81   Ransom 1936c.
82   Bourdieu 1977, 169 (I use Bourdieu's terminology without recourse to the substan-
     tive areas of critique and inquiry to which he applied them). Doxa, in the terminol-
     ogy of Bourdieu, is the "universe of the undiscussed": a "quasi-perfect correspon-
     dence between the objective order and the subjective principles of organization." In
     such a state of affairs, a given order appears self-evident. Under certain circum-
     stances, the doxa is challenged, and the defense of the given order has to be
     assumed by means of referring to "orthodoxy," a weaker form of justification and
     explanation to the order of things. It is here that we enter a universe of discourse in
     which orthodoxy is countered by the principle of "heresy": a competing possible
     (1977, 159–71).
83   Horwitz 1992, 209.
84   The best examples are perhaps Thurman Arnold and Jerome Frank. Arnold, on
     the one hand, established a reputation as one who reduced "the most sacred
     economic and moral beliefs to witty absurdities," and, on the other hand, acted in
     his governmental roles on the premise that duty "overrode inner convictions"
     (Hawley 1966, 423). Frank, on his part, deconstructed the most sacred legal princi-
     ples on the one hand and became one of the administration's most trusted admin-
     istrators on the other.
85   Oliphant 1928.
86   Parkinson and McComb 1935, 293.
87   Yntema 1934, 207.
88   Landis 1934, 124.
89   Landis 1930, 893.
90   Handler 1934a, 138.

91   Irons 1982, 296; See chap. 4 for a more elaborate discussion on the realists' attitude towards the administrative process.

92   Kocourek 1935, 469. For a reading of this stance as a "naive enthusiasm for government" and a failed yet "salutary effort to refocus legal scholarship from the common law to the emergent world of statute-dominated law," see Posner 1991, 33.

93   Hunt 1978, 40–41.

94   Frank 1933a, 101; Frank 1934, 12412; Also see Jackson 1941; Glennon 1985; Duxbury 1991.

95   Glennon 1985, 220, n. 78. The intention to add such a preface may also have reflected Frank's desire to respond to Frankfurter's criticism that he failed to articulate "any substantive program of reform" (ibid., 49). Glennon also discusses a series of letters exchanged between Frankfurter and Frank on the relationship between legal realism and the New Deal (ibid., 87).

96   Auerbach 1976; Irons 1982; Ackerman 1983; Kalman 1986.

97   Dezalay, Sarat, and Silbey 1989, 11–12.

98   An incomplete list of law professors who were engaged in such activities from their academic posts includes Fred Rodell (Harvard), Francis Sayre (Harvard), Karl Llewellyn (Columbia), Robert Hale (Columbia), Walter E. Dodd (Harvard), Walter W. Cook (Johns Hopkins), Walter Nelles (Yale), Charles E. Clark (Yale), Felix Frankfurter (Harvard), Hessel Yntema (Johns Hopkins), Max Radin (Berkeley), and Thomas R. Powell (Harvard).

99   An incomplete list of law professors who assumed governmental positions includes William O. Douglas (Yale) in the Securities and Exchange Commission, James M. Landis (Harvard) in the Securities and Exchange Commission, Thurman Arnold (Yale) in the Agricultural Adjustment Administration and later in the Justice Department's Anti-trust Division, Jerome Frank (Yale) in the Agricultural Adjustment Administration, John Dickinson (University of Pennsylvania) as assistant attorney general, Calvert Magruder (Harvard) in the National Labor Relations Board, Lloyd Garrison (Wisconsin) in the National Labor Relations Board, Howard Marshall (Yale) in the Petroleum Administrative Board, Milton Handler (Columbia) in the National Labor Board, Walton Hamilton (Yale) in the National Recovery Administration, Harry Shulman (Yale) in the Railway Retirement Board, Abe Fortas (Yale) in the Agricultural Adjustment Administration, Felix Cohen (New School of Social Research) in the Department of the Interior, Wesley Sturges (Yale) in the Agricultural Adjustment Board, Herman Oliphant (Johns Hopkins) in the Department of Treasury, and Ruswell Magill (Columbia) as assistant secretary of the treasury on taxation. See: Schlezinger 1958; Hawley 1966; Irons 1982; Kalman 1986.

100   *Fortune Magazine*, Jan. 1936, 63. On Frankfurter's role in placing lawyers and orchestrating drafting projects, see Irons 1982; Auerbach 1976. Both Glennon (1985, 72) and Urofsky (1991, 38) describe Frankfurter at the time as a "one man employment agency."

101 Stevens 1983, 134. I owe the term "contributory relations" to Terrance Halliday (1987).

102 Dean Albert Harno, cited in Brown 1938, 73; Yntema 1934, 207; see also Cohen 1935.

103 Dickinson 1935b, 55.

104 Clark 1933, 18.

105 Green 1934, 1032.

106 Frankfurter 1936, 61.

107 Dworkin 1991, 368. Bealism, named after Joseph Beale of Harvard, has been contrasted to realism, which, arguably, represented the other pole on jurisprudential thought.

108 Ibid.

109 Grey 1990, 590 (cited in Rorty 1991, 89).

110 Fish 1991, 58.

111 Horwitz analyzes the "double gesture" of the realists' reliance on behavioral and positivist social sciences as a movement that "ultimately dulled the critical edge" of legal realism (1992, 210). Horwitz suggests that the positivism of the realists loaded the Is with normative content, thereby leading to a justification of the status quo as "description . . . privileged over prescription" (1992, 211). This view seems to hold true as far as the inward-looking posture of realist legal science had been concerned, but I am not convinced that it explains the decline of realism as an active policymaking agenda (on the distinction between the two faces of the realist constructive project see nn. 84 and 85 above).

112 See Derber, Schwartz, and Magrass 1990 for a discussion of such politics in terms of a "new class" theory.

113 Hunt 1978; Rorty 1991; also see Cotterell (1987), who treats legal realism as "lawyers' law." On the enduring intellectual influence of legal realism, especially on the critical legal studies movement and some currents of thought in the sociology of law, see Hunt 1978; Dezalay et al. 1989; Kairys 1990.

114 Klare 1978; Summers 1982; Ackerman 1983; Posner 1991; Feldman 1991; Horwitz 1992.

7 Lawyers as Servants of Power

1 Halliday 1983, 326. This early literature includes the work of Durkheim [1893] 1957; Marshall 1939; Carr-Saunders and Wilson 1933.

2 Johnson 1972; Larson 1977.

3 Larson 1977, 243, 229.

4 Ibid., 169.

5 Ibid., 172.

6 Domhoff 1970; Radosh 1972; Weinstein 1968.

7 Skocpol 1980. For the "official" theoretical version of this approach, see Miliband 1969.

8   Skocpol 1980.

9   Glennon 1985, 77; Hawley 1966, 423; Auerbach 1976, 171.

10 Kalman 1986, 93–97.

11 This approach seems to be the one currently advocated in Domhoff 1990.

12 Manza 1991, 85.

13 Poulantzas 1973; Block 1977. For a sophisticated class-centered analysis of two New Deal administrative agencies, see Stryker 1990.

14 Skocpol 1980; Skocpol, Reuschemeyer, and Evans 1985.

15 Block 1977, 25.

16 Ibid., 15. The Poulantzian theory posits that the ability of the state to contribute to the reproduction of capitalist relations of production in advanced industrial societies depends on its relative autonomy—on the real separation between capitalists on the one hand and legal and political institutions on the other. In this model the state is treated as a complex of administrative and bureaucratic apparatuses that allows for the emergence of a new breed of experts, technocrats, and civil servants who do not answer directly to concrete capitalist demands and who develop their own agendas and working procedures, often in the guise of science. While Skocpol treats Poulantzas and Block as if they articulated two distinct approaches, the similarities and continuities between them are greater than Skocpol is willing to admit. The main disagreement between the two revolves around the Poulantzian notion of relative autonomy. Block argues that the theoretical implication of positing the state as relatively autonomous is misleading because it assumes that "the ruling class will respond effectively to the state's abuse of that autonomy" (1977, 9). Marxists, Block argues, should not employ a silent assumption that there is a well-organized capitalist class that is able to impose its collective will upon the state when things go wrong. There is no fundamental difference between Block and Poulantzas insofar as both agree that the state is not directly controlled by capitalists and, moreover, that state managers pursue their own interests. Block's reluctance to invoke the notion of relative autonomy is a result of his own particular way of reading the notion to imply the existence of an organized capitalist class. In fact, one does not have to read the concept of relative autonomy in this particular way. The autonomy of the state may be considered relative simply because state managers are objectively constrained in their actions in the very way that Block describes. The debate between Block and Poulantzas, therefore, is to a considerable extent an internal terminological debate between two structural Marxists.

17 Block 1977, 26.

18 Skocpol does not accept Block's assertion that working-class pressure contributed to the state's ability to legislate prolabor measures. Referring to the strike wave of early 1934, Skocpol argues that "it cannot be plausibly argued that these strikes directly produced the Wagner Act of 1935" because they only led to Public Resolution 44, "a measure cautiously designed to offend as little as possible major industrialists and conservative politicians." Further, she shows that following the passage

of the resolution the number of strikes fell off significantly (1980, 187). Indeed, several blows to the labor provisions of the NIRA and the administrative jurisdiction of the National Labor Board, by both the courts and the administration, brought about a growing wave of labor protests. Yet the immediate result of this wave of strikes was not the passage of Public Resolution 44, as Skocpol argues. Rather, it was the labor disputes bill, which Senator Wagner introduced to Congress in February 1934, five months before Resolution 44 was passed as an interim measure. This early Wagner bill met the approval of the Senate Committee on Education and Labor in May, 1934, and, most important, the bill was essentially identical to the Wagner Act of 1935. Thus, it was early 1934, and not 1935, when the idea of a powerful labor board came into being (Cortner 1964, 62). Further, the fact that Skocpol could register a decline in the number of strikes following the passage of Public Resolution 44 is not very meaningful. William Green, for example, the president of the A.F. of L., convinced the steel unionists to agree to a National Steel Labor Relations Board under the aegis of Public Resolution 44 and to suspend their threatened strikes. The point is, however, that Public Resolution 44 was conceived as a temporary measure and did not prevent the ongoing efforts of labor and its friends in Congress to pass a more comprehensive bill. Given that an earlier version of Wagner's bill had been circulating in the halls of Congress since early 1934, Skocpol's critique of Block does not hold. In fact, Skocpol admits that the whole period leading to the Wagner Act of 1935 had been marked by strong rhetorical class conflict and that Block's model seems to fit the general developments. It is due to her own theoretical focus that Skocpol chooses to focus on the role played by "independent" politicians.

19   Skocpol 1980, 176.

20   Domhoff 1990; Allen 1991.

21   This does not mean that the idea of law's autonomy does not have tangible implications. This was a lesson that President Roosevelt learned once he tried to pack the Court. The court-packing plan drew an uproar of protest even from devoted New Dealers and reminded the administration that it had to respect the symbolic significance of law's autonomy.

22   Luhmann 1988.

23   Fish 1991, 69.

24   Stinchcombe 1991.

25   Reuschemeyer 1973; 1989.

26   Reuschemeyer 1989, 306–7.

27   For an application of Weber's distinction between formally rational and substantively rational law to the American case, see Shamir 1993.

28   See Larson 1977, 169.

29   Horwitz 1977, 254.

30   Mensch 1990, 20.

31   Larson 1977, 169.

32   For a different type of correspondence between legal and economic laissez-faire, see Verkuil 1978.

33   McFarland 1934, 620.

34   Brigham and Harrington 1989.

35   This account of the rise of the realists' critical agenda is different from the one suggested by Szelenyi and Martin (1989). Szelenyi and Martin synthesize Larson's treatment of lawyers as servants of power with Gouldner's "new class" predictions and argue that professionals become "radical" under conditions of "deprofessionalization." My account shows that the threat of deprofessionalization led corporate lawyers to vehemently defend their prerogatives, and that the realists' revolt had to do with alienation within the legal field.

36   Gouldner 1979, 86.

37   The *political* decline of realism by no way suggests that the realist critical posture simply disappeared. There is little doubt that legal realism infused legal thinking with new insights and that the critical legacy of the realists is carried out by radical scholars in the critical legal studies movement and the sociolegal community. The point is, however, that this critical and subversive posture is again the domain of intellectuals, free from representaiton functions and, therefore, without a significant impact on state policies.

Bibliography I: General Sources

Abel, Richard L. 1981. Toward a Political Economy of Lawyers. *Wisconsin Law Review* 5:1117–1187.

———. 1989a. *American Lawyers*. New York: Oxford University Press.

———. 1989b. Comparative Sociology of the Legal Profession. In *Lawyers in Society: Comparative Theories*, edited by R. L. Abel and P. S. C. Lewis. Berkeley: University of California Press.

———. 1994. Revisioning Lawyers. Unpublished manuscript.

Abbott, Andrew. 1988. *The System of Professions: An Essay on the Division of Expert Labor*. Chicago: University of Chicago Press.

Ackerman, Bruce. 1983. *Reconstructing American Law*. Cambridge: Harvard University Press.

Allen, Michael P. 1991. Capitalist Response to State Intervention: Theories of the State and Political Finance in the New Deal. *American Sociological Review* 56 (Oct.): 679–89.

Alsop, Joseph, and Turner Catledge. 1938. *The 168 Days*. New York: Doubleday.

Arthurs, H. W. 1985. *"Without the Law": Administrative Justice and Legal Pluralism in Nineteenth-Century England*. Toronto: University of Toronto Press.

Auerbach, Jerold S. 1976. *Unequal Justice*. London: Oxford University Press.

Baker, Ralph H. 1941. *The National Bituminous Coal Commission*. Johns Hopkins University Studies in History and Political Science, no. 59. Baltimore: Johns Hopkins University Press.

Barber, Bernard. 1963. Some Problems in the Sociology of the Professions. *Daedalus* 92:669–88.

Belknap, Michael R. 1992. *To Improve the Administration of Justice: A History of the American Judicature Society*. Washington: American Judicature Society.

Benditt, Theodore M. 1978. *Law as Rule and Principle*. Stanford: Stanford University Press.

Block, Fred. 1977. The Ruling Class Does Not Rule: Notes on the Marxist Theory of the State. *Socialist Review* 33:6–27.

Botein, Stephen. 1983. "What Shall We Meet Afterwards in Heaven": Judgeship as a Symbol for Modern American Lawyers. In *Professions and Professional Ideologies in*

America, edited by Gerald L. Geison, 49–69. Chapel Hill: University of North Carolina Press.

Bourdieu, Pierre. 1977. *Outline of a Theory of Practice.* Cambridge: Cambridge University Press.

———. 1987. The Force of Law: Toward a Sociology of the Juridical Field. *Hastings Law Journal* 38:814–53.

Breslau, Daniel. 1990. The Scientific Appropriation of Social Research. *Theory and Society* 19:417–46.

Brigham, John, and Christine B. Harrington. 1989. Realism and Its Consequences: An Inquiry into Contemporary Sociological Research. *International Journal of the Sociology of Law* 17:41–62.

Brint, Michael, and William Weaver, eds. 1991. *Pragmatism in Law and Society.* Boulder: Westview Press.

Brint, Steven. 1990. Rethinking the Policy Influence of Experts: From General Characterizations to Analysis of Variation. *Sociological Forum* 5:361–85.

Brown, Esther L. 1938. *Lawyers and the Promotion of Justice.* New York: Russell Sage.

Cain, Maureen. 1979. The General Practice Lawyer and the Client: Towards a Radical Conception. *International Journal of the Sociology of Law* 7:331–54.

Calabresi, Guido. 1982. *A Common Law for the Age of Statutes.* Cambridge: Harvard University Press.

Carlin, Jerome E. 1962. *Lawyers on Their Own.* New Brunswick: Rutgers University Press.

Carr-Saunders, A. M., and P. A. Wilson. 1933. *The Professions.* Oxford: Clarendon Press.

Cole, Stephen. 1983. The Hierarchy of the Sciences? *American Journal of Sociology* 89:111–39.

Cortner, Richard C. 1964. *The Wagner Act Cases.* Knoxville: University of Tennessee Press.

Cotterell, Roger. 1987. Power, Property and the Law of Trust: A Partial Agenda for Critical Legal Scholarship. In *Critical Legal Studies*, edited by P. Fitzpatrick and Alan Hunt. London: Blackwell.

Cowan, Thomas A. 1956. *The American Jurisprudence Reader.* New York: Oceana Publications.

Department of Justice. 1941. *Final Report of the Attorney General's Committee on Administrative Procedure.* Washington: Government Printing Office, 1941.

Derber, Charles, William A. Schwartz, and Yale Magrass. 1990. *Power in the Highest Degree: Professionals and the Rise of a New Mandarin Order.* New York: Oxford University Press.

Dezalay, Yves, Austin Sarat, and Susan Silbey. 1989. From Dissident Challenge to Meritocratic Knowledge: Elements for a Social History of American Legal Sociology. Unpublished manuscript.

Domhoff, William G. 1970. *The Higher Circles: The Governing Class in America.* New York: Vintage.

Durkheim, Emile. [1893] 1957. *Professional Ethics and Civic Responsibility.* London: Routledge and Kegan Paul.

Duxbury, Neil. 1990. Some Radicalism About Realism? Thurman Arnold and the Politics of Modern Jurisprudence. *Oxford Journal of Legal Studies* 10:11–41.

———. 1991. Jerome Frank and the Legacy of Legal Realism. *Journal of Law and Society* 18:175–205.

Dworkin, Ronald. 1991. Pragmatism, Right Answers, and True Banality. In *Pragmatism in Law and Society*, edited by Michael Brint and William Weaver. Boulder: Westview Press.

Ernst, Daniel. 1988. Lawyers' Ideals and Labor Relations in the 1920's: The Case of Walter Gordon Merritt. Legal History Program, Institute for Legal Studies, Working Papers Series 2 (May): University of Wisconsin-Madison.

Eulau, Heinz and John D. Sprague. 1964. *Lawyers in Politics*. Indianapolis: Bobbs-Merrill.

Feldman, Stephen M. 1991. An Interpretation of Max Weber's Theory of Law: Metaphysics, Economics, and the Iron Cage of Constitutional Law. *Law and Social Inquiry* 16 (spring):205–48.

Fish, Stanley. 1991. Almost Pragmatism: The Jurisprudence of Richard Posner, Richard Rorty, and Ronald Dworkin. In *Pragmatism in Law and Society*, edited by Michael Brint and William Weaver. Boulder: Westview Press.

Fisher, William W., Morton Horwitz, and Thomas A. Reed, eds. 1993. *American Legal Realism*. New York: Oxford University Press.

Foucault, Michel. 1972. The Discourse on Language. In *The Archaeology of Knowledge*. New York: Pantheon.

Freidson, Eliot. 1983. The Theory of Professions: State of the Art. In *The Sociology of Professions: Lawyers, Doctors and Others*, edited by R. Dingwell and P. Lewis. New York: St. Martin's Press.

———. 1986. *Professional Powers: A Study of the Institutionalization of Formal Knowledge*. Chicago: University of Chicago Press.

Friedman, Lawrence M. 1989. Lawyers in Cross-Cultural Perspective. In *Lawyers in Society: Comparative Theories*, edited by R. L. Abel and P. S. C. Lewis. Berkeley: University of California Press.

Galanter, Marc. 1974. Why the "Haves" Come Out Ahead: Speculations on the Limits of Legal Change. *Law and Society Review* 9 (fall):95–160.

———. 1983. Mega-Law and Mega-Lawyering in the Contemporary United States. In *The Sociology of Professions: Lawyers, Doctors and Others*, edited by R. Dingwell and P. Lewis. London: Macmillan.

Gay, Thomas B. 1971. *The Hunton Williams Firm and Its Predecessors, 1877–1954*. Richmond: privately printed.

Glennon, Robert J. 1985. *The Iconoclast as Reformer: Jerome Frank's Impact on American Law*. Ithaca and London: Cornell University Press.

Goode, William J. 1957. Community within a Community: The Professions. *American Sociological Review* 22 (Apr.):194–200.

Gordon, Robert W. 1984. "The Ideal and the Actual in the Law": Fantasies and Practices of New York City Lawyers, 1870–1910. In *The New High Priests: Lawyers in Post-Civil War America*, edited by Gerard W. Gawalt. London: Greenwood Press.

Gouldner, Alvin. 1979. *The Future of Intellectuals and the Rise of the New Class*. New York: Seabury Press.

Gramsci, Antonio. [1929–35] 1971. *Selections from the Prison Notebooks*. New York: International Publishres.

Grey, Thomas. 1990. Hear the Other Side: Wallace Stevens and Pragmatist Legal Theory. *Southern California Law Practice* 63:1590.

Halliday, Terence C. 1983. Professions, Class and Capitalism. *European Journal of Sociology* 24:321–46.

———. 1987. *Beyond Monopoly: Lawyers, State Crises, and Professional Empowerment.* Chicago: University of Chicago Press.

———. 1989. Legal Professions and Politics: Neocorporatist Variations on the Pluralist Theme of Liberal Democracies. In *Lawyers in Society: Comparative Theories*, edited by R. L. Abel and P. S. C. Lewis. Berkeley: University of California Press.

Harbaugh, William H. 1973. *Lawyers' Lawyer: The Life of John W. Davis.* New York: Oxford University Press.

Harrington, Christine B. 1983. The Political Economy of Administrative Law Practice. Paper presented at the Annual Meeting of the Law and Society Association, June 2–5, Denver, Colo.

Hart, H. L. A. 1983. *Essays in Jurisprudence and Philosophy.* Oxford: Clarendon Press.

Hawley, Ellis w. 1966. *The New Deal and the Problem of Monopoly.* Princeton: Princeton University Press.

Heinz, John P. 1983. The Power of Lawyers. *Georgia Law Review* 17 (summer):891–911.

Heinz, John P., and Edward O. Laumann. 1982. *Chicago Lawyers: The Social Structure of the Bar.* Chicago: American Bar Foundation.

Herget, J., and S. Wallace. 1987. The German Free Law Movement as the Source of American Legal Realism. *Virginia Law Review* 73 (Mar.):399–455.

Himmelberg, Robert F. 1976. *The Origins of the National Recovery Administration.* New York: Fordham University Press.

Holmes, Oliver W. 1897. The Path of Law. *Harvard Law Review* 10:457.

Horwitz, Morton J. 1977. *The Transformation of American Law, 1780–1860.* Cambridge: Harvard University Press.

———. 1992. *The Transformation of American Law, 1870–1960.* New York: Oxford University Press.

Hull, N. E. H. 1987. Some Realism about the Llewellyn-Pound Exchange over Realism: The Newly Uncovered Private Correspondence, 1927–1931. *Wisconsin Law Review* 6:921–69.

———. 1990. Restatement and Reform: A New Perspective on the Origins of the American Law Institute. *Law and History Review* 8 (spring):55–96.

Hunt, Alan. 1978. *The Sociological Movement in Law.* Philadelphia: Temple University Press.

Irons, Peter H. 1982. *The New Deal Lawyers.* Princeton: Princeton University Press.

Jackson, Robert H. 1941. *The Struggle for Judicial Supremacy.* New York: Vintage.

Jaffe, Louis L. 1954. *The Administrative Process.* New York: Prentice Hall.

Johnson, Terence J. 1972. *Professions and Power.* London: Macmillan.

Kairys, David. 1990. *The Politics of Law: A Progressive Critique.* New York: Pantheon.

Kalman, Laura. 1986. *Legal Realism at Yale, 1927–1960.* Chapel Hill: University of North Carolina Press.

Kennedy, Duncan. 1980. Toward an Historical Understanding of Legal Consciousness: The Case of Classical Legal Thought in America, 1850–1940. In *Research in Law and Sociology,* edited by S. Spitzer. Vol. 3. Greenwich: JAI Press.

Klare, Karl E. 1978. Judicial Deradicalization of the Wagner Act and the Origins of Model Legal Consciousness, 1937–1941. *Minnesota Law Review* 62:265–339.

Kritzer, Herbert M. 1991. Abel and the Professional Project: The Institutional Analysis of the Legal Profession. *Law and Social Inquiry* 16 (summer):529–52.

Larson, Magali S. 1977. *The Rise of Professionalism: A Sociological Analysis.* Berkeley: University of California Press.

———. 1989. The Changing Functions of Lawyers in the Liberal State: Reflections for Comparative Analysis. In *Lawyers in Society: Comparative Theories,* edited by R. L. Abel and P. S. C. Lewis. Berkeley: University of California Press.

Lash, Joseph P. 1988. *Dealers and Dreamers.* New York: Doubleday.

Leuchtenberg, William E. 1963. *FDR and the New Deal.* New York: Harper and Row.

———. 1969. Franklin Delano Roosevelt's Supreme Court "Packing" Plan. In *Essays on the New Deal,* edited by W. H. Droze, G. Wolfskill, and W. E. Leuchtenberg. Austin: University of Texas Press.

Lewis, Philip S. C. 1989. Comparison and Change in the Study of Legal Professions. In *Lawyers in Society: Comparative Theories,* edited by R. L. Abel and P. S. C. Lewis. Berkeley: University of California Press.

Lisagor, Nancy, and Frank Lipsius. 1988. *A Law unto Itself: The Untold Story of the Law Firm Sullivan and Cromwell.* New York: William Morrow.

Luhmann, Niklas. 1988. Closure and Openness: On Reality in the World of Law. In *Autopoietic Law: A New Approach to Law and Society,* edited by G. Teubner. Berlin: Walter de Gruyter.

Manza, Jeff. 1993. G. William Domhoff and the Political Sociology of the New Deal. *Berkeley Journal of Sociology* 38:77–91.

Marshall, T. H. 1939. The Recent History of Professionalism in Relation to Social Structure and Social Policy. *Canadian Journal of Economics and Political Science* 5:128–55.

Mensch, Elizabeth. 1990. The History of Mainstream Legal Thought. In *The Politics of Law: A Progressive Critique,* ed. David Kairys, 13–37. New York: Pantheon.

Miliband, Ralph. 1969. *The State in Capitalist Society.* New York: Basic Books.

Millerson, Geoffrey. 1964. *The Qualifying Associations.* London: Routledge and Kegan Paul.

Mills, Wright C. 1966. *Sociology and Pragmatism: The Higher Learning in America.* New York: Oxford University Press.

Minow, Martha. 1987. Interpreting Rights: An Essay for Robert Cover. *Yale Law Journal* 96:1860–1915.

Nelson, Robert L. 1985. Ideology, Practice, and Professional Autonomy: Social Values and Client Relationship in the Large Law Firm. *Stanford Law Review* 37:503–51.

———. 1988. *Partners with Power: The Social Transformation of the Large Law Firm.* Berkeley: University of California Press.

Nelson, Robert L., J. P. Heinz, E. O. Laumann, and R. H. Salisbury. 1988. Lawyers and the Structure of Influence in Washington. *Law and Society Review* 22:237–300.

Nelson, Robert L., D. Trubek, and R. L. Solomon, eds. 1992. *Lawyers' Ideals—Lawyers' Practices: Transformations in the American Legal System.* Ithaca: Cornell University Press.

Nonet, Philippe, and Philip Selznick. 1978. *Law and Society in Transition: Toward Responsive Law.* New York: Octagon.

Osiel, Mark J. 1990. Lawyers as Monopolists, Aristocrats, and Entrepreneurs. *Harvard Law Review* 103:2009–2966.

Parkin, Frank. 1979. *Marxism and Class Theory: A Bourgeois Critique.* New York: Columbia University Press.

Parsons, Talcott. 1964. A Sociologist Looks at the Legal Profession. In *Essays in Sociological Theory.* New York: Free Press.

———. 1968. Professions. *International Encyclopedia of the Social Sciences* 12:536–46. New York: Macmillan.

Pitkin, Hannah. 1967. *The Concept of Representation.* Berkeley: University of California Press.

Posner, Richard A. 1991. What Has Pragmatism to Offer Law? In *Pragmatism in Law and Society,* edited by Michael Brint and William Weaver. Boulder: Westview Press.

Poulantzas, Nicos. 1973. *Political Power and Social Classes.* London: New Left Books.

Powell, Michael. 1993. Professional Innovation: Corporate Lawyers and Private Lawmaking. *Law and Social Inquiry* 18, no. 3:423–52.

Purcell, Edward A. 1973. *The Crisis of Democratic Theory.* Kentucky: University Press of Kentucky.

Radosh, Ronald. 1972. The Myth of the New Deal. In *A History of Leviathan: Essays on the Rise of the Corporate State,* edited by R. Radosh and N. Rothbard. New York: Dutton.

Reuschemeyer, Dietrich. 1964. Doctors and Lawyers: A Comment on the Theory of Professions. *Canadian Review of Sociology and Anthropology* 1 (Feb.):17–30.

———. 1973. *Lawyers and Their Society: A Comparative Study of the Legal Profession in Germany and the United States.* Cambridge: Harvard University Press.

———. 1989. Comparing Legal Professions: A State-Centered Approach. In *Lawyers in Society: Comparative Theories,* edited by R. L. Abel and P. S. C. Lewis. Berkeley: University of California Press.

Rheinstein, Max. 1966. *On Law in Economy and Society.* Cambridge: Harvard University Press.

Richberg, Donald. 1954. *My Hero.* New York: Putnam's Sons.

Root, Elihu. 1916. Public Service by the Bar. *American Bar Association Journal* 2:736–50.

Rorty, Richard. 1991. The Banality of Pragmatism and the Poetry of Justice. In *Pragmatism in Law and Society*, edited by Michael Brint and William Weaver. Boulder: Westview Press.

Schlegel, John H. 1980. American Legal Realism and Empirical Social Science: The Singular Case of Underhill Moore. *Buffalo Law Review* 29:195.

Schlesinger, Arthur M. 1959. *The Coming of the New Deal.* Boston: Houghton Mifflin.

Shamir, Ronen. 1993. Formal and Substantive Rationality in American Law: A Weberian Perspective. *Social and Legal Studies* 2:45–72.

Skocpol, Theda. 1980. Political Response to Capitalist Crisis: Neo-Marxist Theories of the State and the Case of the New Deal. *Politics and Society* 10:155–201.

———. 1985. Bringing the State Back In: Strategies of Analysis in Current Research. In *Bringing the State Back In*, edited by P. Evans, D. Reuschemeyer, and T. Skocpol. Cambridge: Cambridge University Press.

Skowronek, Stephen. 1982. *Building a New American State: The Expansion of National Administrative Capacities, 1877–1920.* Cambridge: Cambridge University Press.

Smigel, Erwin O. 1969. *The Wall St. Lawyer.* Bloomington: Indiana University Press.

Stevens, Robert. 1983. *Law School.* Chapel Hill: University of North Carolina Press.

Stinchcombe, Arthur L. 1991. *An Essay on the Demand for Formality in Laws, Regulations, and Organizations.* Unpublished manuscript.

Stryker, Robin. 1990. Science, Class, and the Welfare State: A Class-Centered Functional Account. *American Journal of Sociology* 96 (Nov.):684–726.

Summers, Robert S. 1982. *Instrumentalism and American Legal Theory.* Ithaca: Cornell University Press.

Sutherland, Arthur E. 1967. *The Law at Harvard.* Cambridge: Harvard University Press.

Szelenyi, Ivan, and Bill Martin. 1988. The Three Waves of New Class Theories. *Theory and Society* 17:645–67.

———. 1989. The Legal Profession and the Rise and Fall of the New Class. In *Lawyers in Society: Comparative Theories*, edited by R. L. Abel and P. S. C. Lewis. Berkeley: University of California Press.

Terdiman, Richard. 1987. The Force of Law: Toward a Sociology of the Juridical Field (translator's introduction). *Hastings Law Journal* 38:814–53.

Tester, Keith. 1992. *Civil Society.* London: Routledge.

Trubek, David. 1972. Max Weber on Law and the Rise of Capitalism. *Wisconsin Law Review* 3:720–53.

Twining, William. 1973. *Karl Llewellyn and the Realist Movement.* University of Oklahoma Press.

Unger, Roberto M. 1983. *The Critical Legal Studies Movement.* Cambridge: Harvard University Press.

Urofsky, Melvin I. 1991. *Felix Frankfurter: Judicial Restraint and Individual Liberties.* Boston: Twayne Publishers.

Urofsky, Melvin I., and David W. Levy. 1992. *Half Brother, Half Son: The Letters of Louis D. Brandeis to Felix Frankfurter.* Norman and London: University of Oklahoma Press.

Vadney, Thomas E. 1970. *The Wayward Liberal: A Political Biography of Donald Richberg.* Kentucky: University Press of Kentucky.

Verkuil, Paul R. 1978. The Emerging Concept of Administrative Procedure. *Columbia Law Review* 78:258–329.

Weber, Max. 1978. *Economy and Society.* Berkeley: University of California Press.

Weinstein, James. 1968. *The Corporate Ideal in the Liberal State, 1900–1918.* Boston: Beacon Press.

White, Edward G. 1972. From Sociological Jurisprudence to Realism: Jurisprudence and Social Change in Early Twentieth-Century America. *Virginia Law Review* 58:999–1028.

White, Morton. 1949. *Social Thought in America: The Revolt Against Formalism.* New York: Viking.

Willensky, Harold L. 1964. The Professionalization of Everyone? *American Journal of Sociology* 70:137–58.

Wolfskill, George. 1962. *The Revolt of the Conservatives.* Boston: Houghton Mifflin.

Bibliography II: Selected Legal and Historical Sources

Legal Sources

American Bar Association. 1933a. Letter from Charles H. Davis to Clarence Martin, Aug. 10, 1933. *Proceedings of the Executive Committee* (Aug.): Exhibit O. Typescript.

———. 1933b. Letter from Rush C. Butler to Mrs. Ricker, the ABA's Executive Committee Secretary, Apr. 24, 1993. *Proceedings of the Executive Committee* (May): Exhibit F–I. Typescript.

———. 1933c. *General Sessions Proceedings* (Aug.):9–15. Typescript.

———. 1934a. Letter from Harry Covington to Earle Evans, Apr. 12, 1934. *Proceedings of the Executive Committee* (May): Exhibit B. Typescript.

———. 1934b. Letter from John O'Connor to Silas Strawn, Aug. 26, 1933. *Proceedings of the Executive Committee* (Jan.): Exhibit N. Typescript.

———. 1934c. *General Sessions Proceedings* (Aug.):178–92. Typescript.

———. 1934d. General Sessions Proceedings. *Reports of the American Bar Association* 59 (Aug.):153.

———. 1934e. *Proceedings of the Executive Committee* (Aug.):115–21, 298–310. Typescript.

———. 1935a. General Sessions Proceedings. *Reports of the American Bar Association* 60 (Aug.):149–94.

———. 1935b. *Judicial Section Proceedings* (July):78–120. Typescript.

———. 1935c. *Proceedings of the Executive Committee* (May):1–17, 30. Typescript.

———. 1936a. Letter from Evan H. Hammett to William Ransom, December 1935. *Proceedings of the Executive Committee* (Jan.):1–2. Typescript.

———. 1936b. General Sessions Proceedings. *Reports of the American Bar Association* 61 (Aug):200–225.

———. 1936c. *Minutes of the House of Delegates* (Aug.):84–92. Typescript.

———. 1936d. *Proceedings of the Executive Committee* (Jan.):1–68.

———. 1936e. *Proceedings of the Executive Committee* (Aug.):82–97; 120–201; 341–44. Typescript.

American Bar Association Journal. 1933a. A New Constitution for Industry. *American Bar Association Journal* 19 (June):314–51.

———. 1933b. Limiting Jurisdiction of the District Courts. *American Bar Association Journal* 19 (July):388.

———. 1933c. NIRA—My Code to Thee. *American Bar Association Journal* 19 (Dec.):737.

———. 1933d. The Law as a Public Profession. *American Bar Association Journal* 19 (July): 398.

———. 1934. Due Process and the Nebbia Case. *American Bar Association Journal* 20 (Apr.):225.

———. 1935a. Professional Ethics Committee Rules Organization and Offer of National Lawyers Committee Not Unethical—Opinion in Full. *American Bar Association Journal* 21 (Dec.):476.

———. 1935b. The NRA Decision. *American Bar Association Journal* 21 (July):430–31.

———. 1936a. Measures Restricting Powers of Federal Courts Disapproved. *American Bar Association Journal* 22 (Oct.):741–42.

———. 1936b. Special Committee to Report on Federal Legislation. *American Bar Association Journal* 22 (Mar.):148.

American Bar Association Resolutions Committee. 1936. Assembly Proceedings. *Reports of the American Bar Association* 61 (Aug.):134.

American Liberty League. 1935a. Extension of the NRA. *American Liberty League* Document no. 34 (May):1–12.

———. 1935b. Potato Control. *American Liberty League* Document no. 64 (Sept.):3–11.

———. 1935c. The Bituminous Coal Bill. *American Liberty League* Document no. 32 (Apr.):3–15.

———. 1935d. The Farmers' Home Bill. *American Liberty League* Document no. 36 (May): 3–10.

———. 1935e. The Holding Company Bill. *American Liberty League* Document no. 21 (Mar.):1–14.

———. 1935f. The Labor Relations Bill. *American Liberty League* Document no. 27 (Apr.): 1–11.

———. 1935g. The National Recovery Administration. *American Liberty League* Document no. 11 (Jan.):1–24.

———. 1935h. The National Labor Relations Act. *American Liberty League* Document no. 66 (Sept.):3–10.

———. 1935i. The Revised AAA Amendments. *American Liberty League* Document no. 45 (June):2–11.

———. 1936. Professors and the New Deal. *American Liberty League* Document no. 91 (Jan.):2–23.

Arnold, Thurman W. 1933. The New Deal Is Constitutional. *New Republic*, Nov. 15, 989–91.

———. 1934. Trial by Combat and the New Deal. *Harvard Law Review* 47 (Apr.):913–47.

———. 1935a. Apologia for Jurisprudence. *Yale Law Journal* 44 (Mar.):729–53.

———. 1935b. *Symbols of Government.* New Haven: Yale University Press.

———. 1937. *The Folklore of Capitalism.* New Haven: Yale University Press.

Association of American Law Schools. 1934. *Handbook of the Association of American Law Schools and Proceedings of the 32 Annual Meeting* (Dec.):154.

————. 1935. Symposium on "The Constitution and Social Progress." *Handbook of the Association of American Law Schools and Proceedings of the 32 Annual Meeting* (Dec.):43–77.

Association of the Bar of the City of New York. 1934. Annual Report of the Committee on Federal Legislation for 1933–34. *Yearbook of the Association of the Bar of the City of New York* (May):231–32.

————. 1936. Annual Report of the Committee on Federal Legislation for 1935–35. *Annual Meeting and Reports for 1935* (May):204–6.

Baker, Newton D. 1935. The Judiciary's Place in Our Democracy. *United States Law Week*, Feb. 26, 5.

Ballantine, Arthur. 1934. Amending The Federal Securities Act. *American Bar Association Journal* 20 (Feb.):85–87.

Beck, James. 1933a. Mr. Beck Speaks on Citizenship. *American Bar Association Journal* 19 (Dec.):689–70.

————. 1933b. The Future of the Constitution. *American Bar Association Journal* 19 (Sept.): 493–501.

————. 1933c. The NRA Is Unconstitutional. *Fortune Magazine*, Dec., 48.

————. 1934. *New York State Bar Association Yearbook*, 614–37.

————. 1935a. *American Bar Association General Sessions Proceedings* (Aug.):160–65.

————. 1935b. The Balance Wheel of the Constitution. *American Bar Association Judicial Section Proceedings* (July):23–25. Typescript.

————. 1935c. What Is the Constitution among Friends? *American Liberty League* Document no. 22 (Mar.):2–11.

Benton, John. 1934. Are the NRA Codes Valid as Regulations of State Commerce? *Public Utilities Fortnightly* 13:213–23.

Biddle, Francis. 1935. Collective Bargaining Under the Labor Board. *United States Law Week*, Feb. 12, 3.

Black, John D. 1936. Present Federal Legislative Tendencies. *Illinois State Bar Association Annual Report for 1935* (May):286–94.

Blair, Edwin F. 1935. Has the Supreme Court Doomed the New Deal? *Fortune Magazine*, Sept., 63.

Boudin, Louis B. 1935. The Supreme Court and Democracy. *Nation* 141, July 10, 40–42.

Bouve, Clement L. The Supreme Court, the Average Reader and Others. *Journal of the District of Columbia Bar Association* 9 (Feb.):9–21.

Brookings Institution. 1934. *The ABC of the NRA*. Washington: Brookings Institution.

Butler, Rush C. 1933. Assembly Proceedings. *Reports of the American Bar Association* 58 (Aug.):129–31.

————. 1934. Assembly Proceedings. *Reports of the American Bar Association* 59 (Aug.):99.

Caldwell, Louis G. 1933. Report of the Committee on Administrative Law. *Reports of the American Bar Association* 58 (Aug.):199.

————. 1935. Report of the Committee on Administrative Law. *Reports of the American Bar Association* 60 (Aug.):138–43.

Caulfield, Henry S. 1933. The Constitution and the Crisis. *Illinois State Bar Association Proceedings and Reports* (June):154–63.

Chamberlain, Joseph P. 1933. Report of the Committee on Noteworthy Changes in Statute Law. *American Bar Association General Sessions Proceedings* (Aug.):213–15.

Chandler, Henry P. 1936. The National Labor Relations Act. *American Bar Association Journal* 22 (Apr.):245.

Chenoweth, R. M., and C. L. Whitehead. 1934. Restriction of the Jurisdiction of the United States District Courts as to Contracts between the United States and Citizens. *Mississippi Law Journal* (Dec.):168–85.

Chicago Bar Association. 1936a. Report of the Committee on Federal Legislation. *Chicago Bar Record* 16 (Feb.):137–38.

———. 1936b. Results on Referendum on Supreme Court Limitation. *Chicago Bar Record* 16 (Mar.):170.

Clark, Charles E. 1933. Law Professor, What Now? *Handbook of the Association of American Law Schools and Proceedings of the 31 Annual Meeting* (Dec.):14–24.

———. 1934a. A Socialistic State under the Constitution? *Fortune Magazine*, Feb., 68.

———. 1934b. Individualism and the Constitution. *New York State Bar Association Annual Meeting and Reports for 1933* (Jan.):325–49.

———. 1934c. Legal Aspects of Legislation Underlying National Recovery Program. *American Bar Association Journal* 20 (May):269–72.

———. 1935a. *Handbook of the Association of American Law Schools and Proceedings of the 33 Annual Meeting* (Dec.):74–75.

———. 1935b. The Supreme Court and the N.R.A. *New Republic*, June 12, 120–22.

Cohen, Felix S. 1933. *Ethical Systems and Legal Ideas.* New York: Falcon Press.

———. 1935. Transcendental Nonsense and the Functional Approach. *Columbia Law Review* 35:809–49.

Cohen, Morris R. 1935. Fallacies about the Court. *Nation* 141, July 10, 39–40.

Colby, Bainbridge. 1933. Maryland State Bar Association Speech of Bainbridge Colby. *New York State Bar Association Bulletin* (Oct.):417–19.

Cross, James T. 1933. Legal Aspects Leading to Milk Control Law. *New York State Bar Association Bulletin* (May):211–23.

Cummings, Homer. 1933. Modern Tendencies and the Law. *American Bar Association Journal* 19 (Oct.):576–79.

———. 1936. The American Constitutional Method. *United States Law Review* 70 (Jan.):10–21.

Davis, John W. 1934. Fundamental Aspects of the New Deal from a Lawyer's Perspective. *United States Law Week*, Dec. 25, 3–4.

———. 1936. The Redistribution of Power. *New York State Bar Association Proceedings and Reports for 1935* (Jan.):245.

Day, L. B. 1935. The Independence of the Judiciary. *Proceedings of the Nebraska State Bar Association* (Dec.):60–68.

Dean, Arthur H. 1933. The Federal Securities Act: I. *Fortune Magazine*, Aug., 50.

Desvernine, Raoul. 1935. Human Rights and the Constitution. *American Liberty League Document* no. 35 (May):1–7.

Dickinson, John. 1933. The Major Issues Presented by the Industrial Recovery Act. *Columbia Law Review* 33 (Nov.):1095–1102.

———. 1935a. Quasi-Judicial Action as an Administrative Function. *Minutes of the Judicial Section of the American Bar Association* (July):78. Typescript.

———. 1935b. The Professor, the Practitioner, and the Constitution. *Handbook of the Association of American Law Schools and Proceedings of the 33 Annual Meeting* (Dec.):54–63.

———. 1936. States and the Nation. *Illinois State Bar Association Annual Report for 1936* (June):268–85.

Diggs, James. 1933. Should the Constitution of Oklahoma Be Amended, If So in What Respect. *Oklahoma State Bar Journal* (Oct.):127–32.

Dodd, Merrick E. 1934. How Not to Amend the Federal Securities Act—Fundamental Purpose Should Not Be Impaired. *American Bar Association Journal* 21 (Apr.):247–49.

———. 1935. Amending the Securities Act: The American Bar Association Committee's Proposals. *Yale Law Journal* 45 (Dec.):199–231.

Dodd, Walter F. 1936. Adjustment of the Constitution to New Needs. *American Bar Association Journal* 22 (Feb.):126–30.

Donworth, Charles T. 1933. A Review of the Securities Act of 1933. *Washington Law Review* (Sept.):61–69.

Douglas, William O., and George E. Bates. 1933. Stock Brokers as Agents and Dealers. *Yale Law Journal* 43 (Nov.):46–62.

Epstein, Henry. 1936. Address. *New York State Bar Association Proceedings and Reports for 1935* (Jan.):394–405.

Farnum, George R. 1934. The New Deal, the Constitution, and the Courts. *Law Society Journal* (Nov.):393–96.

———. 1935. Faith in the Court. *Law Society Journal* (Aug.):725–28.

Faville, F. F. 1935. The Great Contract. *Proceedings of the Nebraska State Bar Association* (Dec.):88–95.

Finkelstein, Maurice. 1933. The Dilemma of the Supreme Court. *Nation* 137, Oct. 18, 428–30.

Fletcher, R. V. 1934. Our Changing Constitution. *Illinois Bar Journal* (June):321–28.

Flexner, Bernard. 1934. The Fight on the Securities Act. *Atlantic*, Feb., 232–50.

Fortune Magazine. 1934. After the NRA—the NRA? June, 91.

Fox, Frank B. 1935 What About Administrative Tribunals? *American Bar Association Journal* 21 (June):376–78.

Fraenkel, Osmond K. 1935a. Five to Four Decisions of the Supreme Court. *United States Law Week*, July 2, 2.

———. 1935b. The Value of Judicial Review. *Nation* 141, July 10, 42–43.

Frank, Jerome. 1930. *Law and the Modern Mind.* New York: Brentano's.

———. 1933a. *Handbook of the American Association of Law Schools and Proceedings of the 31 Annual Meeting Meeting* (Dec.):100–108.

———. 1933b. What Constitutes a Good Legal Education? *American Bar Association Journal* 19 (Dec.):723–28.

———. 1933c. Why Not a Clinical Lawyer School? *University of Pennsylvania Law Review* 81:907–23.

———. 1934. Experimental Jurisprudence and the New Deal. *78 Congressional Record,* 12412–12414.

Frankfurter, Felix. 1933. The Federal Securities Act: II. *Fortune Magazine,* Aug., 80.

———. 1935. Address to the Association of American Law Schools. *Handbook of the Association of American Law Schools and Proceedings of the 33 Annual Meeting* (Dec.):90–96.

———. 1936. The Young Men Go to Washington. *Fortune Magazine,* Jan., 61.

Franklin, Mitchell, 1934. Administrative Law in the United States. *Tulane Law Review* 8 (June):483–506.

Fuchs, Ralph E. 1935. Collective Labor Agreements under Administrative Regulation of Employment. *Columbia Law Review* 135 (Apr.):493–518.

Garrison, Lloyd K. 1934. Results of the Wisconsin Bar Survey. *Handbook of the Association of American Law Schools and Proceedings of the 31 Annual Meeting* (Dec.):58–74.

Gifford, James P. 1933. Lawyers and the Depression. *Nation* 137, Aug. 30, 236–73.

Gilmore, E. A. 1933. What Price Recovery? *American Bar Association* Judicial Section Proceedings (Aug.):94–117. Typescript.

———. 1936. Constitutional Integrity—Changing Concepts. *Nebraska Law Bulletin* 14 (May):403–16.

Goodwin, John. 1936. Assembly Proceedings. *Reports of the American Bar Association* 61 (Aug.):221–25.

Green, Leon. 1934. The Law Professor, the Lawyers' Brain Trust. *American Law Schools Review* 7 (Apr.):1031–1035.

———. 1935. The Administrative Process. *American Bar Association Journal* 21 (Nov.): 708–12.

Griswold, Erwin. 1934. Government in Ignorance of the Law: A Plea for Better Publication of Executive Legislation. *Harvard Law Review* 48 (1934):198–215.

Grogan, William B. 1937. A Note on a Proposal to Establish a Federal Administrative Court. *District of Columbia Bar Association Journal* (Jan.):63–75.

Hanna, John. 1931. The Law School as a Function of the University. *North Carolina Law Review* 10 (Dec.):117–57.

Handler, Milton. 1933. The National Industrial Recovery Act. *American Bar Association Journal* 19 (Aug.):440.

———. 1934a. Analysis of Section 7-A of the National Industrial Recovery Act. *United States Law Week,* May 15, 4.

———. 1934b. *Handbook of the Association of American Law Schools and Proceedings of the 32 Annual Meeting* (Dec.):132–39.

Harvard Law Review. 1933. Some Legal Aspects of the National Industrial Recovery Act. *Harvard Law Review* 47 (Nov.):85–125.

Interim Report of the Committee on Administrative Law. 1935. *American Bar Association: Proceedings of the Executive Committee* (Jan.):Exhibit A 1–26 and Exhibit T 1–3. Typescript.

Interim Report of the Special Committee to Study Federal Legislation and Policies as Affecting the Rights and Liberties of American Citizens. 1935. *American Bar Association: Proceedings of the Executive Committee* (Jan.):14 and Exhibit Z. Typescript.

Isaacs, Nathan. 1933. The Securities Act and the Constitution. *Yale Law Journal* 43 (Nov.): 218–26.

Jackson, John G. 1934. Consolidation of Replies to Unauthorized Practice Questionnaire, with Introductory Note. *American Bar Association Journal* 20 (July):407–9.

Jackson, Robert. 1934. The Bar and the New Deal. *Handbook of the Association of American Law Schools and Proceedings of the 32 Annual Meeting* (Dec.):113–20.

Johnson, Sveinbojrn. 1936. The Fifty-Eight Lawyers. *United States Law Review* 70 (Jan.): 23–30.

Kantorowicz, Herman. 1934. Some Rationalism About Realism. *Yale Law Journal* 43: 1240–1253.

Kennedy, Walter B. 1934. The New Deal in the Law. *United States Law Review* 68 (Oct.): 533–39.

Kocourek, Albert. 1934. Project of an Institute on Legislative Science. *American Bar Association Journal* 20 (July):468–72.

Landis, James. 1930. Statutory Interpretation. *Harvard Law Review* 43 (Apr.):863–93.

———. 1934. *Handbook of the Association of American Law Schools and Proceedings of the 32 Annual Meeting* (Dec.):122–31.

———. 1934a. *Cases on Labor Law.* Chicago: Foundation Press.

———. 1938. *The Administrative Process.* New Haven: Yale University Press.

Lashly, Jacob. 1939. Administrative Law and the Bar. *Virginia Law Review* 25 (Apr.):641–68.

Laski, Harold. 1935. The Decline of the Professions. *Harper's Magazine,* Nov. 676–85.

Ledwith, John J. 1934. Guides to Constitutional Construction. *Proceedings of the Nebraska State Bar Association* (Dec.):76–88.

Llewellyn, Karl. 1930. A Realistic Jurisprudence: The Next Step. *Columbia Law Review* 30:431–65.

———. 1931. Some Realism about Realism. *Harvard Law Review* 44:1222–1259.

———. 1933. Where Do We Go from Here? *Handbook of the Association of American Law Schools and Proceedings of the 31 Annual Meeting* (Dec.):62–66.

———. 1934. The Constitution as an Institution. *Columbia Law Review* 34 (Jan.):1–40.

———. 1935. On What Is Wrong with So-Called Legal Education. *Columbia Law Review* 35 (May):651–78.

Loftin, Scott M. 1935. Maintaining the Independence of the Judiciary. *United States Law Week,* July 23, 6.

Manton, Martin T. 1933. A "New Deal" for Lawyers. *American Bar Association Journal* 19 (Oct.):596–600.

Martin, Clarence E. 1933a. Shall We Abolish Our Republican Form of Government? *American Bar Association Journal* 19 (Aug.):435–39.

———. 1933b. The Growing Impotency of the States. *American Bar Association Journal* 19 (Oct.):547–52.

———. 1934. Report of the President. *American Bar Association: Proceedings of the Executive Committee* (Jan.):Exhibit A 1–4. Typescript.

McCarren, Patrick A. 1933. The Growth of Federal Executive Power. *American Bar Association Journal* 19 (Oct.):587–91.

McFarland, Carl. 1934. Administrative Agencies in Government. *American Bar Association Journal* 20 (Oct.):612.

McGuire, O. R. 1933. Proposed Reforms in Judicial Reviews of Federal Administrative Action. *American Bar Association Journal* 19 (Aug.):471–74.

———. 1935. Labor Disputes and the Federal Government. *American Bar Association Journal* 21 (Apr.):239–42.

———. 1936a. Federal Administrative Court and Judicial Review. *American Bar Association Journal* 22 (July):492–96.

———. 1936b. Sailing Close to the Wind, or the Need for a Federal Administrative Court. *American Bar Association Journal* 22 (Dec.):855–59.

———. 1936c. The Proposed United States Administrative Court. *American Bar Association Journal* 22 (Mar.):197–202.

McLaughlin, James A. 1934. *Handbook of the Association of American Law Schools and Proceedings of the 32 Annual Meeting* (Dec.):144–52.

McNutt, Paul. 1934. *Reports of the American Bar Association* 59 (Aug.):229–31.

Merritt, Walter G. 1937. A Paper by Walter G. Merritt. *New York State Bar Association Annual Meeting and Reports for 1936* (Jan.):170–84.

Miller, Benjamin. 1936. *New York State Bar Association Annual Meeting and Reports for 1935* (Jan.):330–34.

Miller, Nathan. 1934. The Constitution and Modern Trends. *Reports of the American Bar Association* 59 (Aug.):348–61.

Mississippi State Bar Association. 1933. Proceedings of the 28th Annual Meeting of the Mississippi State Bar. *Mississippi Law Journal* 6 (Sept.):77.

Montague, Gilbert. 1933. Confusion Feared over Vague Codes. *New York Times*, Sept. 23, 3.

Morris, Roland. 1935. Address. *New York County Lawyers Association Yearbook* (Jan.):372–77.

National Labor Relations Board. 1936. *First Annual Report*. Washington: United States Printing Office.

National Lawyers Committee of the American Liberty League. 1935. *Report on the Constitutionality of the National Labor Relations Act*. Pittsburgh: Smith Brothers.

National Recovery Administration. 1933. *Release. No. 1.* Washington, D.C.

Nelles, Walter. 1934. Towards Legal Understanding (Pts. I & II). *Columbia Law Review* 34 (May):862–889, (June):1041–1075.

New York County Lawyers Association. 1935. *Report of the Commerce Committee.* (Apr.): 350.

New York State Bar Association. 1935a. *Annual Meeting and Reports for 1934* (Jan.):104–21.

New York State Bar Association. 1935b. Report of the Committee on NIRA. *Annual Meeting and Reports for 1934* (Jan.):167–74.

———. 1936a. Address of Stanley Reed. *Annual Meeting and Reports for 1935* (Jan.):381–84.

———. 1936b. Address of Thurman Arnold. *Annual Meeting and Reports for 1935* (Jan.): 159–76.

———. 1936c. *Annual Meeting and Reports for 1935* (Jan.):326–34.

———. 1937. *Annual Meeting and Reports for 1936* (Jan.):213–14.

Nyce, Peter Q. 1933. National Industrial Recovery Act: Its Administration and Effect on the Petroleum Industry. *Reports of the American Bar Association* 58 (Aug.):633–42.

O'Brien, Quin. 1933. The New Deal and the Old Constitution. *Proceedings of the Nebraska State Bar Association* (Dec.):69–76.

O'Brien, Patrick H. 1933. Address of Welcome. *Proceedings of the 27th Annual Meeting of the National Association of Attorneys-General* (Aug.):3–11.

Oklahoma State Bar Association. 1933. Editorial. *Oklahoma State Bar Journal* 4 (Aug):1.

Oliphant, Herman. 1928. A Return to Stare Decisis (Pts. 1 & 2). *American Bar Association Journal* 14:71–158.

Parker, John J. 1933. Is the Constitution Passing? *American Bar Association Journal* 19 (Oct.):570–75.

Parkinson, Thomas L. 1935. Are the Law Schools Adequately Training for the Public Service? *American Law School Review* 7 (Dec.):291–98.

Phillips, Orie L. 1934. Our Faith in Democracy. *Proceedings of the Nebraska State Bar Association* (Dec.):89–97.

Podell, David L. 1934. Essential Factors in Determining Constitutionality of Recovery Act. *American Bar Association Journal* 20 (May):281–83.

Pound, Roscoe. 1931. The Call for a Realist Jurisprudence. *Harvard Law Review* 44:697.

———. 1934. Law and the Science of Law in Recent Theories. *Yale Law Journal* 43 (Feb.): 525–36.

Powell, Thomas R. 1935a. Fifty-eight Lawyers Report. *New Republic,* Dec. 11, 119–21.

———. 1935b. Would the Supreme Court Block a Planned Economy? *Fortune Magazine,* Aug., 48.

Rabinowitz, Herbert. 1933. Amend Section 7-A. *Nation* 137, Dec. 27, 732–34.

———. 1934. Senator Wagner's New Labor Bill. *Nation* 138, Mar. 26, 356–58.

Radin, Max. 1935. The Courts and Administrative Agencies. *Minutes of the Judicial Section of the American Bar Association* (July). Unreleased version. Typescript.

Ransom, William. 1936a. Government and Lawyers. *Illinois State Bar Association Journal* (May):295–302.

———. 1936b. Memorandum for the Executive Committee as to the Resistance to Various Legislative Acts and Administrative Regulations Tending to Abridge the Independence of the Profession of Law. *American Bar Association: Proceedings of the Executive Committee* (Jan.):1–2. Typescript.

———. 1936c. The Profession Should Face Its Problems. *American Bar Association Journal* 22 (Aug.):519–25.

———. 1936d. Which Road for the Legal Profession? *American Bar Association Journal* 22 (Jan.):21–23.

Reed, Stanley. 1936. The Constitution of the United States. *American Bar Association Journal* 22 (Sept.):601–8.

Report of the Committee on Commerce. 1935. *American Bar Association: Proceedings of the Executive Committee* (May):1–4. Typescript.

Report of the Committee on Jurisprudence and Law Reform. 1934. *Reports of the American Bar Association* 59 (Aug.):74.

———. 1936. *Reports of the American Bar Association* 61 (Aug.):193–98.

Report of the Committee on Proposed Amendments to the Federal Constitution. 1937. *New York State Bar Association Annual Meeting and Reports for 1936* (Jan.):165–70.

Report of the Committee on Unauthorized Practice of Law. 1936. *Reports of the American Bar Association* 61 (Aug.):74.

Report of the Special Committee on Administrative Law. 1933. *Reports of the American Bar Association* 58 (Aug.):407–27.

———. 1934. *Reports of the American Bar Association* 59 (Aug.):539–64.

———. 1936. *American Bar Association Advance Program* (Jan.):209–82.

Report of the Special Committee on Amendments to the Federal Securities Act of 1933. 1934. *Reports of the American Bar Association* 59 (Aug.):565–87.

———. 1936. *Reports of the American Bar Association* 61 (Aug.):795–96.

Report of the Standing Committee on Commerce. 1933. *Reports of the American Bar Association* 58 (Aug.):339–45.

———. 1934. *Reports of the American Bar Association* 59 (Aug.):439–49.

———. 1935. *Reports of the American Bar Association* 60 (Aug.):439.

Report of the Special Committee to Study Federal Legislation and Policies as Affecting the Rights and Liberties of American Citizens. 1936. *American Bar Association Advance Program and Reports for 1936* (Mar.):367–86.

Report of the Standing Committee on Jurisprudence and Law Reform. 1933. *Reports of the American Bar Association* 58 (Aug.):378–80.

———. 1936. *Reports of the American Bar Association* 61 (Aug.):656–63.

Report of the Standing Committee on Noteworthy Changes on Statute Law. 1933. *Reports of the American Bar Association* 58 (Aug.):386–403.

Report of the Sub-committee to Consider and Report Upon the Report of Special Committee to Study Federal Legislation and Policies as Affecting the Rights and

Liberties of American Citizens. 1935. *American Bar Association: Proceedings of the Executive Committee* (July):1–3. Typescript.

Richberg, Donald. 1934. *New York State Bar Association Annual Meeting and Reports for 1933* (Jan.):286–99.

Riley, Fletcher. 1935. Judicial Liberalism. *Proceedings of the Nebraska State Bar Association* (Dec.):96–109.

Ritchie, Albert. 1935. The American Bar: The Trustee of American Institutions. *American Liberty League* Document no. 48 (June):1–8.

Robinson, Edward S. 1934. Law: An Unscientific Science. *Yale Law Journal* 44 (Dec.):823–47.

Robinson, William H., Jr. 1935. Lawyers and Practitioners: A Study in Contrasts. *American Bar Association Journal* 21 (May):277–80.

Rodell, Fred. 1933. Regulation of Securities by the Federal Trade Commission. *Yale Law Journal* 43 (Dec.):277–80.

Rogers, James G. 1934. *Handbook of the Association of American Law Schools and Proceedings of the 32 Annual Meeting* (Dec.):106–13.

Rogers, Remington. 1935. Administrative Agencies in Government and Effect Thereof on Constitutional Limitations. *Oklahoma State Bar Journal* (May):26–33.

Rowell, Chaster. 1933. Has the NRA Killed the Constitution? *Proceedings of the Sixth Annual Meeting of the State Bar of California* (Sept.):62–71.

Rush, Orville F. 1933. Constitutionality of the Emergency Relief Measures. *Mississippi Bar Law Journal* 5 (Aug.):292–319.

Schelegel, Jerald H. 1985. Between the Harvard Founders and the American Legal Realists: The Professionalization of the American Law Professor. *Journal of Legal Education* 35:311–25.

Securities and Exchange Commission. 1941. *Judicial Decisions, 1934–1939*. Washington: United States Printing Office.

Shouse, Jouette. 1934a. Progress vs. Change. *American Liberty League* Document no. 7 (Nov.):8.

———. 1934b. Recovery, Relief, and the Constitution. *American Liberty League* Document no. 8 (Dec.):3–15.

Smith, Hal H. 1934. The National Industrial Recovery Act: Is It Constitutional? *American Bar Association Journal* 20 (May):273.

Stevens, Morgan J. 1935. The Constitution of the United States. *Mississippi Law Journal* 7 (Jan.):338–50.

Stone, Harlan F. 1934. The Public Influence of the Bar. *Harvard Law Review* 48 (Nov.):1–14.

Sturges, Wesley A. 1933. National Legislation of the Depression. *Washington Law Review* 3 (Oct.):51–60.

Sutherland, Arthur E. 1936. Should Recent Economic Developments Lead Our Courts to Relax the Traditional Restrictions of the Federal Constitution? *New York State Bar Association Proceedings and Reports for 1935* (Jan.):146–58.

Thatcher, Thomas D. 1934. Need of Administrative Tribunals to Review NRA Decisions. *United States Law Week*, May 15, 3.

———. 1935. Invasions of Judicial Powers. *New York State Bar Association Proceedings and Reports for 1934* (Jan.):94–104.

Thomas, William K. 1935a. Collective Bargaining since the New Deal. *Ohio Law Journal* 1 (May):214–47.

———. 1935b. Supreme Court: Organized Labor vs. Capital. *Ohio Law Journal* 1 (Apr.): 102–16.

United States Law Review. 1934a. Notes and Comments. *United States Law Review* 68 (July):337–41.

———. 1934b. The Minnesota Moratorium Case and NIRA. *United States Law Review* 68 (Jan.):1–4.

———. 1935a. Saviors of the Constitution. *United States Law Review* 69 (Dec.):617–21.

———. 1935b. The Decision in the NIRA Cases. *United States Law Review* 69 (June):281–92.

———. 1935c. The Fifty-eight Lawyers. *United States Law Review* 69 (Oct.):355–57.

Vanderbilt, Arthur. 1937. Whither the Bar. *Proceedings of the Nebraska State Bar Association* (Dec.):389–96.

Vaught, Edgar S. 1935. The Commerce Clause of the Constitution. *Oklahoma State Bar Journal* (Feb.):222–30.

Vold, Lawrence. 1936. The NRA and the AAA Experiments in Government, Economics, and Law. *Nebraska Law Bulletin* 14 (May):417–57.

Whitman, Charles. 1934. The Bar and the Future. *Proceedings of the Nebraska State Bar* (Dec.):104–11.

Wickersham, Cornelius. 1935. The NIRA from the Employers' Viewpoint. *Harvard Law Review* 48 (Apr.):954–77.

Wickersham, George. 1933. Address to the American Bar Association. *American Bar Association Journal* 19 (May):327–29.

———. 1934. Address to the American Bar Association. *American Bar Association Journal* 20 (Oct.):634.

———. 1935. Address to the American Bar Association. *American Bar Association Journal* 21 (June):344.

Williston, Samuel. 1933. The Judge and the Professor. *Reports of the American Bar Association* 58 (Aug.):598–611.

Wood, Frederick H. 1934. Some Constitutional Aspects of the National Recovery Program. *American Bar Association Journal* 20 (May):284.

Yale Law Journal. 1934a. Impact of the Courts upon the NRA Program: Judicial Administration of NIRA. *Yale Law Journal* 44 (Nov.):90–109.

———. 1934b. Limitation of Lower Federal Court Jurisdiction over Public Utility Rate Cases. *Yale Law Journal* 44 (Nov.):119–33.

Yntema, Hessel E. 1934. Legal Science and Reform. *Columbia Law Review* 34 (Feb.):207–29.

U.S. Congressional Hearings

U.S. Congress. House Committee on Interstate and Foreign Commerce. 1933. *Federal Securities Act: Hearing before the Committee on Interstate and Foreign Commerce.* 73d Cong., 1st Sess., 1, Apr. 4–5.

U.S. Congress. House Committee on Ways and Means. 1933. *National Recovery Act: Hearing before the Committee on Ways and Means.* 73d Cong., 1st. Sess., May 18–20.

U.S. Congress. Senate Committee on Banking and Currency. 1933. *Securities Act: Hearing before the Committee on Banking and Currency.* 73d Cong., 1st Sess., Mar. 31–Apr. 8.

U.S. Congress. Senate Committee on Finance. 1933. *National Industrial Recovery: Hearing before the Committee on Finance.* 73d Cong., 1st Sess., May 22, 26, 29, 31, June 1.

U.S. Congress. Senate Committee on the Judiciary. 1933. *Limiting Jurisdiction of Federal Courts: Hearing before a Sub-committee of the Committee on the Judiciary.* 73d Cong., 1st Sess., May 26.

U.S. Congress. House Committee on Interstate and Foreign Commerce. 1934. *Securities Exchange Regulation: Hearing before the Committee on Interstate and Foreign Commerce.* 73d Cong., 2d Sess., Feb. 14–Mar. 24.

U.S. Congress. House Committee on Judiciary. 1934. *Jurisdiction of U.S. District Courts over Suits Relating to Orders of State Administrative Boards: Hearing before the Committee on Judiciary.* 73d Cong., 2d Sess., Feb. 27–Mar. 1.

U.S. Congress. Senate Committee on Banking and Currency. 1934. *Stock Exchange Practices: Hearing before the Committee on Banking and Currency.* 73d Cong., 1st Sess., Feb. 26–Mar. 16. (pt. 15), and Mar. 23–Apr. 5 (pt. 16).

U.S. Congress. Senate Committee on Education and Labor. 1934. *To Create a National Labor Board: Hearing before the Committee on Education and Labor.* 73d Cong., 2d Sess., Mar. 26–Apr. 3 (pt. 2), Apr. 4–9 (pt. 3).

U.S. Congress. Senate Committee on Interstate Commerce. 1935. *Public Utility Holding Company Act: Hearing before the Committee on Interstate Commerce.* 74th Cong., 1st Sess., Apr. 16–29.

U.S. Congress. Senate Committee on Education and Labor. 1935. *National Labor Relations Board: Hearing before the Committee on Education and Labor.* 74th Cong., 1st Sess., Mar. 21–Apr. 2.

U.S. Congress. House Committee on the Judiciary. 1936. *To Amend the Federal Register Act: Hearing before Sub-committee no. 2 of the Committee on the Judiciary.* 74th Cong., 2d Sess., Feb. 21.

Statutes

Act to Amend Section 24 of the Judicial Code. Statutes at Large. 1934. Vol. 48, sec. 283, 775.
Administrative Procedure Act. Statutes at Large. 1946. Vol. 60, sec. 324, 237.
Agriculture Adjustment Act. Statutes at Large. 1933. Vol. 48, sec. 25, 31.
Bituminous Coal Conservation Act. Statutes at Large. 1935. Vol. 49, sec. 824, 991.

Federal Register Act. Statutes at Large. 1935. Vol. 49, sec. 417, 500.
Home Owners' Loan Act of 1933. Statutes at Large. 1933. Vol. 48, sec. 64, 128.
National Industrial Recovery Act. Statutes at Large. 1933. Vol. 48, sec. 90, 195.
National Labor Relations Act. Statutes at Large. 1935. Vol. 49, sec. 372, 449.
Public Utility Holding Company Act. Statutes at Large. 1935. Vol. 49, sec. 687, 803.
Securities Act of 1933. Statutes at Large. 1933. Vol. 48, sec. 38, 74.
Securities Exchange Act of 1934. Statutes at Large. 1934. Vol. 48, sec. 404, 881.

Table of Cases

Index

Lawyer(s) (*cont.*)
  tion, 93–113; Wall Street, 46, 112, 148.
    See also National Industrial Recovery
    Act (NIRA): opposition to *and* sup-
    port of; Solo practitioners
League for Industrial Rights, 89
LeBoeuf & Winston, 86
Lee, George, 48–49
Legal autonomy. *See* Autonomy: of law
Legal field, 35, 76; concept of, 5–8, 35,
    136
Legal realism: and the New Deal, 134–
    137, 141–157, 162, 164–165, 168–174, 213
    n.18, 213 n.24, 214 n.42, 222 n.37
Litchfield, P. W., 21
Llewellyn, Karl, 141, 144, 146, 148, 151, 213
    n.24
Loftin, Scott, 53, 55, 78
Logan bill, 109
Louisiana State Bar Association, 26
Lund, Robert L., 22

MacBarnes, Albert, 110
MacLane, John, 42–43
Magruder, Calvert, 148
Market control, 93–94, 96–99, 113–124.
    See also Professionalism
Martin, Charles E., 53, 55–58
Martin, Clarence, 27, 48–49, 52
McFarland, Carl, 100–101, 172
McGuire, O. R., 45–46, 108–109
McLaughlin, James, 146
Merritt, Walter Gordon, 44, 89
Miller, Benjamin, 95–98
Miller, Justin, 110
Miller, Nathan, 77, 92, 100, 186 n.26
Mississippi State Bar Association,
    25–26
Mitchell, William, 53–57, 60
Monopoly. *See* Market control
Moore, Justin. *See* MacLane, John
Moore, Underhill, 149

National Association of Manufacturers
    (NAM), 22, 67
National Bar Program, 78–79
National Electrical Manufacturers Asso-
    ciation (NEMA), 21
National Industrial Recovery Act
    (NIRA), 15–35, 54, 161, 176 n.1, 177 n.7,
    178 n.10, 180 n.38, 189 n.63; admin-
    istrative features of, 18–21; effects on
    industry, 21; internal contradictions
    of, 17–18, 32; opposition to, 18–24; as
    response to emergency, 24–27; sup-
    port of, 16–18, 21–24, 72. *See also* Na-
    tional Recovery Administration
    (NRA); *Schechter Poultry Corporation
    v. United States*
National Labor Board (NLB), 176–177
    n.1
National Labor Disputes Board. *See* Na-
    tional Labor Relations Board
National Labor Relations Act, 18, 39, 41,
    42, 66–67, 74, 95–99, 164; opposition
    to, 44, 85–86
National Labor Relations Board, 39, 41,
    100
National Lawyers Guild, 92
National Recovery Administration
    (NRA), 16, 60, 83, 108; powers of, 18–
    19, 180 n.41. *See also* Johnson, Hugh;
    National Industrial Recovery Act
    (NIRA)
Neagle, Francis E., 24
Nebraska State Bar Association, 78
Nelles, Walter, 133
New Deal, 1–6, 15, 19, 134–135, 167–169;
    and administrative agencies, 205 n.44;
    role of lawyers during, 3–6, 169–172.
    See also Capitalism: New Deal legisla-
    tion; Legal realism; National Indus-
    trial Recovery Act; National Labor
    Relations Act
New York State Bar Association, 17, 20,

Ronen Shamir is Assistant Professor of Sociology at Tel Aviv University.

Library of Congress Cataloging-in-Publication Data
Shamir, Ronen.
    Managing legal uncertainty : elite lawyers in the New Deal / Ronen
Shamir.
        p.   cm.
    Includes bibliographical references and index.
    ISBN 0-8223-1650-1 (cloth). — ISBN 0-8223-1662-5 (pbk.)
    1. Corporate lawyers—United States—History—20th century.
2. Law—United States—Interpretation and construction—
History—20th century.   3. Sociological jurisprudence.   4. New
Deal, 1933–1939.   5. United States—Politics and
government—1933–1945.   I. Title.
KF299.I5S53   1995
340'.115—dc20   95-6279